A TREATISE ON THE POLICE AND CRIMES OF THE METROPOLIS

Patterson Smith Reprint Series in Criminology, Law Enforcement, and Social Problems

A listing of publications in the Series *will be found at rear of volume*

PUBLICATION NO. 128: PATTERSON SMITH REPRINT SERIES IN CRIMINOLOGY, LAW ENFORCEMENT, AND SOCIAL PROBLEMS

A TREATISE ON THE POLICE AND CRIMES OF THE METROPOLIS

BY

JOHN WADE

REPRINTED FROM THE 1829 EDITION
WITH A NEW INTRODUCTION BY
J. J. TOBIAS

MONTCLAIR, N. J.
PATTERSON SMITH
1972

Originally published 1829
Reprinted 1972 by
Patterson Smith Publishing Corporation
Montclair, New Jersey 07042

Library of Congress Cataloging in Publication Data

Wade, John, 1788—1875.
A treatise on the police and crimes of the metropolis.
(Patterson Smith reprint series in criminology, law enforcement, and social problems. Publication no. 128)
Reprint of the 1829 ed. with a new introduction.
Includes bibliographical references.
1. London — Police. 2. Law enforcement — London. 3. Crime and criminals — London. I. Title.
HV8198.L7W3 1972 364'.9'421 71-129306
ISBN 0-87585-128-2

This book is printed on
three-hundred-year acid-free paper.

INTRODUCTION
TO THE REPRINT EDITION

JOHN WADE, the author of this book, was a man of many talents. He was first a journalist, being leader-writer on the *Spectator,* a non-party but reformist weekly, for the first thirty years of its life (1828–1858). Next he was a political writer, author of a violent attack on the Crown, the Government, the Church and everything else; the work's flavour can best be given by setting out its title: *The Extraordinary Black Book: An Exposition of the United Church of England and Ireland; Civil List and Crown Revenues; Incomes, Privileges, and Power, of the Aristocracy; . . . Profits, Influence, and Monopoly of the Bank of England and East-India Company, with Strictures on the Renewal of their Charters; Debt and Funding System; Salaries, Fees, and Emoluments in Courts of Justice, Public Offices, and Colonies; Lists of Pluralists, Placemen, Pensioners, and Sinecurists; . . . Presenting a Complete View of the Expenditure, Patronage, Influence, and Abuses of the Government, in Church, State, Law, and Representation.* This work, which first appeared in serial form in 1820–23, sold 50,000 copies, and other editions were published between 1831 and 1835. The book is perhaps Wade's greatest claim to fame, earning him passing mentions in histories of the early nineteenth century. The Oxford History of England describes it—in a footnote—as "amusing, though not very reliable,"[1] and though its general level was

[1] E. L. Woodward, *The Age of Reform, 1815–1870,* Oxford History of England, vol. 13 (New York: Oxford University Press, 1938), p. 27n.

not very high it was an important contribution to the writings of that period of intense political activity. (It is ironic that Wade, author of this violent attack on the Civil List, was dependent in his later years on a Civil List pension of £50 a year, granted in 1862; he died in great poverty in 1875, at the age of 87 years.)

In another sphere of his life Wade was an historical writer, producing a number of works of popular appeal. A general history of Britain appeared in 1839 and ran through five editions, and other books at the same level had a moderate degree of success. However, his attempt at a more serious work, a study of the authorship of the *Letters* of Junius, was badly received. It was perhaps as an historian, too, that Wade became Vice-President of the Institut d'Afrique at Paris; at this time, of course, Africa was still "the dark continent," only the fringes having been opened up to European contact. Still another sphere of Wade's activity was as a writer on legal subjects, and it was in this field that his most solid piece of work was done. He wrote *The Cabinet Lawyer,* a volume of legal advice—to be kept in one's cabinet, the title implied. The book was first published in 1826 and was reprinted many times, the 25th edition coming out in 1885 after the author's death. This was not his only book in the field; he published other guides on legal and commercial subjects.

Wade's *Treatise on the Police and Crimes of the Metropolis,* the book the reader now has in his hands, was obviously connected with his work as legal writer, historian and reformer. The note of shrill indignation that marked the *Extraordinary Black Book* is absent from the *Treatise,* perhaps because there was no great abuse or vested interest to attack, perhaps also because there was already a move in the direction Wade was advocating. Indeed, as will be seen, Wade refers in the opening words of his prefatory "Advertisement" to the attention his subject was receiving in 1829, and as the book went through the press in that year he inserted an Appendix discussing the bill introduced into Parliament by Robert Peel, the bill which was to lead to the establishment of the Metropolitan Police. It was no doubt this bill, and the transformation of the whole subject-matter of the book to which it led, that prevented the *Treatise* from having the success of most of Wade's other works. It was not reprinted (as far as I know), and indeed the book is very scarce. But this accident of timing makes the *Treatise* all the more valuable today, for it means that we have a survey of the police and crimes of London, a survey made just as the old system of watch and police was about to be abolished, and presented by an experienced writer not afraid to say what he thought. It is, I think, true to say that historians of the Metropolitan Police and the forces based on it, dazzled by the undoubted virtues of the new system and its manifold and manifest advantages over the old, have been overly critical of the watch and police that existed before the Metropolitan Police was established on 29 September, 1829. With all its faults, the system replaced by the Metropolitan Police was far from useless. John Wade gives us an invaluable picture of the system on the eve of reform.

As Wade portrayed a system at the end of its life, readers may like to have an outline of the way in which the system originated and developed. Its basis was the nightly watch in the streets of the metropolis—what

Wade calls the "parochial police" because the parish was the unit of organisation over most of the country. The nightly watch was one of the ancient institutions of the country, mentioned in—but not, I think, founded by—the Statute of Winchester of 1285. The streets of every city and borough were to be patrolled nightly throughout the summer months, from Ascension Day to Michaelmas. At first each householder was required to perform this duty in person or by substitute, but by Wade's day this had long been abolished. In place of personal service each householder paid a rate (Americans would call it a local tax), from the proceeds of which were maintained, throughout the year, the paid forces of watchmen described by Wade.[2] Each of the twenty-six wards of the City of London had its own watch force, and so did the individual parishes of the City of Westminster and the other parishes of the metropolitan area. As Wade makes clear, one great defect of the watch system was precisely this piecemeal form of organisation. He explains that there was no single administrative body for the metropolitan area as a whole. Apart from the City of London, the ancient centre which already in 1829 was the financial and commercial core of a vast metropolis with a diminishing residential population, the remainder of the built-up area was, as far as we are concerned, just a miscellaneous collection of parishes each governed by its own vestry.[3]

The parish was the unit of organisation of another vital piece of constitutional machinery in the field of law enforcement, the constable. The parish constable, from the time of the Statute of Winchester to Wade's

[2] Pp. 48, 52–55, 80–81, 362.
[3] P. 28.

day, was an unpaid officer, holding his position for a year as his turn came round and expected to abandon his shop or other means of livelihood to arrest felons, suppress a riot, serve a summons or perform any one of a whole host of other duties. Very often the householder whose turn it was to hold the office chose to pay a deputy to perform the duties for him rather than act in person, but this was by no means an invariable rule. Each metropolitan parish had several constables each year, and the one whose night it was for duty was supposed to see the watch go out in the evening, to supervise its operation and to inspect the men on their return to the watchhouse in the morning. Part of the night was to be spent at the watchhouse receiving charges as the watchmen brought in their prisoners, and part on patrol around the district. To assist them the constables had the beadles of the parish, minor salaried officials who kept order in the streets by day (with the assistance of subordinates called street-keepers) but who were mainly concerned with the prevention of street-begging. (They had other responsibilities in connection with the Poor Law; it will be recalled that Mr. Bumble's activities in this respect brought him into contact with Oliver Twist.) The beadles also took turns of night-duty as well, acting as subordinate to the constable of the night—and, it seems, very often having to do the whole duty in the absence of the constable, who preferred to spend the night in his bed to fit him for his work in the morning. There were also patrols or sergeants, first-line supervisory officers who were entrusted with the oversight of the watchmen in a part of the district. This whole system of constable, beadle, patrol and nightly watch is what Wade calls the "parochial police." As his evidence shows, at its best it could work well, but often it was far from satisfactory.

In addition to the parochial system, there had developed by Wade's day an impressive set of other law-enforcement bodies, organised on a larger basis. The City of London, in addition to the watches and patrols of each ward, had centrally organised patrols under the direct control of the Lord Mayor, together with some detectives attached to the two daily magistrates' courts held at the Mansion House (the official residence of the Lord Mayor) and the Guildhall (the centre of the City's administration).[4] The remainder of the metropolis had a more elaborate system, which indeed the City had copied, which had developed from the court at Bow Street.

Though the Bow Street Magistrates' Court was the foundation on which rested much of the law enforcement of Wade's day, it was established by chance rather than by conscious decision. The chance event which led to all that followed was the appointment in 1748 of Henry Fielding to be a salaried justice of the peace of Westminster. There had been for many years someone known as the Court Magistrate, a justice of the peace on whom the king's court and the Government put their reliance and who discharged, for a salary paid out of Secret Service funds, confidential business needing a magistrate's powers but unworthy of the personal attention of a Secretary of State. Henry Fielding, however, gave the office a new twist by giving great attention to something his predecessors had not concerned themselves with—the active and disinterested pursuit of criminals. The story of his activities has often been told.[5] He gathered around him a group

[4] Pp. 45–46.

[5] See, for example, P. Pringle, *Hue and Cry* (London: Museum Press, 1955), chap. 5.

of active men, former parish constables; they became known as the Bow Street Runners (the police officers mentioned by Wade). The Bow Street Court became, in Fielding's day and after his death, the place to which victims of crime turned and from which was directed the pursuit of the criminals. Thus far the role of the Government had been merely to sanction what had been done by the initiative of others, footing the bill out of Secret Service funds. In 1780 or thereabouts the Government took a positive step—it established a Foot Patrol under the control of the Bow Street Magistrates. A handful of men was employed to patrol the streets of the centre of the metropolis (apart from the City) as an addition to the parochial watch. A Horse Patrol was added in 1805, with the duty of patrolling the turnpikes in the environs of London, the danger-spots where highwaymen operated. The oddly-named Dismounted Horse Patrol—in reality a foot section of the Horse Patrol—was added in 1821 to cover the area between the Foot and the Horse Patrol. All three forces operated only at night; the first to do duty by day was the Day Patrol, set up in 1822, and it covered the central area only. These patrols were all under the supervision of the Chief Magistrate at Bow Street and were known collectively as the Bow Street Patrols.[6] Their existence did not affect the parochial watch, which continued to operate as before.

Bow Street was thus the centre of patrol policing in London, but this was not its only contribution to future developments. Note was taken of the success of the Bow Street Court and its Runners in providing for the investigation of crime, which at that time was a respon-

[6] Pp. 59–62, 68.

sibility of the justice of the peace, who acted much like the district attorney of today in superintending the enquiries of the detectives. In 1792 seven other police offices were established, each, like Bow Street, headed by three magistrates and having attached to it a number of police officers (this being the general name for the detectives who at Bow Street were given the name "Runners"). Wade very rightly calls attention to the enormous improvement in policing that the establishment of these offices, or courts as we should call them, brought about. In 1800 London's ninth police office, the Thames Police Office, was established; this was rather different from the others in that it had, in addition to the usual staff, a body of river police patrolling in boats. These nine police offices, with all their detectives and patrols of various kinds, made up what Wade calls the "stipendiary police."[7]

The preceding section has described the evolution of the police of London to 1829, the year in which Wade's *Treatise* was published and the year in which the system was drastically altered. Many people at the time knew that reform was required. Select Committees of the House of Commons had investigated the police of London in 1812, 1816–18, and 1822, and another was at work in 1828, when Wade was engaged in the preparation of the *Treatise*. It was this latter Committee which recommended a drastic overhaul of the police of the metropolis and hence gave Robert Peel, the Home Secretary, the welcome opportunity to suggest a new system. However, the exact nature of the reforms was far from settled, and Wade's informed and shrewd survey may well have played its part in

[7] Pp. 37–39, 55–59, 67–68, 214.

determining the final shape of what became the Metropolitan Police Act of 1829 and of the Metropolitan Police itself. Wade, like most other writers of the time, saw the need for some sort of central police authority for London, and he went further than some others in wanting to strip the parishes of their powers in this field. He was perceptive enough, too, to realise that the new police should supplant not merely the nightly watch but the inefficient day police as well. Indeed, as he points out in the Appendix, his ideas on this question went further than those on which the bill was based.[8] Fortunately, however, the new system when it was put into operation went as far as Wade wished on this point. The Metropolitan Police was a day-and-night force, replacing within its area the whole parochial police; constable and beadle ceased to have any function in this field, and the watchman became simply a privately employed additional safeguard for vulnerable premises. The Foot Patrol, the Day Patrol and the Dismounted Horse Patrol were terminated. The new force did indeed have to continue for a time in unhappy co-existence with the Horse Patrol, the Thames Police and the detectives attached to the nine police offices, but this anomaly was ended by 1839. The Horse Patrol and the Thames Police were finally absorbed into the Metropolitan Police and the detectives of the police offices lost their function, which too passed to the Metropolitan Police. The police offices became merely police courts—a title which today has been changed yet again to magistrates' courts.

Obviously the system established in 1829 was not exactly that which Wade had suggested. He was not alone, however, in being unable to see exactly what

[8] Pp. 86–90, 371.

shape the new organisation should take, and a great deal of the final solution was only hammered out by Peel and the two first commissioners after the scheme had been approved in outline. We cannot of course claim for Wade that he was right in every detail or that all his suggestions have won subsequent approval, though it is fascinating to find in the *Treatise* one proposal that still today passes as modern thinking. Wade advocates that the new police should provide householders with expert advice on the security of their premises;[9] this idea was not adopted for over a century, but recently crime prevention, as it is called, has been seen as a new but important part of police duty!

One can find other passages in the book which are as true today as when they were written. Wade's comments on the problem facing the police officer of distinguishing "the innocent from the guilty, the virtuous man from a burglar, or a belated female from a street-walker"[10] will have an echo in many quarters today. Police officers on both sides of the Atlantic would cry "Hear, hear" to his conclusion: "If mistakes are committed in the execution of laws, it is more fair to ascribe them to misapprehension or defects inseparable from their administration than a premeditated invasion of public liberty; and the reflective mind, instead of entering into futile altercations with the agents of power, will consider his personal annoyance a trifling sacrifice to the general safety."[11]

Thus we can find much to applaud and more to interest us in the portions of the *Treatise* which deal with police; the portions dealing with crime are not of

[9] P. 194. [10] P. 25. [11] P. 26.

such great value. They do indeed give us testimony as to the state of crime which is useful when added to that from other sources,[12] but the analysis is not so careful as on police topics. Wade's views on the causation of crime and on methods of punishment, too, are mainly of interest to the specialist as typical of the times; he was not so far ahead of the others of his day on these themes. Even the general reader, however, may like to be reminded that a humane and forward-looking man, one who was in the vanguard of the attack on old ideas, could put forward views today rejected by all. Such a man could express doubts about the abolition of branding, could write that "regular and continued hard labour, in the eye of the public, with coarse fare and strict subordination, would in time break the spirit of the fiercest burglar," could declare that "of all punishments devised, that is the best which perpetually ejects the delinquent from the bosom of the society he has offended . . . For our part, we cannot see why exile should not be applied to almost every description of offence, short of those demanding capital execution."[13]

The general reader will, it is to be hoped, also find much to interest him in the mass of information about London in 1829 that Wade lays before him. At this time London and all Britain were on the threshold of a period of world dominance. The Industrial Revolution had been under way for three-quarters of a century, and was now permeating much of British life. The defeat of Napoleonic France and the end of the generation-long wars was fourteen years in the past;

[12] I used Wade's evidence with that of others in my *Crime and Industrial Society in the Nineteenth Century* (London: Batsford; New York: Schocken, 1967).

[13] Pp. 17–18, 20, 21.

the railway era was about to commence with the opening in 1830 of the Liverpool-Manchester line. The fifty years ahead of Britain when Wade wrote were a period of great progress, which transformed many of the nation's institutions beyond recognition. John Wade captures for us a world about to be violently changed.

—J. J. TOBIAS

The Police College
Bramshill House
Basingstoke, Hants.
England
May 1971

A

TREATISE

ON THE

POLICE AND CRIMES

OF THE

Metropolis;

ESPECIALLY

JUVENILE DELINQUENCY,
FEMALE PROSTITUTION,
MENDICITY,
GAMING,
FORGERY,
STREET-ROBBERIES,
BURGLARY AND HOUSE-BREAKING,
RECEIVING OF STOLEN GOODS,
COUNTERFEITING THE COIN,
EXHUMATION,
CHEATING AND SWINDLING,
ADULTERATION OF FOOD, &c.

ALSO AN ACCOUNT OF THE

COURTS OF JUSTICE AND PRISONS OF LONDON;

AND

AN INQUIRY

INTO THE

CAUSES OF THE INCREASE OF CRIME;

THE

Tendency of the Debtor Laws;

AND INTO THE

PRESENT STATE OF THE LICENSED VICTUALLERS' TRADE:

WITH

SUGGESTIONS FOR THE IMPROVEMENT OF THE PROTECTIVE INSTITUTIONS OF THE METROPOLIS,

AND THE

PREVENTION OF OFFENCES.

BY THE EDITOR OF "THE CABINET LAWYER;" OF "A DIGEST OF FACTS AND PRINCIPLES ON BANKING AND COMMERCE;" OF "AN ACCOUNT OF PUBLIC CHARITIES," &c.

LONDON:

LONGMAN, REES, ORME, BROWN, AND GREEN.

1829.

[*Title page of the original edition*]

ADVERTISEMENT.

It may be thought, from the present work appearing rather opportunely, when the Police and Crime of the Metropolis are obtaining an unusual share of attention, that it has been prepared on "the spur of the occasion;" but this is not the case: it has been announced for publication upwards of a twelvemonth, and has engaged our attention for the last two or three years, and the only reasons of the delay have been the difficulty of completing our inquiries and maturing our judgment on the important matters to which it relates.

Fielding has observed that a writer does not usually treat a subject the worse for knowing something of its bearing; and, we believe, those who have directed their inquiries into the state of crime, and the protective institutions of the Metropolis, will admit, in the present instance, we have not entirely neglected the precaution of that sagacious monitor, by providing ourselves, at least, with some preliminary information for the task. A residence of considerable duration in London—a somewhat miscellaneous intercourse in society—some little vicissitudes in life—leisure and partiality for the pursuit—and access to valuable public information, form our chief pretensions to the office we have undertaken.

To our conclusions on the Police of the capital we have little fear of obtaining the Reader's concurrence, after perusing CHAPTERS IV. and V., exhibiting the defects in the present system, and the advantages which would result from a general and consolidated establishment, acting under one head, for a common purpose, and subject to real responsibility for the lives and property of nearly two millions of persons. The existing system is both corrupt and inefficient; and, after the evidence of these facts, daily afforded, and the still more alarming testimony of a rapidly increasing calendar, it can only have been the difficulties of the undertaking that have so long delayed the introduction of an effective remedy. In the reform of our criminal administration, generally, no want of zeal has been manifested of late years; but, unfortunately, perhaps, our approaches have not been directed to the most advantageous extremity: for while occupied in establishing penitentiaries, in improving the discipline of gaols, and in devising better measures for the reform, the trial, and punishment, of delinquents, we have too long neglected the means by which prisons may become less necessary, and the commission of offences prevented. Our mode of proceeding may be likened to that of a person whose dwelling is inundated, and who vainly endeavours to stem the flood by baling out the water that constantly returns, instead of stopping the inlets through which the torrent is admitted. To grapple with the abuses that exist demands an energy, perseverance, and tact of no ordinary kind, and a mind that shall not shrink from new expedients, or fear to depart from old ones, to which long usage and associations have granted almost chartered immunities.

One reason, probably, that may be assigned for the imperfect state of the police in this country is, the singular fact that scarcely a magistrate or writer of eminence has thought it worth while to bestow the least attention on the subject: on general legislation, on laws, on the theory of crimes and punishments, on prison discipline, on the execution of offenders, and all the ulterior proceedings of criminal administration, we have treatises without number; but, on the institutions of preventive justice we have not a single author (the late Dr. COLQUHOUN excepted) to explain their organization, or the general principles upon which they ought to be established.

The plan we have ventured to submit for organizing the metropolitan police appears, to our apprehension, practicable and efficient, and to secure the chief ends sought—co-operation—mutual dependence of parts—and, in the agents, a well-defined responsibility. Our suggestions for destroying a vile combination between those who ought to protect the community from depredations and those by whom depredations are committed may not be unworthy attention.

Our exposition of the Crimes of the Metropolis forms another division of our labours not, perhaps, the least interesting and valuable. As regards our suggestions for the prevention of Offences, and our remarks on the causes of the Increase of Crime—on the tendency of the Debtor-Laws—on Anatomical Legislation—and other matters of great importance and difficulty, of course different opinions will be entertained:—the Reader is not bound to adopt our conclusions; we have faithfully submitted to him the data, and we expect he will exercise his own judgment, as we have done ours, on the evidence brought before him: having taken pains to inquire, we thought we might be allowed to submit an opinion; and, being convinced the wisest and best are liable to error, we freely partake of the growing spirit of the age, in freedom from dogmatism and tolerance of dissent. We claim some merit in not having suggested any sudden or extensive alterations; for we think experience has demonstrated that the most enlightened reformers are those who are content with mitigating positive evils, without risking the uncertain issues of undefined innovations. Amidst the intelligence and discussion which now pervade society, the propagation of an erroneous sentiment cannot do much harm,—at most it must be short-lived and of limited influence; but the withholding of an useful truth is a misprision of social duty, the consequences of which no man can appreciate.

To complete our exposition, we have given an account of the Courts of Justice and Prisons of London; also a brief notice of the Public Sewers, of Gas and Water Companies, and of the Fire-Police. These form part of the establishments connected with the security and health of the inhabitants of the Metropolis, and could not have been properly omitted in an account of its protective institutions.

The chapter on the history and present state of the Victualling-trade, in London, is, in our opinion, of great importance to the public interests, and intimately connected with its general police.

Before concluding, we wish to point out an inconsistency into which we have fallen: in Chap. VI. p. 101, we seem to have argued as though the more atrocious crimes against the *person* had diminished; but, in Chap. IX. p. 208, we have shown that offences against the person, as well as those against property, have increased in a greater ratio than the population. We were led into the error from having adopted the conclusion of others; but, when we came to examine the criminal returns submitted to Parliament, we found no authority for the more gratifying inference. The number of personal injuries is, we believe, proportionably less in this country than in most other European communities; but the assertion is incorrect that they have not increased of late years,—though not so fast as offences against property.

April 16, 1829.

CONTENTS.

CHAPTER I.

GENERAL PRINCIPLES OF POLICE, AND PREVENTIVE PUNISHMENTS.

CHAPTER II.

EXTENT AND MUNICIPAL DIVISIONS OF THE METROPOLIS.

CHAPTER III.

POLICE ESTABLISHMENTS.

CHAPTER IV.

DEFECTS IN THE POLICE.

CHAPTER V.

GENERAL PLAN OF POLICE.

CHAPTER VI.

CRIMES IN THE METROPOLIS.—GAMING.—BANKRUPTCY, INSOLVENCY, AND IMPRISONMENT FOR DEBT.—PRIVATE CREDIT.

CHAPTER X.

COURTS OF JUSTICE.

CHAPTER XI.

PRISONS OF THE METROPOLIS.

CHAPTER XII.

PUBLIC SEWERS.—WATER COMPANIES.—GAS-LIGHT ESTABLISHMENTS.—FIRE-POLICE.

CHAPTER XIII.

BREWERS — LICENSED VICTUALLERS — HOTEL, COFFEE-HOUSE, AND TAVERN KEFPERS.

CHAPTER XIV.

CONCLUDING REMARKS ON METROPOLITAN POLICE, CRIMES, FRAUDS, AND MANNERS.

APPENDIX.

A TREATISE,

&c. &c.

PART I.

POLICE OF THE METROPOLIS.

CHAPTER I.

GENERAL PRINCIPLES OF POLICE, AND PREVENTIVE PUNISHMENTS.

General Objects of Police defined.—Limits of the Ministerial and Judicial Powers.—Different Constitution of the Police in large and small Towns, Daily Newspapers.—Qualifications proper to Magistrates and Officers in the Police Department.—Objects of their Jurisdiction: Licensed Places, Mendicity, Vagrancy, the Coin, Violation of Penal Statutes, &c.—Ought to supersede Informers.—Gaming more hurtful to the Industrious than Higher Classes.—Punishments best adapted to deter from Crime and promote the Reform of Offenders, Penitentiary Schemes.—Punishments, if public, ought to be terrible in the Exhibition.—Solitary Confinement.—Transportation, or Perpetual Exile, best adapted to a civilized Society.—Inadequacy of the best-organized Police without Individual Precau-

B

tion and Co-operation.—Jealousy of the Police as inimical to Public Liberty.—Recent Examples show the Necessity of an efficient Police Establishment for the Metropolis.

THE police is a branch of that extensive system instituted to protect the community from fraud, annoyance, violence, and depredation. While the courts of administrative justice ascertain the guilt and prescribe the punishment of actual delinquents, the business of the police is more especially directed to prevent the commission or apprehend the perpetrators of offences.

The functions of police, however, are not limited to mere purveyance to the judicial powers, they extend to whatever interferes with internal security, order, comfort, and economy; to the removal of nuisances and obstructions, the repression of disorders, the protection of the peaceful citizen in his daily and nightly vocations, the maintenance of the public health and of a due observance of the local and general laws intended for municipal government and regulation.

The great problem in preventive justice is to obtain the most economical and efficient establishment with the least possible infringement of civil liberty. Every abridgment of personal freedom is, abstractedly, an evil, justifiable only on the ground of greater compensating advantages to the community, and the question that occurs on every suggestion for improving this branch of civil polity is, how far it is compatible with existing feelings, usages, and institutions. In despotic countries people are accustomed to the exertions of authority in its most repulsive forms, and the police may be armed with all the powers essential to the prompt and efficient discharge of its duties; but in countries aspiring to free institutions, where the persons, property, habitations, and even amusements of the people are guarded by so many barriers, which no one with impunity can violate without legal and adequate occasion, a much more scrupulous and circuitous process is required. Consequently, in England the business of police is chiefly confided to the people themselves; there are few stipendiary officers, who assume no distinctive garb or character, constituting a sort of invisible power, which moves unseen, and, though usually at hand when occasion requires its interference, the eye is never offended by the parade of surveillance and coercion.

Whether our system is adequate to the purposes of its establishment, or what improvements it requires, will form a subject for future consideration. At present our intention is briefly to indicate the general principles of police, and the circumstances which ought to influence its formation. It is a branch of inquiry on which we do not purpose long to detain the reader; for, in the first place, we feel some diffidence in trusting ourselves with the general discussion of a question which, so far as we know, has not obtained particular notice from juridical writers; in the next, we have our doubts whether the police of any place can ever be reduced to general principles: it seems one of those practical questions which, like most others having relation to the social state, must be determined by cotemporary incidents—the institutions, occupations, and feelings of the people for whom it is intended; and, therefore, any attempt to establish an abstract system of preventive justice would be void of utility, as well as inconsistent with the more useful and less pretending objects of our publication.

The only points which admit of general observation are,—1. The connexion between the preventive, or ministerial, and the judicial, or administrative, branch of justice. 2. The peculiarities in society which ought to determine the character and formation of a police establishment. 3. The persons and instruments proper to be employed in the functions of police. 4. Their power and the objects of their jurisdiction and surveillance. 5. Punishments best calculated to deter from crime and prevent the repetition of offences. 6. Concluding observations on the inadequacy of the best organized system of police unless aided by individual precaution; and on the jealousy of the police as inimical to public liberty.

Each of these propositions would admit of lengthened discusion, but we shall treat them briefly, and principally with a view to their bearing on the Police of the Metropolis.

As to our first position, we may begin with observing that it is generally admitted a separation of the ministerial and judicial powers is essential to a temperate and equitable administration of the laws, and they cannot be advantageously exercised by the same individual. The duties of the ministerial or police officer is to search out and collect evidence of guilt, and to take precautions, warranted by previous information, against the perpetration of offences: his great ambition ought to be to prevent crimes, and, by vigilance, produce a conviction that criminality cannot exist without danger of detection. On the other hand, the duty of the judicial magistrate is to watch over the conduct of the police officer, to judge of the value of his evidence, and proceed only on legal proofs; his business is not only to see the law duly enforced, but enforced in such manner as no doubt can arise as to its impartial administration.

The union of powers so distinct would obviously remove a salutary check against the abuse of authority in the first stages of execution. Every one must have remarked how quickly men become interested in a pursuit in which they are engaged and anxious about the result. A delinquent is no sooner apprehended than the apprehender is conscious of a stake in his guilt or innocence: to acquit the accused impugns his discrimination, his judgment, and the propriety of his conduct. The law, therefore, has wisely precluded him from the adjudication of the offence, and, by interposing the authority of the magistrate, submits it to the arbitration of a less biassed tribunal. The same precaution is observable through the whole course of a criminal suit; every step in the proceeding is checked and overlooked by a next superior power: the charge before a night constable is, next morning, re-heard by the committing justice; his award is brought before the grand jury; and, finally, the whole is submitted to the inquisition of a petit-jury and the judges of session or assize. These are wise precautions; such relays in prosecution operate like the zig-zag turnings to a crowded assembly, they check the force of the current, and, by interposing points of obstruction and consideration, prevent the errors which might ensue from acting on a continuous and accelerated impulse.

Notwithstanding the utility of separating the ministerial and judicial offices, an union of the two is often unavoidable and even justifiable. Our justices of the peace act both ministerially and judicially; the former, in preserving the peace, hearing charges, and issuing summonses and warrants thereon, examining witnesses, binding over parties to prosecute and give evidence, accepting bail or committing for trial; the latter, in convicting for offences. Their judicial powers, however, only extend to minor offences, the more serious crimes being sent to a higher tribunal, which has had no share in the preliminary proceedings against the accused. The only class of officers whose duties are strictly ministerial are constables, watchmen, patrols, gaolers, &c.

We shall next advert to the peculiarities in society which ought to determine the character of a police establishment.

Besides the general influence, to which allusion has already been made, of free institutions and opinions, the formation of the police must greatly depend on the number, habits, and vocations of the inhabitants over which its powers extend. The differences observable between small and moderately-sized towns, consisting of a settled population, and great capitals, a large proportion of whose inhabitants are migratory, are very striking. In the former, the retreats and opportunities for delinquency are few and limited; the pursuits and even character of each person are matters of notoriety and interest; not to be known is to be an object of inquiry or suspicion: in a word, every one is the police of his neighbour, and unconsciously exercises over him its most essential duties. But this is widely different from the mode of living in a great city, especially in London. Here there is no such thing as vicinage,—no curiosity about neighbours,—every one is engrossed in his own pursuit, and neither knows nor cares about any human being except the circle to which he has been introduced and with which he is connected by ties of business, pleasure, or profit. It is from this circumstance London affords so many facilities for the concealment of criminality. In the smaller towns offenders live as it were in the open champaign, always liable to be observed and detected by the agents of justice. But the metropolis is like an immense forest, in the innumerable avenues of which they may always find retreat and shelter. A person desirous of so doing may insulate himself, like the "last man," and, though in the midst of a million of people, create for himself a social solitude.

This is only one of the peculiarities in London society. A spirit of gaiety, recklessness, and adventure, animates the inhabitants, which is never observed in provincial towns. It is proverbially the resort of opulence, talent, and enterprise, as well as of those who, having lost *caste* in the places of their birth, seek to hide themselves amidst its multitudinous population. Among such busy elements there is little of stagnant life; every one being intent upon some object of ambition, profit, or deception. The magnitude of the place, and consequent ignorance of individuals of many by whom they are necessarily surrounded, precludes all nice scrutiny into motives and purposes; even the distinctions of wealth and rank are almost lost in the crowd; and all that can be relied upon are certain external indications and appearances which may be either genuine or counterfeit. Many have no fixed domicile: they live in lodging-houses, hotels, or taverns, and, forming moving bodies with no determinate orbits, are removed from the restraint and observation which a settled abode and known circle of acquaintance impose on individual conduct.

With such a floating, unknown, and stirring population to watch over and control, it is obvious the police requires corresponding powers and authority. Its numerical force ought to be proportionately greater, as well as its power of inquisition, over both persons and places. A vigilance and suspicion which would be wholly superfluous in a provincial town are indispensable to the safety and regulation of a vast metropolis.

Another peculiarity and auxiliary to crime distinguishes the capital in the circulation of the daily newspapers; while the journals are of the utmost utility in giving publicity to offences and offenders, and in making known the artifices of cheats and impostors, they, on the other hand, afford great facilities to the designs of unprincipled men. They offer the ready means of publishing any insidious project, and bringing it under the notice of the highest as well as the lowest in society. In the advertizing department of a daily paper is a complete exposition of the wants and the ways and means of the metropolis. This, no doubt, is regularly consulted by the adventurer, who here learns the address and circumstances of individuals, and hence forms his scheme of fraud and depredation. The cases of Howard and other miscreants are too recent to require citing, as examples of this mode of proceeding. It is an evil, however, without remedy; all that can be expected of the proprietors of newspapers is to exclude paragraphs openly immoral or illegal; they cannot institute inquiries into persons and motives; they can only proceed on the principle of the common carrier, who lends his vehicle to whoever can pay the fare. Individuals alone can be their own safeguard, and those who advertize money to lend or borrow, or a furnished house to be let, must be aware that such notice will pass under the eye of those who will apply only for a sinister purpose, as well as of those who, *bonâ fide*, require such accommodation. They must also be aware of the principle on which newspapers are conducted: that, generally, all who pay may insert, and that they are the common highway of publicity to the nefarious as well as honest part of the community.

We proceed to the third proposition,—the persons and qualifications proper to be employed in the police department, reserving some further observation on the peculiarities of metropolitan society to a subsequent chapter.

The first requisite to a police officer is an acquaintance

with the laws, in the preliminary stages of whose execution he is employed. This knowledge ought not to be confined to the committing magistrate, but in a more limited degree extend to the subordinate functionaries. It frequently happens points of great legal nicety occur in the execution of warrants, in the suppression of affrays, the removal of nuisances, the making of seizures, and the laying of informations. Unless an officer has clear ideas of his duty, in these cases, he necessarily acts with diffidence;—he over-steps his powers, or does not act up to them;—he is too officious or too lax in his movements. Probably, in a majority of cases, the parties against whom he proceeds are equally ignorant, but this presumption ought not to be acted upon; he will always be liable to encounter individuals who have correct notions of his duties, and when an ignorant discharge of them will lead to the exposure and obloquy of the establishment to which he belongs.

But not only is considerable knowledge of law requisite to the police, but also an *acquaintance with life.* A mere lawyer from the chambers or inns of court forms an indifferent police magistrate; and a man, as Mr. Bentham has remarked, may have been a barrister in full practice, and yet know no more of the business of a police magistrate than if he had graduated in the army or navy. They ought to be men of the world, as well as of sufficient professional attainments to secure them from the imputation of legal incompetence. With the localities of their jurisdiction, and the prevailing character of the population, their occupations, amusements, and habits, they ought to be intimately acquainted. A general knowledge of all the arts of fraud, imposture, and depredation, is also indispensable. Next to this is a qualification which can hardly be derived from education, and can only result from observation, or perhaps natural gift. The qualification to which I allude is the power of discriminating criminal character. Magistrates have much discretionary authority, and according as they possess this endowment will their decisions be just or unjust, expedient or hurtful. Some there are who can read, almost infallibly, in the face and manner, incorrigible vagrant, hardened thief, or accomplished swindler; while others are without this tact and blind to the indications which distinctly mark the criminal by nature from one by *accident*. The London justices have a wide field for observation, and to some the opportunity has not been lost; but we cannot always expect Fieldings to occupy the benches. To be a perfect criminal judge, it is almost essential to have previously mingled in scenes of delinquency; for the criminal mind has motives of action, habits of thinking, and is influenced by circumstances, which those who have always felt and acted honestly can never enter into or appreciate.

The inferior officers of police, as well as their superiors, ought to be well acquainted with life, in order to an efficient discharge of their duties. Some qualities are, *prima faciæ*, so essential to both descriptions of functionaries that it has hardly been thought necessary to enumerate them; such as general knowledge, acuteness, presence of mind, probity, command of temper, and freedom from political or religious bias in the examining magistrate—sobriety, courage, personal strength, and activity in the operative officer. Reformed rogues, no doubt, if one could trust them, would make the best thief-takers; and the whole establishment from the highest to the lowest be most ably filled by men who are themselves honest, though versant in all the arts of fraud and depredation. A parish or district is indeed badly *policed* if there is not one officer, at least, acquainted with every brothel, every disorderly house, and every suspicious person and place it contains.

Another indispensable qualification of the police is *responsibility*. To the police is confided the security of persons and property ; and, where the trust is so momentous, there ought to be an adequate guarantee it will not be betrayed. This can only be safely obtained by acting on the common principles of human nature, and rendering it more advantageous to perform than neglect duty. If the emoluments of police are mean, so will be the candidates for them. Beside a good salary, contingent rewards, either honorary or pecuniary, proportioned to desert and exemplary service should be added. Under such a system there would be sufficient responsibility ; the employment would be sought by men of character, who would not forfeit that and a profitable and honourable situation for slight temptations.

In England, it is usual to undervalue the department of police, and think meanly of its functionaries. It is not easy to see the grounds of this prejudice ; the utility and importance of the employment will be readily admitted, and we have just shewn that the qualifications requisite, both natural and acquired, are very considerable. It can only then be the inadequacy of the pecuniary remuneration which degrades the office, and this, in a community where the idolatry of wealth is paramount to every other species of worship, is quite sufficient to account for the prevalent opinion. Lately the incomes of the metropolitan justices were augmented, but they are still barely commensurate with the situation ; they ought to be sufficient to enable them to mingle with every class in life, as well as to place them in dignified independence of those among whom their duty chiefly lies, and to whom, in many instances, they necessarily become personally obnoxious.

We proceed to the fourth proposition—namely, the powers of the police and the proper objects of their jurisdiction and surveillance.

As a general principle it may be first stated that neither the persons, avocations, nor amusements of the people ought to be interfered with, unless publicly hurtful to the community; and next, that this interference should be exercised in a manner as little annoying and offensive as is compatible with the discharge of the prescribed duty.

Among objects which fall fairly under the jurisdiction of the police are all licensed places, whether for amusement or the sale of commodities subject to the duties of custom or excise. The fact of a license being granted shows such places only exist by sufferance, and consequently subjecting them to the inspection of the police adds little to the hardship of their tenure. Theatres and other places of public amusement, being the resort of numerous and promiscuous bodies, are specially liable to crime and disorder requiring the control of authority. Hotels, wine-houses, inns, ale-houses, and even coffee-shops and oyster-shops, seem all to fall within police jurisdiction. They are all places of public resort, and the hours of entertainment being different from the ordinary hours of business they are proper subjects of jealousy and suspicion. For the same reason hackney-coaches or light carts, plying at unusual hours, or persons travelling or being abroad at unusual hours, either on foot or horseback, are proper objects of inquiry and inspection. It is the unseasonableness of the hour and the facilities such hours afford for depredation, as well as the little probability the parties are engaged in any honest pursuit, that brings them within the cognizance of the police. In like manner, all vagrants, chapmen, as hawkers, pedlers, and travelling auctioneers; also, trades carried on without settled connexions, and in which buyers and sellers are unknown or indifferent, such as dealers in second hand goods, marine-stores, furniture-brokers, pawnbrokers, &c. are proper for the visitation and superintendence of the police.

How far gaming-houses should be subjected to the police requires consideration. The pleasures of the people are entitled to protection as well as their persons and properties. By gaming is not meant mere play for recreation, but that which is systematically pursued for the purposes of gain or livelihood, than which nothing can be more fatal to virtuous habits and productive of crime. Mr. Hume has remarked that the same actions are not equally bad in the rich and the poor. Idleness and drunkenness are completely ruinous to the private economy of a mechanic or tradesman; while to the opulent, however personally degrading, they are comparatively innoxious. On this principle it may be urged that low gaming ought to be rigorously suppressed. Time and money are alike valuable to the industrious classes; neither can be wasted without detriment to their business and domestic comforts. For this reason, all sedentary games in public-houses and the lesser gaming-houses, by mechanics, clerks, and tradesmen, are public evils, and ought to be suppressed. No good can result from such pursuits; they are not conducive to health or rational recreation, and a propensity to them increases on their votaries like addiction to intoxicating liquors, till it terminates in the extinction of the personal qualities most conducive to utility and happiness.

With respect to the higher classes, the mischiefs resulting from gaming are less pernicious. These are chiefly personal to themselves, by extinguishing the nobler traits of character and a thirst for honourable distinction. Removed by birth and fortune from the obligations of others, neither a strict economy of money or time, nor habits of order and application, are indispensable to the discharge of their social duties. If large fortunes be broken up by play, the public may be benefited by the power of wealth being distributed in channels where it may be more beneficially employed than in the hands of the former possessors. Add to this, the consideration that in every opulent community exists a numerous class without intellectual resource, and whose large incomes leave them without motive to exertion; pleasure is the chief business of their lives, and gaming one of the few stimulants left them to diversify the torpid monotony of existence. The mode in which their wealth is dissipated neither affects the cultivation of the soil nor the prosperity of trade; the national resources are undisturbed, whether the rents of the nobility and gentry pass from them by the shuffling of cards and dice or by the parchment instruments of the legal practitioner.

In England, more than in any European community, is a numerous class enjoying, or, rather, labouring under, a plethora of wealth, the produce of vast colonial possessions, of agricultural improvements, and the successful pursuit of commerce and manufactures. Grand dinners, concerts, operas, and balls; the encouragement of the arts of painting, sculpture, and architecture; foreign tours and election contests; are all insufficient to absorb the immense incomes derived from rents, profits, tithes, and taxes. The surplus cannot go on accumulating for ever; younger children have a resource in the army, navy, public offices, and learned professions; and the eldest, whatever the vicissitudes of *hazard* or *blind hookey*, cannot impair the ancestral stem,—he can at most only lop off the branches, the roots of the parent tree being fast locked in the soil by the eternal law of primogeniture.

While, therefore, gaming is chiefly confined to the landed and monied aristocracy, however much its personal consequences may be lamented, it is not such a source of public disorder as demands the cognizance of the civil power, more especially if carried on as in the metropolis, principally in club-houses, from which all below a certain grade are excluded.

A more important duty than the last devolves on the police, in looking to the observance of the laws made for the public benefit. The legislature, in making a new law, only performs half its duty, unless it also takes precautions to enforce an impartial observance by all those on whom it is intended to operate. A law laxly executed, observed by some, and evaded by others, becomes at once an instrument of oppression or unmerited advantage; oppression to the conscientious upon whom it imposes restraint and sacrifice,—and advantage to the unprincipled who escape the restrictions to which their neighbours are subjected.

The persons chiefly engaged in looking to the execution of penal statutes are mostly voluntary informers, unprincipled pettifoggers, with no recognized authority, and who pursue their vocation not for justice, but for gain. With them it is a matter of indifference whether they receive a penalty for the infraction of a law, or an equivalent bribe for connivance at its provisions; their purpose being not to carry the laws into impartial operation, but to fill their pockets. Hence their office is a nuisance, not one of public utility; an instrument of individual extortion, caprice, and tyranny.*

To avoid these evils, the whole, or a branch, of the police, qualified for the undertaking by previous instruction, should be specially employed in watching over the execution of penal statutes, and who should be the public prosecutors for their violation. No odium would attach to them in consequence, since it would be deemed merely a discharge of part of their official duty incumbent on them to perform. The laws more particularly requiring their superintendence are all local and public acts relative to old and decayed buildings; to street nuisances and disorders; all acts relative to licensed houses; to stage-coaches, carts, carriages, and other vehicles; to counterfeit coin, frauds in weights and measures; adulteration of provisions; evasions of the customs, excise and stamp duties.

Mendicity and vagrancy form two other objects falling within police jurisdiction. Fluctuations in trade, changes in the seasons, the operation of the debtor laws, the arts of impostors, and the profligacy of parents, continually pour into the streets and outskirts of the metropolis a crowd of miserable objects, painful to the spectator and inconsistent with social order. Some of these merit punishment; others are the victims of misfortune, requiring temporary aid, or, perhaps, only advice, to enable them to obtain the assistance which individual benevolence or the law of the country has provided. In

* In the metropolis, a number of persons and places are kept under regular contribution by the informers, who take their rounds every Christmas, to collect annual sums, as hush-money. This is called "keeping them sweet." But it is obvious such a system defeats the purpose of legislation, and whether a law is a living or dead letter—a partial or general enactment—depends on the pleasure of such irresponsible agents as the Byers, the Stringers, and Johnsons!

an opulent and populous community, this mass of wretchedness can only be analysed and disposed of by public authority; it is too extensive an evil to be dealt with by individuals, or even by societies supported by voluntary subscriptions.

The remaining objects of police are too well known to require enumeration,—such as preserving the peace, the prevention of offences, and the apprehension of offenders. We pass on to the fifth proposition, namely, the punishments best calculated to deter from crime and promote the reform of offenders. This is an extensive subject, and might be branched out into many others; but, waiving the more general discussion, we shall restrict our remarks to such points as have occurred to our own observation.

The criminal mind approximates nearest to that of man in a natural state, being more under the influence of feeling than reason, and requires corresponding treatment. With such an organization the precepts of the moralist are mostly unavailing; his reasoning on the superior advantages of virtuous courses is not felt or understood; the moral principle being lost, it is appealing to a sense which has ceased to exist. The only motives which hold out allurements are pleasures to be enjoyed; the only evils dreaded are pains to be endured. Hence, punishments should be corporal rather than mental, and if publicly inflicted, more solemn and appalling they are in the exhibition, and more likely to counterbalance temptations to crime.

In England, the prevalent opinion is, that punishments ought to be softened as a nation advances in refinement; and on this principle painful inflictions, as embowelling, branding, whipping, and the pillory, have been wholly or partially abolished. That such applications ought to be seldom resorted to, and with a due regard to the character of the offender, must be admitted; but doubts may be entertained on the wisdom of their entire removal. However much the general mass of a community may improve, it does not change the nature of the offences committed; murder and robbery continue the same outrages against society, indicate the same depravity, and merit the same punishment, whether perpetrated in a savage or civilized state. Experience, however, will best determine the wisdom of recent ameliorations in the criminal code: if milder inflictions have been found sufficient to prevent crime or its increase, the expediency of the change is proved; if not, the contrary inference must be conceded. Late returns to parliament show that the more atrocious offences against the person have diminished, while those against property have increased: but a longer experience may be necessary to determine whether these are accidental or permanent changes in the character of the criminal calendar. The business of the legislator, in a country where justice is chiefly administered by the people, is to consult the public sentiment; for if his punishments are so exemplary that they excite sympathy for the offender rather than admiration of the justice of the law, they defeat their purpose, like an overcharged gun; on the other hand, he cannot forget that the great purpose of his enactments is not to frame them in accordance with the feelings of those unaware of the precautions essential to their own security, but to protect society at large and diminish crime.

In the task of reforming offenders recent experience begins to evince little success is to be expected. Penitentiary schemes have proceeded on the opinion that the criminal acts from ignorance of his real interests, and that he only requires to be enlightened by precept or example, in order to be reformed. But constituted as he is from nature or previous habits, his own course is probably most conducive to his enjoyment. The pride of a good character, industry, order, and economy, have no charms for him: he lives under a different dispensation; indolence, drinking, and noisy dissipation being his delight, and the praise of associates, as guilty as himself, the only objects of his ambition. Among the vicious and improvident that have fallen under our cognizance, we do not remember having conversed with one who could not assign some reason for his conduct, either in his own natural unfitness for better things, or in urging some sneer or pretext, showing the hypocrisy and folly of more honourable courses. Like every other *caste* of society, criminals have their peculiar code of ethics, which stifles remorse, and makes them self-satisfied. Choice as much as chance has given them their position in the social scale, and we fear that the best precautions society can adopt towards them is in the certainty of punishment, in the strength of our prisons, and in the vigilance of a well-organized police.

Example has, doubtless, some influence on the less hardened offenders. It has been observed above that criminals are generally more accessible to feeling than reason, and hence the spectacle of good or evil acts more forcibly on them than other men. For this reason the classification of prisoners, if pursued on a right principle, cannot fail to be advantageous. In a promiscuous intercourse the old offenders are not only sure to instruct the less initiated, but they usually demean themselves in a way highly pernicious; knowing they have forfeited beyond redemption the esteem and confidence of society, they assume a tone of defiance, recklessness, and gaiety, fascinating and encouraging to the young and less practised delinquent.

Of the kind of punishments likely to be most salutary,

we shall say a few words. Those which inflict corporeal suffering and are terrible in the exhibition are best. Punishments that strike the senses of the multitude, divested of all circumstances that serve to show off the hardihood or mock-heroism of the culprit are likely to make the most useful impression. Above all things, let them be degrading, and such as deprive the criminal of self-esteem. Thieves are the vainest of God's creatures; the applause of their companions for adroitness, cleverness, and boldness, serve them in lieu of the consolations of religion and the admiration of the good. Hence, whatever in dress or treatment tends to exhibit them in a ridiculous light, as subdued or humiliated, is beneficial. Regular and continued hard labour, in the eye of the public, with coarse fare and strict subordination, would in time break the spirit of the fiercest burglar,—it would divest him of insolent pretensions, and though it might not work a reform, would leave a lasting dread of being subjected to similar inflictions.

Mere imprisonment, whether solitary or open, is not calculated to produce much effect on the generality of offenders. Vulgar minds, and of such the great majority of criminals consist, only sink into torpor and inaction when secluded. Divested of their usual excitements, they do not reflect on the past and conceive reformatory resolves for the future,—they only become sluggish and stupid, and on the expiration of their term of imprisonment return, with energies refreshed rather than otherwise, to their old vocation. Labour, order, cleanliness, low fare, strict subjection, limited society,—habits the reverse of those to which they had been accustomed, are much more efficacious.

In the treatment of juvenile offenders, we agree in the correctness of the opinion generally expressed by the magistrates examined by the Police Committee.

These, more particularly than old delinquents, are the creatures of feeling rather than reason; therefore, summary and corporal punishment is the best, administered under such responsible authority as precludes the possibility of abuse. Imprisonment before or after trial can produce nothing but evil to the young fry of depredators, it leads to no salutary reflection, and, if opportunities are afforded for communication with older villains, (as is too often the case in the London prisons) they are inducted into a mere school of delinquency.

Of all punishments devised, that is the best which perpetually ejects the delinquent from the bosom of the society he has offended. Transportation not only holds out the best chance of criminal reform, but is in most accordance with the feelings of a civilized community. For our part, we cannot see why exile should not be applied to almost every description of offence, short of those demanding capital execution. In England this mode of punishment would have two advantages; first, it would prevent the criminal calendar being swelled, as it so frequently is, by the names of delinquents committed for a second or greater number of offences; and, secondly, it would tend to reduce the redundant population, by removing some of the worst members of society.

Advantages would also result to the criminal himself from perpetual banishment. In the first place, he would be severed for ever from his old haunts and associates; and, in the next, by being cut off from all hope of returning to the parent state, he would become identified in interest, feeling, and prospect, with the colony to which he had been transported. The return of convicts from transportation, or even imprisonment, is seldom productive of benefit either to themselves or society. Without character or pecuniary resource, they have scarcely an option between good or evil, and necessity, if not choice, compels them to resort to their former or more aggravated crimes.

Prior, however, to this change being introduced, we would recommend some alteration in the present system of transportation. The punishment itself might be graduated according to the degree of criminality, by different kinds of treatment and labour. We would suggest a new mode of treatment in cases of minor delinquencies,—namely, that an offender be sentenced for a limited term to convict treatment in a penal settlement, and after the expiration of that term, be made a free colonist, subject to the condition of perpetual residence therein, and exile from the mother country.

These seem the chief points connected with preventive punishment: it may be thought our strictures on criminal character are tinctured with harshness and precipitancy; but it is a subject we have often considered, and we do not see how a writer can be useful or conduce to right thinking, unless he honestly states the results of his inquiries. We may be mistaken: the vicissitudes of our own life have afforded some opportunities for judging the dispositions of those classes from whom the criminal ranks are chiefly recruited, and what we have advanced is hazarded merely as the conclusions of our own experience. As reformers, we have not been very successful; we have occasionally mingled with the victims of vice and crime, and have sometimes essayed to warn them of the folly and wretchedness of their course; we obtained acquiescence, but cannot boast of conversions. The experience of others unhappily leads to similar results. The book of Mr. Cunninghame, the failure of the Milbank Penitentiary, the testimony of police justices before parliamentary committees, the late Report to the Surrey Magistrates, and the history and re-committal of returned transports,—all tend to show the hopeless and incorrigible nature of the criminal mind.

Having adverted to the chief matters included under the head of general principles of police, we shall conclude this introductory chapter with some remarks; first, on the insufficiency of the best organized system of police without the aid of individual precaution and co-operation; and, secondly, on the jealousy of the police as inimical to public liberty.

As a general principle, it may be stated that whatever can be done by the ordinary prudence and precaution of individuals, ought never to be left to public authority or regulation. However numerous and vigilant the police, they cannot have the gift of ubiquity, and be present at all times and all places, for the protection of persons and property. The treachery of domestics, and the extraordinary ingenuity of depredators will occasionally lay open the property of individuals in a manner that no watchfulness nor establishments can prevent.

To protect the community from all the offences to which it is exposed; from robbery, theft, fraud, swindling, imposture, adulterations, &c. would require one half of society to watch the other half. Hence, the powers of preventive justice must always be imperfect, and in the great majority of cases individuals must be their own police, and take care of themselves. Such robberies, for example, as those of Grimaldi's, Lund's, Hatton's, and the bankers, which recently excited so much attention,—how could they have been averted under any imaginable system of prevention? Or, again, if individuals will be guilty of the monstrous imprudence of frequenting in a great capital strange company and places, displaying their money, and talking of their private affairs, can it be expected some guardian angel of the police should be always present, to protect them from fraud and violence. All that can be expected from the authorities is the repression of the more open and organized outrages; the lesser and multifarious delinquencies must be left to individuals.

Besides using precaution in protecting their persons and property, it is incumbent on individuals to lend their aid to the civil power in the punishment and apprehension of offenders. In this country the chief criminal administration is confided to the people in the capacity of magistrates, jurors, peace-officers, prosecutors, and witnesses; and, unless they zealously co-operate, it is obvious the most vigilant police and wisest penal code must frequently prove unavailing. Owing either to mistaken humanity, the undistinguishing severity of the criminal law, or to a mere vulgar prejudice against authority, it rarely happens prosecutors and witnesses receive the commendation they deserve for exertions in furthering the ends of justice. But it is obvious they are performing a public duty of the utmost importance, and justly meriting the thanks of the community. For our part, when we hear of a thief or a swindler, or even a brutal coachman or waterman brought to justice by individual efforts, we feel thankful for the service, and think the parties well entitled to the gratitude of their fellow-citizens. It ought never to be forgotten that the mendicant—impostor, sharper, pickpocket, and thief are the natural foes of the really unfortunate, the honest, and industrious, and of that mutual confidence and benevolence which are the great charms of society; and whoever contributes to exterminate them is as much entitled to civic honour as those worthies of antiquity who devoted their lives to rid the world of beasts of prey.

Notwithstanding several defects in metropolitan police, which will be shown in the sequel, it possesses important advantages. Considering the immense wealth and population to be protected, it is hardly possible to imagine a system more economical, or one which interferes so little with individual freedom. In few places the public peace is better preserved, persons and property more generally secure; and, if the prisons are crowded with delinquents, it at once argues the vigilance of the ministerial power and the defects in the ulterior proceedings by which individuals are deterred from the commission of offences. Crimes have multiplied from peculiarities in our condition—the extremes of indigence and opulence—the commercial and enterprising character of the population—the fluctuations in employment and subsistence—the enormous increase in property and population—the uncertainty, and, in many cases, leniency of criminal punishment—reluctance to prosecute offenders—decline of domestic power and superintendence—the avidity of gain—the temptations to luxury and dissipation—and the rivalry in individual expense and ostentation which peculiarly marks the present period.

Of the difficulty of reconciling a more perfect system of preventive justice with the feelings of the people, we have frequent examples in the metropolis, where the rights of individuals are more scrupulously watched than in any other part of the kingdom, and where any infringement of them is promptly visited by public exposure and animadversion. The magistrate is thus often placed in the unpleasant dilemma of either incurring popular odium or a lax discharge of his ministerial duties. While, however, one cannot too highly commend the active jealousy of those who are constantly on the alert to guard against the encroachments of authority, it must be allowed that this feeling may be carried to an extreme, so as to interfere with those precautions essential to the safety of the community. It is impossible, under every circumstance, to distinguish the innocent from the guilty, the virtuous man from a burglar, or a belated female from a street-walker; but it is obvious that regulations made to restrain the vicious will seldom be intentionally applied to the honest citizen ; it follows, if mistakes are committed in the execution of laws, it is more fair to ascribe them to misapprehension or defects inseparable from their administration than a premeditated invasion of public liberty ; and the reflective mind, instead of entering into futile altercations with the agents of power, will consider his personal annoyance a trifling sacrifice to the general safety.

However great the improvements in the condition of society, we are still far from the millenium in which poverty, ignorance, and the violence of the passions are excluded ; and so long as these fruitful sources of crime exist there must always be a portion of the population whose conduct can only be restrained by strict surveillance and the dread of punishment. A great change has, undoubtedly, taken place in the character of the people within the last fifty years, but no one can contemplate the mass of delinquency annually brought before the tribunals of the country without being convinced of the lamentable extent of depravity which still remains. Knowledge, virtue, and order have not so extended their domain as to supersede the necessity of a numerous and energetic police. Indeed, scenes are constantly occurring in London which transcend all preceding instances of daring atrocity, and which one is at a loss to reconcile with the general diffusion of intelligence. Brutal sports have declined more from the coercive interference of the magistrate than any want of encouragement and popular support. So recently as in 1825, numerous bands of desperate characters assembled in the heart of the metropolis, and openly plundered the shops of the inhabitants ; and it was only by the prompt interference of government that the lawless rabble was suppressed. The excesses committed by " Lady Holland's mob," as it is termed, in 1822, and the robberies perpetrated in open day, in a crowded street, only last November, amply show that the ancient leaven of violence and ferocity is not extirpated; and so long as these traits are observable in the character of the populace, every considerate mind must be sensible of the necessity of a powerful police to the safety of the community, and the wisdom of bearing the occasional inquisition of constables, watchmen, and patrols, for the sake of the greater compensating advantages such institutions confer.

While the proceedings of judges and magistrates are open to public observance, and the press so vigilantly and ably exercises its powers, the people are amply secured against the caprice and oppression of authority. To the scrutiny and animadversion of this tribunal, no individual, however high, can be indifferent. Moreover, the magistrates are drawn from the people, with whom, in the private relations of life, they are in constant intercourse, so that any remarkable aberration in their ministerial duties would not only be liable to the cognizance of their immediate friends and connexions, but, also, draw upon them the notice of that superior power by which they are appointed.

Leaving, however, these general observations, we shall come to the more immediate object of the present publication, and, in the following chapters, proceed to develope the actual state and organization of the police of the metropolis. It is a subject little understood by a great portion of the inhabitants, and though not established upon any general principles, or reduced to systematic organization, but resulting from partial and irregular legislation, originating in local circumstances and necessity, and totally unequal to the present wants of the capital, yet it will be found less defective than might have been apprehended from the antiquity and mode of its institution.

CHAPTER II.

EXTENT AND MUNICIPAL DIVISIONS OF THE METROPOLIS.

Population and local Limits of the Metropolis.—Increase of Population since the Census in 1821.—*Municipal and Magisterial Divisions.—Districts of the Public Police Offices.—Hours and Mode of Application.—Superiority of the Metropolitan over the Country Magistracy.*

It is necessary, in order to comprehend our arrangement, and also the police and government of the capital, to be previously informed of the local distribution of its immense population, and the several magisterial jurisdictions into which its civil administration is divided.

The metropolis of the British empire is situated in the two counties of Middlesex and Surrey, and comprehends, within its entire limits, 152 parishes. Of this number, 97 parishes are within the boundary of the ancient walls of the city of London, 16 parishes are without the walls, but under the jurisdiction of the city; 24 are termed the out-parishes in Middlesex and Surrey; 10 parishes are within the city and liberties of Westminster; the remaining 5 parishes are without the bills of mortality, and consist of St. Luke, Chelsea, Kensington, St. Mary-le-bone, Paddington, and St. Pancras.

The terms metropolis, capital, and London, without city annexed, will be invariably used, in the following pages, as synonymous, and understood to comprehend these 152 parishes.

The walls of the ancient city of London included a

space, now in the middle of the metropolis, about one mile and a half in length from east to west, and rather more than half a mile in breadth. The population, within these limits, has diminished three-fifths since the beginning of the last century; many streets have been widened, and public buildings and warehouses erected, whereby the number of inhabited houses has been lessened; independently of which the inhabitants have decreased in a much larger proportion, from the less crowded manner of residence which has gradually taken place.

The city of London, *without* the walls, is an extension of the same ancient boundary and jurisdiction.

The city of Westminster, once an episcopal see, and now the seat of government, adjoins the city of London, extending westward.

The appellation of the Out-Parishes is taken from the London Bills of Mortality, which were first used in the year 1562; and, from 1603, have been kept in regular series. They were intended to afford timely notice of the plague from which London was then seldom free. They purport to exhibit the number of christenings and burials, and the diseases occasioning death, in each parish; but are very defective; some of the largest parishes being excluded; the births and deaths of Dissenters are not mentioned, and the description of diseases, from the reports of the searchers, is inaccurate and unscientific. In these bills, the number of out-parishes is made to amount to 29, by including, under that designation, Kennington, Brixton, Norwood, West Hackney, and Poplar, which are merely hamlets appertaining to the parishes of Lambeth, Hackney, and Stepney. A portion of three of the out-parishes is within the city jurisdiction.

The five parishes without the bills of mortality,

though omitted in the return of the parish-clerks, form an integral part of the capital, and are usually included in acts of parliament, regulating its general police and government.

The following is an alphabetical list of the parishes according to these divisions, and with which it may be useful for residents in London to be acquainted, so that they may know the civil jurisdiction under which they live, and to which they can resort in case of necessity. The population of the parishes is taken from the parliamentary census in 1821.

I.—CITY OF LONDON WITHIN THE WALLS.

Parish	Population
Alban, St. Wood-street	631
Allhallows, Barking	1664
Allhallows, Bread-street	320
Allhallows-the-Great	526
Allhallows, Honey-lane	137
Allhallows-the-Less	98
Allhallows, Lombard-street	580
Allhallows, London-wall	1677
Allhallows-Staining	577
Alphage, near Sion-College	1206
Andrew, St. Hubbard	287
Andrew, St. Undershaft	1161
Andrew, St. by-the-Wardrobe	690
Anne and Agnes, St. Aldersgate	561
Anne, St. Blackfriars	2938
Anthony, St. vulgarly Antholin	365
Augustine, St.	307
Bartholomew, St. Royal Exchange	339
Benedict, St. vulgo Bennet-Fink	511
Bennet, St. Gracechurch-st.	290
Bennet, St. Paul's Wharf	552
Bennet, St. Sherehog	142
Botolph, St. Billingsgate	191
Christchurch	2002
Christopher, St.	84
Clement, St. Eastcheap	273
Dionis, St. Backchurch	791
Dunstan, St. in the East	1155
Edmund, St. the King	442
Ethelburga, St.	704
Faith, St. the Virgin, under St. Paul's	999
Gabriel, St. Fenchurch	343
George, St. Botolph-lane	215
Gregory, St. by St. Paul's	1468
Helen, St. Bishopsgate	696
James, St. Duke's Place	732
James, St. Garlick-hythe	473
John, St. Baptist	417
John, St. Evangelist	86
John, St. Zachary	322
Katharine, St. Coleman	712
Katharine, St. Creechurch (otherwise Christchurch.)	1814
Lawrence, St. Jewry	702
Lawrence, St. Pountney	352
Leonard, St. Eastcheap	307
Leonard, St. Foster-lane (part of.)	377
Magnus, St	227
Magaret, St. Lothbury	331
Magaret, St. Moses	149
Margaret, St. New Fish-st.	344
Margaret, St. Pattens	135
Martin, St. Pomroy, Ironmonger-lane	132
Martin, St. Ludgate	1200
Martin, St. Orgars	350
Martin, St. Outwich	252
Martin, St. Vintry	205
Mary, St. Abchurch	505
Mary, St. Aldermanbury	883

Parish	Population
Mary, St. Aldermary	429
Mary, St. le-Bow	368
Mary, St. Bothaw Dowgate	295
Mary, St. Colechurch	275
Mary, St. at-Hill	818
Mary, St. Magdalen, Old Fish-street	721
Mary, St. Magdalen, Milk-st	300
Mary, St. Mountshaw	358
Mary, St. Somerset	270
Mary, St. Staining	221
Mary, St. Woolchurch-Haw	206
Mary, St. Woolnoth	511
Matthew, St. Friday-street	228
Michael, St. Bassishaw	714
Michael, St. Cornhill	492
Michael, St. Crooked-lane	576
Michael, St. Queenhithe	716
Michael, St. le Quern	252
Michael, St. Paternoster Royal	181
Michael, St. Wood-street	433
Mildred, St. Bread-street.	329
Mildred, St. Poultry	271
Nicholas, St. Acons	180
Nicholas, St. Cole-Abbey	228
Nicholas, St. Olave	350
Olave, St. Hart-street	1012
Olave, St. Old Jewry	239
Olave, St. Silver-street	1135
Pancras, St. Soper-lane	190
Peter, St. Cornhill	731
Peter, St. Paul's Wharf	346
Peter, St. le-Poor, Broad-st.	576
Peter, St. Westcheap	266
Stephen, St. Coleman-street	3062
Stephen, St. Walbrook	278
Swithin, St. London-stone	508
Thomas, St. the Apostle	565
Trinity-the-Less	502
Vedast, St. Foster-lane	398

II.—CITY OF LONDON, WITHOUT THE WALLS.

Parish	Population
Andrew, St. Holborn	6234
Bartholomew, St. the Great	2931
Bartholomew-the-Less	823
Botolph, St. without Aldersgate	4003
Botolph, St. Aldgate	9067
Botolph, St. without Bishopsgate	10140
Bride, St. alias Bridget	7288
Dunstan, St. in-the-West	3549
Giles, St. without Cripplegate	13038
George, St. the Martyr, Southwark	36368
John, St. Horselydown, Southwark	9163
Olave, St. Southwark	8420
Saviour's, St. Southwark	16808
Sepulchre, St. without Newgate	8271
Thomas, St. Southwark	1807
Trinity in the Minories	680

III.—CITY AND LIBERTIES OF WESTMINSTER.

Parish	Population
Anne, St. Soho	15215
Clement, St. Danes	10753
George, St. Hanover-sq.	46384
James, St.	33819
John, St.	16835
Leonard, St. Foster-lane (site of New Post-Office.)	
Margaret, St.	22387
Martin, St. in the Fields	28252
Mary, St. le-Strand	1784
Paul, St. Covent-Garden	5834

IV.—OUT-PARISHES IN MIDDLESEX AND SURREY.

Parish	Population
Andrew, St. Holborn above Bars (part of) with St. George the Martyr	26492
Bermondsey, St. Mary	25235
Bethnal Green, St. Matthew	456676

Botolph without Aldgate .. 6429
Christchurch, Spitalfields . 18650
Christchurch, Surrey 13339
Clement, St. Danes (part of) 4010
Clerkenwell, St. James and St. John 39105
Giles, St. in the Fields, and St. George, Bloomsbury, 51793
George, St. in the East .. 32528
Hackney, St. John 22494
Islington, St. Mary...... 22741
Katharine, St. near the Tower 2624
Lambeth, St. Mary...... 57638
Limehouse, St. Ann 9805
Luke, St. Middlesex 40876
Newington Butts, St. Mary 33047
Rotherhithe, St. Mary .. 12523
Sepulchre, St. (part of) .. 4750
Shadwell, St. Paul 9557
Shoreditch, St. Leonard .. 52966
Stepney, St. Dunstan.... 49163
Wapping, St. John...... 3078
Whitechapel, St. Mary .. 29407

V.—PARISHES WITHOUT THE BILLS OF MORTALITY.

Chelsea, St. Luke 26860
Kensington 14428
Mary-le-Bone, St. 96040
Paddington 6476
Pancras, St............. 71838

The total population of the parishes is less than that of the metropolis exhibited below, because many places are extra-parochial, and not included in the parochial enumeration; such are the inns of court, the royal palaces, and various liberties and precincts: these omissions are included in the subjoined table. It also includes what may be termed the floating population of the metropolis, consisting of strangers from the country and foreign parts, and which are supposed, by Mr. Rickford, to form an addition of one twenty-fifth part to the whole of the resident inhabitants.*

THE METROPOLIS.	1700	1750	1801	1811	1821
1.—City of London *within* the Walls.	139,300	87,000	78,000	57,700	58,400
2.—City of London *without* the Walls	69,000	57,300	56,300	68,000	72,000
3.—City and Liberties of Westminster	130,000	152,000	165,000	168,600	189,400
4.—Out-parishes within the Bills of Mortality..	326,900	357,600	477,700	593,700	730,700
5.—Parishes *not* within the Bills of Mortality..	9,150	22,350	123,000	162,000	224,300
Total of the Metropolis ..	674,350	676,250	900,000	1,050,000	1,274,800

* Population Returns for 1821, Appendix, p. 159.

The erection of new buildings and extensive commercial and other improvements in the metropolis render it highly probable that nothing has occurred to check the progressive addition to the population since 1821; supposing during the last seven years it has increased in the same ratio as in the interval from 1811 to 1821, the number of inhabitants now in the metropolis amounts to 1,492,228.

The population of all the parishes, whose churches are situated within a radius of eight miles round St. Paul's Cathedral, amounted, in 1821, to 1,481,500, the parish of Woolwich not included. This was double the population ascribed to Paris, included in a circle of the same diameter. The same circular area round St. Paul's must now, supposing the same ratio of increase as in the last paragraph, comprise a population of 1,669,741.

The burials have absolutely decreased within the bills of mortality, while the population has increased as three to two. The average deaths in London are about one-fifth less than those in Paris; and the average mortality in the former, a vast and luxurious metropolis, differs only by a small fraction from that of the whole of France.*

Although the population of the suburbs has rapidly increased since the beginning of the century, it has not increased so fast as the kingdom in general. In 1700, the metropolis contained almost one-eighth part of the inhabitants of England and Wales; in 1750 and 1801, about a tenth part; in 1811 and in 1821, about a twelfth part.

Some objections may be made to the limits assigned to the metropolis. For example, there is no good reason why Clapham, Deptford, Greenwich, and other parishes

* Quarterly Review, No. 75, p. 153.

in the environs, and which are connected by almost continuous lines of houses with London, should not be included, as well as the five parishes without the bills of mortality, in the number of metropolitan parishes. In any general system of police no doubt this distinction would be disregarded, and all parishes within a certain lineal distance be included within its operation. A radius of eight miles round St. Paul's seems as expedient a circuit as could be assigned to the metropolis for police purposes, comprehending the most populous places adjoining to it, and beside being a distance capable of patrol by horse or foot, and of ready communication with the public offices.

MUNICIPAL DIVISIONS OF THE METROPOLIS.

Having endeavoured to assign the local limits and population of the metropolis we come next to its magisterial divisions; and first of the city of London, which forms the ancient nucleus of this great capital.

The city of London, as before explained, comprehends within its jurisdiction 113 parishes, and is governed by its own corporation, whose authority is derived from ancient charters, public statutes, and acts of common council. The corporation is chosen, directly or indirectly, from the freemen; and, beside acting generally in the government of the city, it also acts subordinately in the government of the several wards or precincts into which the city is divided. The whole civil and municipal government is vested in this body, no other magistrate or power has any right to interfere, and in all public statutes of the realm the ancient rights, privileges, and customs of the city of London are specially guaranteed.

The borough of Southwark, though anciently an independent corporation, is united to, and within the jurisdiction of, the city of London. Its steward and high-bailiff are appointed by the corporation of the city, and the expense of its justiciary administration is defrayed by an annual grant out of the chamber of London.

The city of Westminster forms an independent jurisdiction, under the superintendence of the dean and high steward of Westminster; these nominate annually the burgesses, who have separately the government of the twelve wards into which this city is divided. The authority of the dean and high steward is only exercised on particular occasions, and the functions of the burgesses have fallen into disuse; the whole of the magisterial duties of Westminster being now discharged by the public police offices.

The parishes beyond the limits, and contiguous to the cities of London and Westminster, may be considered as forming separate municipalities, where the inhabitants regulate the police of their respective districts under the authority of numerous acts of parliament, enabling them to raise money for paving the streets, for watching, cleansing, and removing nuisances. These funds, as well as the execution of the powers of the different acts (except where the interference of magistrates is specially directed), are placed in the hands of trustees, or commissioners, of whom, in many instances, the church-wardens or parish officers for the time being are members, ex officio; and by these bodies all matters relative to the immediate government, safety, and convenience, are managed and regulated. They appoint the beadles, constables, and watchmen of their respective parishes, and fix the rates to be levied for lighting, watching, paving, &c.; their powers, however, are merely parochial; all matters of a civil or criminal character, requiring the interference of a magistrate, being brought to one of the public offices, of which we shall next speak.

The jurisdiction of the police offices extends throughout the metropolis (the city of London excepted). These offices are nine in number, situated in different sections of the capital; and belonging to each office are three magistrates, appointed and paid by the crown. By these twenty-seven magistrates, aided by the aldermen of the corporation of London, who act in rotation within the city jurisdiction, nearly the entire ministerial and judicial duties of the metropolitan magistracy are discharged. Every complaint or offence demanding magisterial interference falls within the jurisdiction of the city or of one of the police offices, and to which an application should be made depends on the locality of the offence, being within or without the bounds of the city.

The police districts, including the city of Westminster, the out-parishes and the five parishes without the bills of mortality, embrace the greatest portion of the metropolis; the number of inhabitants in these districts amounted, in 1821, to 1,071,834; the number in the city jurisdiction at the same period to 202,966. But these numbers do not express the relative proportion of business in the two jurisdictions; that must be influenced by other circumstances,—the description as well as the number of the inhabitants—the vigilance of their respective police—the amount of property—and the extent and activity of commercial dealings. A vast mass of business to the public offices arises from nocturnal offences connected with the theatres, gaming-houses, houses of ill-fame, night-houses, and hackney-coaches. On the other hand, the city business preponderates in the class of offences originating in property, in bill transactions, in forgeries, frauds, banking, shipping, bankruptcy, and insurance. Whoever has attended the public offices, either within or without the city, cannot fail to have remarked that abundance of questions daily occur in this vast metropolis fully to occupy the magistrates of each establishment.

In the year 1792, when seven of the police offices were established, the justices then appointed described limits, comprising a certain space surrounding each office, without regard to the parishes. The object of this was to promote the convenience of the public, and also the magistrates, by an equal apportionment of business to each office; and the general practice is to discourage the applications of persons preferring complaints where the offence was committed, or the parties resided out of the district so described. This rule is not invariably observed; still, as applicants are frequently sent from one office to another, on account of this agreement of the magistrates, it will be useful to insert in this place the local districts of the several police offices. The districts are not very accurately defined below, though founded on a return made by the magistrates to parliament:* the same parish, in one or two instances, being placed in the limits of different offices.

Queen-square Office, Westminster.

The district of this office comprises the south side of Piccadilly, in the parish of St. James; also the south side of the western road, in the parishes of St. George, Hanover-square; St. Luke, Chelsea; and Kensington; that part of the parish of St. Martin-in-the-Fields west of Leicester-square to Coventry-street; and the whole of the parishes of St. Margaret and St. John the Evangelist.

Great Marlborough-street Office.

St. James, Westminster.
St. George, Hanover-square.
St. Giles-in-the-Fields and St. George, Bloomsbury.

* Report on the Nightly Watch and Police of the Metropolis, A.D. 1812, p. 30.

St. Mary-le-bone.
St. Pancras west of Tottenham-court-road.
St. Anne, Westminster.

Hatton-garden Office.

St. James, Clerkenwell.
St. John, Clerkenwell.
St. Luke, Old-street.
St. Martin-le-Grand.
St. Sepulchre (Middlesex).
United Parishes of St. Andrew, Holborn, and St. George the Martyr.
Liberty of Saffron-hill.
United Parishes of St. Giles-in-the-Fields and St. George, Bloomsbury.
St. Clement Danes, including Duchy Liberty and Westminster Liberty.
St. Pancras.

Worship-street Office.

St. Leonard, Shoreditch.
St. Luke, Middlesex.
St. Mary, Islington.
St. John, Hackney.
St. Mary, Stoke Newington.
St. Matthew, Bethnal-green.
Christchurch (Middlesex), Spitalfields.
Hamlet of Mile-End New Town.
Liberty of the Old Artillery-ground.
Liberty of Norton Falgate.

Whitechapel Office.

St. Mary, Whitechapel.
St. Botolph without Aldgate.
Trinity, Minories.
St. Mary, Stratford-le-Bow.
Bromley, St. Leonard.
Hamlet of Mile End Old Town.
Hamlet of Mile End New Town.
Precinct of St. Katharine.
Precinct of Tower Without.
Precinct of Wellclose.

Shadwell Office.

St. George, Middlesex.
St. John, Wapping.
St. Paul, Shadwell.
St. Anne, Limehouse.
Hamlet of Ratcliff, }
Hamlet of Poplar, } in the parish of St. Dunstan, Stepney.
Hamlet of Blackwall, }

Union-hall Office.

St. Saviour.
St. George.
St. Olave.
St. John.
St. Thomas.
Newington.
Lambeth.
Christchurch.
Bermondsey.
Rotherhithe.
Camberwell.
Clapham.
Streatham.
Manor of Hatcham.

Thames Office, Wapping.

The district of this office is confined to the river, and the quays, docks, wharfs, and shores adjacent. It has three principal stations; one at Somerset-House, the centre station at Wapping, and that below at Blackwall. The line of river under its more immediate look-out extends from Vauxhall to Woolwich, but its officers frequently go beyond these points. Three boats are constantly out at night plying on the river between each station. Its powers extend to both banks of the river, with the exception of the space from Tower-stairs to the Temple, which is in the jurisdiction of the city. The office is kept open during the whole of the night, and one of the surveyors attends to be ready in case of fire or other emergency. The district patrolled by the land-officers comprises the parishes of Wapping, Shadwell, and St. Botolph-without-Aldgate, the hamlet of Ratcliffe, and the precinct of St. Katharine.

Bow-street Office.

This office has not any defined district; it will be seen, in the next chapter, that its duties are of a more extensive and diversified character than those of the foregoing establishments, and its officers are frequently despatched into the country, to Scotland and Ireland, and even to the Continent, for the apprehension of offenders. Two of the patrol, in rotation, keep nightly watch at this office, and, in case any application is made during the night relative to any atrocious offence or serious occurrence, they call up one of the principal officers, who gives advice and assistance, and acts according to the best of his judgment.

From the above description of the municipal and magisterial divisions of the metropolis, individuals will be apprized to what office it is proper to apply under circumstances requiring judicial cognizance or the aid of the civil power. If the occurrence is within the jurisdiction of the City, application must be made either at the justice-room, Guildhall, or at the Mansion-house, according as it is on the east or west side of King-street. Without the city, application must be made to one of the police offices situated in the district in which the offence or complaint originated. On the Surrey side of the metropolis application must be made to the sitting alderman at the Town-hall, if in any of the five parishes of the borough of Southwark; if not to the magistrate at Union-hall. But if the case in the Borough requires the presence of two magistrates, application had better be made at Union-hall, as two magistrates are required to attend there daily, and they have concurrent jurisdiction in the borough with the city magistrates.

The usual hours of business are from eleven in the morning till three in the afternoon. One of the police magistrates is required by statute to attend each office by ten o'clock in the morning, but we have never found them at so early an hour; the deficiency being generally made up by prolonged attendance in the afternoon. Should the case require the presence of two magistrates to determine, application ought not to be made earlier than twelve o'clock.

Strangers, without business requiring their attendance, are not usually admitted into the police offices, but, with business, access to the magistrates is easy, and advice or assistance readily afforded. Should the case be a public offence, requiring magisterial interference, as a nuisance, or the like, the best mode of proceeding is to acquaint the beadle or street-keeper of the parish, who will bring the matter before the proper tribunal. Criminal offences on the river, the docks, and wharfs, must be brought before the magistrates of the Thames-street office, Wapping; but if the complaint refers merely to the conduct of watermen, or any violation of the act by which they are regulated, it will be heard by the court at Watermen's-hall, the lord mayor, or any justice of the district in which the transaction occurred.

Bow-street and Thames-street offices are alone open for applications through the night, and these only for occasions of such importance as the watchmen or patrol on the spot are inadequate to meet.

As regards police and judicial administration, the inhabitants of the metropolis have many advantages over those residing in the country. Criminal trials are more frequent, and they have a permanent magistracy, always to be found at a certain place and a certain time, and who render their services not as a gratuitous offering, but a duty they are bound to perform. Moreover, they enjoy the inestimable advantage of having every justiciary act performed in the most open and public manner, and, by the agency of the press, of having it brought, within a few hours after adjudication, under the comment and observation of an intelligent and almost innumerable population. With such publicity, the caprice, delay, and oppressions of authority can hardly have place: it is alike advantageous to magistrates and applicants—to the former in securing them the just rewards of talent and probity in the esteem of their fellow-citizens; and to the latter, in the consciousness that, however the result of their application may have been contrary to their own pre-conceived opinions, justice has been promptly and fairly administered.

CHAPTER III.

POLICE ESTABLISHMENTS.

Origin and Progress of the Police of the Metropolis.—Number, Salaries, and Organization of the Police of the City of London.—Police of the City of Westminster.—Police of the Out-Parishes and Vicinity of the Metropolis.—Government Police, including the Nine Public Offices and the Bow-Street Patrol.—Borough of Southwark.—Total Number and Expense of the Metropolitan Police.

LEGISLATION may either proceed on general principles, with a view to prospective contingencies, or it may act under present circumstances, and its measures be framed solely to control existing evils. Which of these modes of procedure is best adapted to meet the exigencies of society, forms too theoretic an inquiry to be entertained in this place. The measures applicable to the police of the metropolis appear to have been generally framed on the latter principle, and intended to control existing inconveniences rather than to establish a general and permanent system of civic regulation. It follows that changes in manners, the increase in commerce and population, and the extension of local boundaries, have constantly required new measures of regulation, and that from an early period the government of the capital has formed an important subject of legislative inquiry and interference.

The earliest police enactment is the 13th Edward I. A.D. 1285, called *Statuta Civitatis*, London, and which, among other preventive measures, enjoins that no one shall appear abroad, with sword and buckler, or in any other manner, after curfew tolled at St. Martin's-le-Grand.* This act applies only to the city, which then comprised the whole of the metropolis. In the 27th of Elizabeth, the city of Westminster became a subject of preventive legislation, and to the statute of that year Lord Burleigh appended a variety of regulations affecting the exercise of trades, nuisances, and other annoyances, and directed that every inhabitant should, at night, keep a lantern at his door. Passing over several charters and statutes, the next important epoch in metropolitan regulation was the establishment of the police offices, whose local jurisdiction embraced the extreme limits of the metropolis. It has, also,

* This statute is omitted in the common edition of the statutes, but is reprinted in the statutes of the realm, under the authority of the commissioners on the state of the public records, and is inserted in the Appendix to the Police Report of 1812, page 9. The following is an extract from this magna charta of city jurisprudence:—

"Whereas, many evils, as murders, robberies, and manslaughters have been committed heretofore in the city by night and by day, and people have been beaten and evil entreated, and divers other mischiefs have befallen against his peace; it is enjoined that none be so hardy as to be found going or wandering about the streets of the city after curfew tolled at St. Martin's-le-Grand, with sword or buckler, or other arms for doing mischief, or whereof evil suspicion might arise, nor any in any other manner, unless he be a great man, or other lawful person of good repute, or their certain messenger, having their warrants to go from one to another with lantern in hand. And if any be found going about, contrary to the form aforesaid, unless he have cause to come late into the city, he shall be taken by keepers of the peace, and be put into the place of confinement appointed for such offenders; and on the morrow he shall be brought and presented before the warden or mayor of the city for the time being, and before the aldermen, and according as they shall find he hath offended, and as the custom is, he shall be punished." The statute also directs that taverns shall not be kept open after curfew; that none shall teach fencing and buckler within the city, on pain of twenty days' imprisonment; and that foreigners shall not be innkeepers, nor brokers, unless made free of the city.

formed a frequent subject of parliamentary inquiry: in 1772, Sir John Fielding was examined by a committee of the House of Commons on the increase of robberies and burglaries in London. But during more recent periods, in 1812 and succeeding years, the subject has been explored in all its ramifications, and the investigations of the committees of the House of Commons extended not only into the state of the police, but, also, into every collateral inquiry, including the state of education, mendicity, female prostitution, juvenile delinquencies, the licensing of public-houses, prison discipline, parliamentary rewards for the apprehension of criminals, the effects of the penetentiary system, &c. The reports of these committees comprise an immense mass of information on the state of this great capital to which we shall often refer: in the present chapter we shall give an account of the different establishments for the maintenance of the public peace and the detection and prevention of crime. They may be classed under the following heads:—

1.—*Police of the City of London.*
2.—*Police of the City of Westminster.*
3.—*Police of the Out-Parishes and Vicinity of the Metropolis.*
4.—*Public Police Offices and Patrol Establishment.*
5.—*Borough of Southwark.*

1.—POLICE OF THE CITY.

The police of the city of London consists of the general police for the city, subject to the immediate superintendence of the Lord Mayor and Aldermen, and paid by the chamber of London, and the police of each separate ward, under the immediate control of the alderman, deputy, and common-councilmen, of the respective wards, and paid by a rate upon each ward. The act which principally regulates the nightly watch is the 10 Geo. II. c. 22, under which the corporation is directed yearly to make regulations on the subject, and the alderman and common council in each ward are to carry these regulations into effect, and to make such minor regulations, as to details, as they may judge necessary. The act also specifies the duties of constables and watchmen and prescribes the mode of punishment for neglect. Morning reports, on the state of the police, are made to the lord mayor, as the chief magistrate; deficiencies are noticed, as well as any disorder, irregularity, or material occurrence, in the night.

Two offices are appropriated to the purposes of police; and, for the greater convenience of the magistrates, the city is divided into two districts. All cases which occur to the eastward of King-street are taken to the lord mayor, at the Mansion-house; and all cases to the westward to the sitting alderman at Guildhall. The lord mayor always presides in his own court; and the aldermen take it in rotation to preside at Guildhall. The weekly rota of the aldermen at Guildhall is fixed at the commencement of each mayoralty; they usually sit from twelve o'clock till the business requiring their attendance is concluded, and on every day, except Sunday, Good Friday, and Christmas-day. The aldermen receive no pecuniary compensation for the discharge of their magisterial duties.

The officers of police, under the lord mayor and aldermen, are the upper and under marshals, marshalmen, day-patrol, night-patrol, and Smithfield-patrol.

The business of the two marshals is to attend the lord mayor on all public occasions; to attend all courts of aldermen and common-council, also the sessions at the Old Bailey; and to superintend the general direction of the city police. They are appointed by the lord mayor, aldermen, and common-council. The yearly salary of the upper marshal is £500, of the under marshal £450; but the amount of their other emoluments is uncertain.

The business of the marshalmen is similar to that of the marshals, but they are solely under their directions, and serve the summonses and the warrants issued from the offices. They have a salary of £130 per annum, and are appointed by the same authority as the marshals.

The day-patrol are twenty-three in number, and appointed by the lord mayor. Their pay, with some small emoluments incident to their appointment, averages £1 : 15 per week. Their duties are to patrol the streets from ten o'clock in the morning until eight o'clock in the evening; to apprehend all thieves, rogues, and vagrants, and to act generally under the orders given by the magistrates. Two of them attend daily at the Mansion-house, and two at the justice-room, Guildhall; the remainder patrol in pairs the several districts to which they are weekly appointed. A portion of them patrol the city on Sundays, and receive extra pay.

The night-patrol are sixteen in number, and appointed by the lord mayor; they are paid £1 : 11 : 6 per week, and patrol the streets from six in the evening until one in the morning; visiting each watch-house, and reporting to the marshals the misconduct of any, and the state of the public-houses. They come on duty again at six in the morning, and continue until they are relieved by the day-patrol.

The Smithfield-patrol are appointed by the lord mayor; they are eight in number, and paid 10*s.* a-week each. Their only duty is to attend at Smithfield on Mondays and Fridays, during the time of the market.

Besides the corporation police, which, from the nature of its establishment, has a general superintendence, each ward appoints a certain number of beadles, watchmen, patrol, constables, and street-keepers, who are paid by a rate levied upon the inhabitants of the ward, and are appointed to patrol the streets, and to fulfil the duties of a nightly watch within their respective wards. The number of these officers varies according to the size of each ward; but their respective duties and mode of appointment are much the same, and may be thus described.

The beadle is an officer annually elected by the inhabitants of each ward, with a salary varying from £50 to £90 a-year, according to the extent of his duties; his office is to set the nightly watch, to collect the watch-rate, to attend the alderman and common-council upon all ward business, and to superintend the constable of the night and the watch.

The constables are elected in rotation from the inhabitants of the ward, who sometimes serve in person, but generally provide substitutes, which substitutes, however, must be approved of by the alderman and common council of the ward, and who receive from their principals a sum varying from £8 to £15 a-year. They must attend in rotation during the night at the watch-house; and the whole body is under the orders of the city marshals on any public occasion. They serve without salary, but when called out on any particular occasion, receive 3*s*. a-day. The same persons are mostly chosen for deputies every year, from the smaller class of shop-keepers.

In most of the wards a patrol is established, varying in number, whose duty is to patrol the ward from four or five in the afternoon until the watch is set. In some wards the patrol is continued through the whole night, and acts as a check upon the watch. The salary varies according to the duty performed by them.

The watchmen are appointed by the alderman and common-council of the ward, on producing a certificate of good character, signed by two respectable housekeepers; no person above forty years of age can be appointed; and care is taken to employ none but able-bodied men. Their pay, as well as the number of hours they remain on watch, vary with the season of the year. As in most of the wards watch-boxes are not allowed, the men must be constantly on the alert, and are relieved, in succession, at certain periods of the night. A watchhouse-keeper is employed, in some wards, to keep the watchhouse clean and in good order, and is occasionally employed as a constable. In some wards, too, besides the regular watchmen, there is an extra number, who attend every night, to supply the place of any regular watchman who may be ill, or unable to attend: these men, if employed, receive the regular pay; if not wanted, they receive three pence, and are dismissed.

Almost every ward has a street-keeper, who attends from eight in the morning till the patrol comes on duty, and whose peculiar business is to remove any nuisances from, and to prevent any impediments in, the streets, from carts and coaches. In some wards they have an additional officer, called the night-sergeant, for the purpose of perambulating the ward in a private manner, at intervals during the night, to look after the watch.

The inquest-jury may be also mentioned as forming a part of the police of each ward. It consists of a certain number of persons, chosen annually at a ward-mote, by the inhabitants, from among themselves; they cannot perform this office by deputy, but, upon refusal to serve, are liable to indictment. The general duties of the inquest are to present all nuisances, disorderly houses, brothels, persons who are carrying on trade, not being free of the city, or liverymen; to superintend weights and measures; and to make a presentment of these objects of their jurisdiction to the court of aldermen. It is also said the right of appointing individuals eligible to the city juries is vested in the inquest.

The preceding account of the city police is chiefly founded on the Report of a Committee of the House of Commons, in 1822, (Parl. Papers, vol. iv. No. 440); since then, some alterations have been made which it will be proper shortly to notice.

Owing to the alarming increase of burglaries and other depredations, in 1827, efforts were made to improve the night-watch of the city. The number of the night-watch, including patrols, beadles, &c. was 758; the charge was £35,240. Great defects prevailed in the mode of watching and patrolling; the watch, in different wards, was disproportionate to their size, and long intervals occurred in the twenty-four hours, during which there was no protection either for persons or property. With a view to improvements, a committee was appointed, which, on the 20th September, made a report to the common-council, stating the defects of the existing practice, and recommending certain alterations: the substance of the "Report on the Nightly-Watch" was as follows:—

That the day-patrol do not come on duty before nine o'clock in the morning, nor remain on duty later than seven o'clock in the evening; during the intervals between these hours and those when the nightly watch is on duty, which intervals consist, in some cases, of eight, and in no case less than four hours, out of twenty-four, the city is left entirely without protection.

That a number of patrols, not exceeding one-fourth, nor less than one-eighth of the number of watchmen, in each ward, be appointed to patrol in the intervals of the day-patrol and nightly-watch being on duty; and that these districts, for this purpose, be accurately defined by the alderman, deputy, and common-council of each ward. Such patrols to come on duty in November, December, January, and February, at five in the evening, and remain till the watch is set, and to come again one hour before the watch leave, and remain till eight o'clock, when the day-patrol should come on.

That the general watch should remain on duty during the following hours:—

From	Nov. 10 to Feb. 10,	from	8	in the evening	to 7	in the morning.
,,	Feb. 10 to May 10,	,,	8	,,	6	,,
,,	May 10 to Aug. 10,	,,	9	,,	5	,,
,,	Aug. 10 to Nov. 10,	,,	8	,,	6	,,

That the stations of the watchmen should be decided by lot, in every ward, nightly; and no watchman should be two nights, in succession, on the same beat.

That a system of relief, of two hours out upon duty and one hour in, should be adopted.

That the regulations of 10 Geo. II. requiring the alderman, &c. to set down, in writing, the stands of the watchmen and the number of rounds, so that each beat should be traversed, at least once every quarter of an hour, should be enforced.

That a superintendent of every six, or at most ten watchmen should be appointed to see the watch in all respects do their duty.

That one fixed rate of payment, at two-pence-halfpenny per hour, be adopted.

That no watch-boxes be allowed.

That notice of the discharge of any watchman, for neglect of duty, be given to the marshals, to prevent him being employed by any other ward.

These propositions were adopted by the common-council of the City, and, with some unimportant modifi cations, have been generally carried into effect through the wards of the city.

II.—CITY OF WESTMINSTER.

In the police of the city of Westminster the same gradation of the different officers of police and the same subdivision of districts do not prevail, and, consequently, there is not that unity of action upon which the maintenance of public order depends: it was attempted to be introduced in the different acts for the regulation of the police, but, owing to the city of Westminster never having been incorporated, the means for introducing efficiency and control throughout this great district have failed. At present, however, there is a general police, under the superintendence of the dean and high steward of Westminster; and a parochial police, maintained by the different parishes.

By the 27th of Elizabeth, confirmed by the 29 Geo. II. c. 25, the city of Westminster is divided into twelve wards; and the dean or high steward nominates, annually, on Thursday, in Easter week, twelve persons, being merchants, artificers, or persons carrying on trade within the city, to be burgesses. Every person chosen a burgess is obliged to serve, under a penalty of £10, and take upon himself the government of a ward. After his first election, he is regularly nominated from year to year, and is not removable, unless for misconduct. The dean or high steward, with the assistance of these burgesses, chooses twelve other persons, who are called assistant burgesses, and form the court called the Court of Burgesses. The statute gives them the power to act as magistrates within the city and liberties, but, since the establishment of the public-offices, that power has fallen into disuse, and they exercise no magisterial function at present, except in the regulation of weights and measures, and removing nuisances and annoyances.

The act of Elizabeth also empowers the dean or high steward to issue his precept to the high bailiff to summon a court leet annually. That court returns the names of 160 tradespeople to the court of burgesses, and the court, out of the number, choose 80 to act as constables. All persons carrying on trade are liable to perform this duty, (except victuallers,) under a penalty of £8. The duties, however, of persons, so nominated, are mostly performed by deputy, but this permission is only granted upon satisfactory excuse being made by the principal, and all deputies are reported to and must be approved by the court of burgesses. The allowance to a deputy, from his principal, appears not to exceed £5 or £6.

The constables are liable to be called out on all public occasions; they attend constantly at the House of Commons during the sitting of Parliament; they attend, also, during elections in the city of Westminster; since the establishment of the police-offices they are not employed in the detection of offenders; they receive no salary from the dean of Westminster, but, when employed on any public occasion, such as attending the King on the opening of Parliament, or attending at a drawing-room or levee, they receive from the Board of Green Cloth a gratuity, at the rate of 5*s.* or 2*s.* 6*d.* a-day. They also receive an annual gratuity of £6 : 6 from the Speaker of the House of Commons.

The dean and chapter have no control over the parochial police and nightly watch. With respect to this branch of police, the same kind of establishment almost prevails in every parish, varying, of course, according to the extent and population of the district. The establishment consists generally of beadles, constables, headboroughs, street-keepers, and watchmen. The general duties of these officers are similar to those in the city of London; and they are appointed sometimes by the inhabitants in vestry assembled, sometimes by trustees under local acts, or at a court-leet. The watch is regulated by the 14 Geo. II. c. 90, which extends to the city and liberties of Westminster and certain parishes named therein, and prescribes, with great detail, the duties, numbers, and rate of wages of the persons to be employed as watchmen in such parishes. No alteration has been made in the act, except in the power given to the police-magistrates to suspend a watchman in case of misconduct, and making any one ineligible to the appointment above forty years of age.

In some of the parishes the nightly police is better regulated than others, chiefly by the exertions of individuals. In the parish of St. James, they employ chiefly Chelsea pensioners for watchmen, who, from habits of discipline imbibed in the army, and, from the allowance of their pensions, being not obliged to work in the day-time, make the best guardians of the night. In St. George's, Hanover-square, they have eighty watchmen under forty years of age, and an early watch of fifty more during the four winter months, besides patrols and supernumeraries.

III.—POLICE OF THE OUT-PARISHES AND VICINITY OF THE METROPOLIS.

The police of the out-parishes in Middlesex and Surrey is similar to that of the parishes in the city of Westminster, consisting mostly of beadles, constables, watchmen, and headboroughs. These parishes are governed by local acts of parliament, authorising the raising of rates for watching and lighting, and vesting powers in certain commissioners, or in vestries, for carrying these purposes into effect: but, in many cases, the execution of these local acts is extremely defective; in some, the power of raising money is inadequate; in others, the full amount is not levied; the mode of watching is generally bad, and the men employed, both in number and ability, wholly inefficient for the purpose. In short, their police is very defective, though forming a large part of the metropolis; not having been brought into municipal organization, there is no gradation of officers, co-operation, or uniformity; and the security of the persons and property in these opulent districts is left to the caprice and abuse of unpaid and irresponsible authorities, who are only partially interested in the neglect of the power and trust confided to them.

In some of the five parishes without the bills of mortality the police is well regulated. In St. Pancras, there are 161 watchmen employed, of good character, not exceeding forty years of age, and twenty-four sergeants of night, or patrols, who have each a proportion of watchmen to muster and superintend every night. In St. Mary-le-bone, they have also sergeants of the night and 180 watchmen; each watchman must be under forty, have served his Majesty, and produce a character of good conduct from an officer. The cost of the parochial police of this parish, paid out of the poor-rates, averaged, during the last three years, £9,160. The watch-rate in St. Pancras is raised, by commissioners, under local acts.

In parishes not forming part of the metropolis, but in its immediate vicinity, the parochial government and police is inferior to what prevails in the metropolitan parishes. In some of these parishes is no night police whatever; in others, only one or two watchmen are kept during winter months, and paid out of voluntary subscriptions collected from the inhabitants. In Deptford, containing a population of 20,000 inhabitants, and almost connected with the metropolis by continuous lines of houses, there is not a single watchman or other authority charged with the distinct duty, during the night, of preventing crime or apprehending offenders.* In the parish of Edgware, only a few watchmen are employed during winter, and they are paid by subscriptions. Fulham, including Hammersmith, contains

* Report on the Police of the Metropolis, p. 26. A.D. 1828.

upwards of 15,000 inhabitants, and there are neither watchmen nor patrols. In Croydon, containing 11,000 inhabitants, there are only a few private watchmen and inefficient constables; and, from a singular parsimony, the inhabitants lately ceased lighting the town. No magistrate resides here; and those in the neighbourhood are gentlemen in business, difficult to meet with. The petty sessions for the hundred, consisting of thirteen parishes, ought to be held weekly, in Croydon, but are often adjourned, for want of justiciary attendance; in consequence of which, an order of affiliation or removal cannot be signed, and persons detained in the gaol, on mere charges, may be kept there a fortnight, or more, before the least inquiry into their guilt or innocence.

These, and many others in the vicinity, may be considered part of the metropolis, for the purposes of police, differing as to their circumstances, the character of their population, and the frequency of crime from country parishes.

IV.—PUBLIC OFFICES OF POLICE AND PATROL.

The nine boards of magistracy have a concurrent jurisdiction, not only in the metropolis, but through the counties of Middlesex, Essex, Surrey, and Kent. Of these boards, that at Bow-street is the oldest established, and considered the chief both from the superior experience of its magistrates, and the skill and address of its officers. Seven of the remaining boards were established in 1792, and were intended to remedy the inconvenience felt in many parts of the metropolis, from the want of some regularly constituted tribunals for the distribution of justice; where the system should be uniform and where the purity of the magistrates and their regular attendance might insure to applicants a prompt and economical adjudication of their complaints and gratuitous advice, as well as official aid, in all cases within their respective districts. The Thames-office was established in 1800, to check depredations and other unlawful practices committed on the river.

Prior to the institution of the regular offices, the greatest abuses prevailed in the metropolitan police. Without the jurisdiction of the city there were no authorities to which the inhabitants could resort with confidence; the attendance of the resident magistrates was uncertain, and their decisions frequently contradictory. Moreover a gross system of pecuniary corruption had become notorious in the proceedings of the acting justices: persons of opulence and character were unwilling to be burthened with magisterial duties, and the office fell into the hands of those who sought it, merely as a means of subsistence. The salaries of these were inadequate, and their chief emolument arose from fees levied on the applicants. Hence arose the opprobrious appellation of *trading justices*;* the magistrates seeking to swell their incomes by sinister exactions, and encouraging litigation. All such impure stimulants to exertion were abolished under the new act; the police justices were paid a fixed salary, and the fees were carried into one fund, to be applied to the general expense of their establishments. The beneficial effects of the new system were soon apparent, by a decrease of nearly one half in the number of recognizances in the year following their establishment.†

Three magistrates are attached to each office, who may be assisted by such of the country magistrates as think proper to attend; and they have a suitable establishment of clerks, constables, office-keepers, messengers, gaolers, and door-keepers. The offices have no connexion or communication with each other; each acting independently in its own jurisdiction, unless par-

* Annual Register, vol. xxxiv. page 157.

† Lambert's History and Survey of London, vol. iii. page 524.

ticular circumstances require a general co-operation. With the exception of Bow-street office, one or more magistrates are required by act of parliament, to attend every day from ten o'clock in the morning until eight o'clock in the evening; and not fewer than two justices are to attend every day at each office, from twelve o'clock at noon until three in the afternoon. Their duties embrace the ordinary functions of justices of the peace, being empowered to convict and punish with fine or imprisonment, in the various cases of vagrancy—excise, stamp, hackney-coach, game or poor laws, disorderly houses, or apprentices—friendly societies—journeymen leaving their employment—quakers, or others, refusing to pay tithes. Their duties also extend to licensing public-houses, charging, instructing, and swearing-in parochial constables—issuing summonses—binding over to prosecute—considering cases of poor persons applying for admission into workhouses—attending general and quarter sessions of the peace—and visiting prisons and houses of correction. In addition to which many criminal cases occur in the course of a year which are examined for the purpose of being sent before superior tribunals for trial; such as charges of treason, murder, coining, forging, burglary, rape, &c.

The constables, or police officers, as they are more frequently termed, have extensive duties to discharge; and may act as constables in the four counties of Middlesex, Essex, Kent, and Surrey. Two are mostly in attendance at each office; others are employed in serving summonses, in apprehending and searching after delinquents, and occasionally in visiting public-houses and patrolling the streets. The duties of these belonging to Bow-street are of more general and diversified character. They are frequently despatched to different parts of the kingdom, to apprehend offenders, and even to the Continent or America. They are also allowed, on the application of private individuals or country magistrates, to aid them in the discovery of crime. Two of them are in constant attendance about the royal household ; they attend occasionally at the Custom-house, Excise, Stamp, and Post-offices ; and one attends at the Bank of England every quarter when the dividends are paid.

Each magistrate receives a salary of £800 per annum. The chief magistrate at Bow-street has additional allowances for attending at the Home-office ; and for superintending the patrol. The chief-clerk has a salary of £240 per annum, and £60 for editing the Hue and Cry Gazette ; the second Clerk £200. The constables are paid 25*s*. weekly ; this, however, is deemed only a retaining fee, their chief emoluments being derived from other sources. The officers attending the king's court have each a salary of £200 ; those attending the public offices or the theatres are paid one guinea per day. They receive considerable sums from individuals employing them in town or country. They have also their regular perquisites on serving summonses, the rewards allowed by parliament on the conviction of offenders, and their expenses for attending trials as witnesses.

The appointment to nearly all offices in the police is vested in the secretary of state for the home department. He appoints the magistrate and chief-clerk ; and the subordinate officers, with the exception of the door-keepers, gaolers, and an assistant-messenger, are nominated by the justices, subject to his approval.

Nearly the same number of individuals is on the establishment of each office. The total number of magistrates is twenty-seven ; there are three clerks at Bow-street, and two at each of the remaining offices ; eight police officers are attached to each office with the exception of Union-hall and Great Marlborough-street, at which there are twelve officers each. The establishment of the Thames-police is different from the rest; besides the three magistrates and two clerks, it comprises seventeen surveyors, six land constables, and forty-five river constables, with an additional establishment of six surveyors and twenty watermen above bridge and at Blackwall. There are, also, sworn in and acting under the authority of these magistrates sixty-seven persons paid by the several dock-companies and Regent's canal-company.

Connected with the office at Bow-street, and under the superintendence of the chief magistrate of that office, are the horse-patrol, mounted and dismounted, and the several bodies of the foot-patrol.

The *horse-patrol* was first established in consequence of the frequency of highway robberies committed on the roads round London, and formed in the year 1805, by Sir Richard Ford, who was then chief magistrate at Bow-street. The patrols were stationed on the great roads leading to and within twenty miles of the metropolis; and the immediate environs, within the distance of four or five miles, were patrolled by the foot patrol. In 1821, the alarming increase of street robberies within the metropolis, and the consequent necessity of confining the exertions of the foot-patrol within narrower limits, led to a considerable and beneficial change in the establishment of the horse and foot patrol. The horse-patrol still continued the performance of the duties originally assigned to it on the principal roads; but the establishment of *dismounted* patrol was connected with them, on whom the charge of patrolling the environs of London devolved. The foot-patrol by whom that duty had been previously executed were confined to the streets of the metropolis. By these means a general reconnoissance is maintained over the area of a circle of forty miles diameter, first by the street-patrol, in the streets of the metropolis; and next by the dismounted patrol, who, from the environs, keep up the chain of communication with the horse-patrol, whose range extends twenty miles into the country.

In all appointments to the mounted and dismounted patrol the individual appointed must not exceed thirty-five years of age, unless he has served in a cavalry regiment, nor in that case if he be above forty years of age. Such of the dismounted men as are qualified supply the vacancies that occur in the mounted branch; the number of the former, including inspectors, is 101; of the latter 60. The dismounted are divided into parties of five, one of whom is leader, and each party has a line of road to watch, extending from the town to the junction with the horse-patrol. There are four inspectors to see the latter perform their duty, and who go on uncertain roads at uncertain hours, to see the men are on the alert.

These establishments are under the immediate superintendence of Mr. Day, the conductor; to whom a salary of £250 is allowed. The dismounted men have each 3*s*. per day; the mounted 4*s*. per day, with additional allowances for length of service. The latter have also cottages, with suitable stables provided on the roads, against which tablets are fixed, denoting the service and number of the station. The annual expense of this establishment is £16,000. The business relating to it was formerly carried on at the Home-office; it is now transacted at No. 8, Cannon-row, Westminster.

The Bow-street *Night Foot-Patrol* establishment consists of one inspector, conductors, and eighty-two patrol. It is under the direction of the chief magistrate of Bow-street, assisted by Mr. Stafford, the chief clerk, and was first formed by the late Sir John

Fielding. The metropolis, exclusive of the city of London, is divided into sixteen districts; and a party of five patrol, one of whom commands the others, is attached to each district. They have the power of constables, and may act as such within the counties of Middlesex, Surrey, Essex, and Kent, and within the royal palaces, and ten miles thereof. They usually go on duty about dusk, and continue to patrol till twelve or one o'clock, according to the season; the object of this force being to protect the streets during the time the public is stirring. Each patrol is armed with a truncheon, a cutlass, and a belt, and a certain number of them carry pistols in addition. Six of the patrol attend the theatres, and there is also an unattached party at Bow-street during the night, disposable for any casual service. The pay of each patrol is 3*s*. per night, and no one is appointed whose age exceeds thirty-five, or who is not five feet five inches high.

The Bow-street *Day Patrol* was established by Mr. Peel, in 1822, and consisted of three inspectors and twenty-four men, under the same direction and inspection as the night patrol. It is divided into three divisions, consisting of one inspector and eight men; the first division meet every morning, at nine o'clock, at Bow-street office; the other divisions meet at other places, according to directions given by their inspectors; they patrol all the principal streets and thoroughfares in Westminster, and around the city of London, for the prevention of offences, until about the time the night-patrol come on duty. They have 3*s*. 6*d*. a day each, and vacancies that occur in this service are supplied by men selected from the night-patrol establishment.

The several patrols are all well armed, and may be mostly known when on duty by their scarlet waistcoats, blue coats, and Wellington boots. The horse-patrol are not allowed to appear abroad at any time without their uniform, nor while on duty to enter any public or other house, except in the search of offenders. The foot-patrol are required to reside near the districts allotted them to patrol, with which they are to make themselves well acquainted, and report all public-houses, coffee-shops, and other places frequented by rogues, vagabonds, and disorderly persons. They are also required to be prompt and active when fires happen in their districts, not only in preserving the property of the sufferers from depredation, but in protecting their persons, and rendering every assistance to stop the progress of the flames. There are several other salutary regulations for promoting an efficient discharge of duty, and an effective co-operation, and interchange of intelligence between the several patrol establishments. The regulations are printed and read to the men monthly, on the day preceding their inspection.

During the present winter the number of the foot-patrol was augmented, but this we believe is only a temporary measure preliminary to more important and general changes in the police of the metropolis.

V.—BOROUGH OF SOUTHWARK.

Southwark was an independent corporation till the reign of Edward VI. when it was united to the city of London, and formed into a twenty-sixth ward, under the title of Bridge-ward Without. In consequence of this union, its police is merged in that of the city, and the corporation of London appoint the steward and high bailiff. The inhabitants of Southwark made frequent applications, to the court of common council, to revive the magistracy of the city in the Borough ; and, in 1815, the sum of £1300 was directed to be annually placed in the chamber of London for that purpose. Out of this sum £500 is yearly allowed to a magistrate appointed to do constant duty in the borough.

The sitting alderman has not power to commit to the county gaol of Surrey, but must commit to the Borough compter; and the individual, when he comes to trial, is removed by habeas; the Borough, however, contributing to the county rate, the alderman may commit to Brixton house of correction.

The five parishes of Southwark are included in the Union-Hall district, which, by placing the inhabitants under two jurisdictions, subjects them to inconvenience in justiciary proceedings. The regular practice, however, is, to take all cases that can be heard by one magistrate before the sitting alderman at St. Margaret's Hill, and those requiring two magistrates to Union-hall. But this does not prevent the evil altogether, and applicants are frequently annoyed by being sent from one office to the other, either from ignorance of the rule, or of the jurisdiction, or perhaps, sometimes, to suit the momentary convenience of the magistrate to whom they first apply.

The justices of the county of Surrey seem also to have concurrent jurisdiction with the city magistrates in the Borough. It was so decided in *King* v. *Sainsbury;* the question arose out of the latter licensing an alehouse, when Lord Kenyon decided there was not a *non-intromittant* clause in the charters excluding the Surrey justices from interfering with the city justices.*

Though the Borough forms a ward of the city, it is not represented in the common council.

VI.—TOTAL NUMBER AND EXPENSE OF THE POLICE.

It is impossible to state accurately either the total number or expense of the metropolitan police. Very

* 4 Term Reports, 431.

copious returns of the number of the day and night police and the parochial expense thereof were laid before the police committee of last year, but these returns do not include the city of London; and returns from some of the Middlesex and country parishes appear not complete. In the Appendix to the Police Report of 1822, are returns of the number of the police and nightly watch; but these, too, are defective. From the best data we can collect, the following appears the most authentic statement of the civil force of the metropolis.

General or Corporation Police of the City of London.

City Marshals	2	Night-Patrol	16
Marshalmen	8	Smithfield-Patrol	8
Day-Patrol	23		
			57

Ward and Parochial Police paid out of a Rate on the Ward or Parish.

Day Police:—Constables, Headboroughs, Beadles, Street-keepers, &c.	1149	Nightly Watch: Watchmen, Patrols, Superintendents, &c.	2510

Government Police, including the Nine Public Offices and Patrol.

Magistrates	27	Day Foot Patrol	27
Police Constables	79	Surgeon	1
River ditto	64	Clerks, Messengers, Office-keepers, &c.	100
Ditto Surveyors	23	Dock and Canal Watch	67
Bow-street Patrol:—Horse Patrol	60		
Dismounted ditto	101	Total Civil Force of the Metropolis	4365
Night Foot Patrol	100		

To this estimate may be added 1000 justices of the peace in Westminster and Middlesex; of which number about 150 in Westminster have taken out their *dedimus potestatem*, and reside near the spot.

The total expense of this force cannot be precisely stated. The parish constables are mostly deputies, paid by their principal, at an average rate of about £10 each. The parochial street-keepers, beadles, patrol, and watchmen, may cost their parishes. on an average, about 14*s.* weekly. The annual expense of the nine public offices is limited, by act of parliament, to £68,000, exclusive of sums for repairs, new buildings, &c. In the City the charge for the night-watch alone amounted, in 1827, to £35,240. The total expense of the metropolitan police may be estimated at about £207,615 per annum.

This is the *direct* charge: how much the police may cost the public indirectly, from defects in the existing system, it is impossible to conjecture. The contributions levied by deputy constables and informers are very considerable, and the expense of criminal prosecutions, of the support of hulks and penitentiary establishments, the cost of transporting convicts, and the immense loss of property by depredations, all chiefly arising from the inadequacy of the present system, are incalculable. In 1827, the expense of the maintenance, prosecution, and conveyance of prisoners, cost the city of London, £22,206 : 12 : 7; and the county of Middlesex £33,677 : 4 : 5¾,* which together amount to nearly the charge of the nine public offices instituted for the protection of seven-eighth parts of the metropolis, and the whole of the vicinity.

The late Dr. Colquhoun estimated the annual amount of the depredations committed on property in the metropolis and its vicinity, in one year, at £2,000,000.† This may appear an exaggerated statement, but if we reflect on the number of criminals who are known to live upon the public, and the vast extent of property exposed to their attacks, from London being the centre of wealth and great *entrepôt* of foreign and domestic trade, we shall be inclined to think the estimate rather under than above the truth. The police of the metropolis has not materially improved since Colquhoun wrote, while the number of houses, inhabitants, and the value of chattel property have greatly augmented.

* Report on the Police of the Metropolis, 1828, pp. 339–40.
† Treatise on the Police of London, 7th edit. p. 613.

CHAPTER IV.

DEFECTS IN THE POLICE.

People not generally acquainted with the Constitution of the Police.—Improvements introduced since 1792.—*Defects in the present System:* 1. *Want of co-operation and dependence, Inconsistencies in the Parochial Police, and Obstructions to Magisterial Process.*—2. *Inadequacy of its Numerical Force through every Grade.*—3. *Want of Classification and correspondent Scale of Remuneration.*—4. *General Defect in the State of the Parochial Constabulary.*—5. *Obstacles arising out of the local Division of Parishes and Authorities.*—6. *Constables, Watchmen, and Patrols not instructed in their Duties, and no General Rules established for watching and patrolling.*

HAVING set forth the municipal and magisterial divisions of the metropolis, the amount of population, and the number, expense, and organization of the police, it seems a proper time to enter on the consideration of the adequacy and fitness of the preventive powers of the capital for the purposes of their institution.

The first reflection which must arise from the preceding exposition is that the metropolitan police is a subject that has hitherto been only imperfectly understood, and much that has been urged against its efficiency has been either greatly exaggerated or totally void of foundation. It is not correct, as has been commonly stated, that *we have no police,* that is, no established authority for the prevention of crime. It is true we have no *espionnage* corps for mingling in social intercourse; we have no registry-office for recording the name, abode, and occupation of every inhabitant; nor have we any barriers round the metropolis at which every stranger may be arrested, measured, and catalogued before he can enter its boundaries. These precautions may be necessary in some countries; but, numerous and flagrant as are the delinquencies of London, we are very far from having attained that pitch of general depravity which renders such encroachments on individual freedom essential to public safety.

Many statements in respect of the police of the metropolis apply to a period anterior to numerous and important reforms which have been introduced within the last thirty-six years. The fact is, not one of our institutions has been so frequently an object of legislative inquiry and improvement; and, if more has not been effected, it has not arisen from a conviction that the present system was perfect, or a more efficient one could not be established, but from reluctance to risk the uncertain results of new establishments, or excite alarm respecting them, so long as the present were tolerably adequate to their purposes, and public opinion had not been very generally expressed against them.

Among the reforms introduced within the period mentioned, the first and principal undoubtedly was the establishment of seven public offices of police in different parts of the town, in 1792. This measure was viewed with considerable jealousy at the time, as augmenting, in a dangerous degree, the patronage of the crown; and some alarm was also felt at the power more definitively given to arrest suspicious characters who could not give a satisfactory account of themselves. In practice, however, these fears were found to be groundless, and the advantages of the new system were soon so manifest that the public, in a few years, was reconciled to the establishment of an additional office for the prevention of depredations on the river Thames.

Next followed the establishment of the horse-patrol, in 1805, by Sir Richard Ford; which was adopted from the French, who have always preceded us in police-improvements, and who had a horse and foot patrol establishment prior to the Revolution. This proved a salutary measure, by completely exterminating the race of mounted highwaymen, which, at the time, were extremely numerous in the environs of London, and rendered travelling across Bagshot or Hounslow Heath almost as perilous as a journey in Tartary. In 1821, the dismounted patrol was instituted for the protection of the environs, while another body of patrol was appointed to the protection of the streets and squares; by which means, the whole of the metropolis, during the night, in and out, to the distance of twenty miles, was placed under a certain degree of surveillance and protection.

In 1822, Mr. Peel established the day-patrol, which has proved of the utmost utility in preventing depredations, in the day-time, on shopkeepers and passengers till the watch and night-patrol come on duty; but the number of men employed is much too small for the service allotted to them.

Some important improvements have been introduced by the late Police Acts; one, in empowering two police magistrates to suspend or discharge any watchman or patrol who misbehaves or is incompetent to his duty; another, in prohibiting any person to be appointed watchman or patrol who is above forty years of age. These regulations extend to the *whole* of the metropolis; and the beneficial effects resulting from them must be apparent to those who compare the description of men now employed in these capacities with their predecessors. In a few years, when the watchmen engaged prior to the new law have been removed by death or otherwise, there will not be one on any beat against whom the hackneyed imputation of age and infirmity can be justly alleged.

The late Police Act also limits the hours during which coffee-shops, or places for the sale of ready-made liquor, may be open: it empowers the constables of the night to take bail for the appearance of persons, charged with petty misdemeanour, before the magistrate next morning, and allows the aldermen and common council of the wards in the city to grant superannuation allowances out of the watch-rate to watchmen, beadles, and patrols.*

Besides the reforms introduced by Government several have been made by parochial and ward authorities which have been partially adopted; such as the institution in several parishes of a double watch—an early and late watch, by which the duty in the winter months is divided; in others watch-boxes have been abolished: this regulation has been adopted through the whole of the city, with the exception of the ward of Bishopsgate; in nearly all parishes superintendents of the watch have been appointed, who patrol the beats at uncertain times, to keep the men on the alert and attentive to their duty.

It is satisfactory to think all these reforms have proved beneficial, and consequently hold out encouragement to proceed in the work of improvement. The police of the metropolis is still in a very imperfect state, and of which the public who suffer thereby are now convinced, and ready to listen to proposals for its amendment. We will, therefore, in the next place, point out the specific defects of the existing system; having laid

* 3 Geo. IV. c. 55, sections 18, 26, 27, 28.

before the reader all the preliminary information which is necessary to enable him to judge as well as ourselves of the value of any suggestion we may be able to offer.

Defects in preventive justice are of two kinds; those which originate in the mal-organization and inefficient constitution of police establishments themselves; and, secondly, those originating in the process and enactments of the penal code, instituted to deter from the perpetration of criminal offence. It is to the former class of defects we shall limit the observations of this chapter, reserving the latter to a subsequent occasion till after we have given an exposition of the predominant crimes of the metropolis.

The *first* and most obvious defect in the metropolitan police is the want of co-operation and dependence between the several parts of which it consists, resulting from the various independent jurisdictions into which its civil government is divided. The area of the metropolis is comprehended within an ellipsis, of which the longest diameter does not exceed eight miles, and there is certainly nothing in this extent which precludes the whole being under the control of one uniform and dependent chain of authority. The disadvantages resulting from the present discordant powers are,—

1. A want of union and subordination in public emergencies requiring a concentrated force.

2. An absence of uniformity and consistency in the police and preventive regulations of the parishes and districts of which the metropolis consists.

3. The existence of numerous obstacles to the prompt execution of legal process in districts without the magistrate's immediate jurisdiction.

With respect to the first of these, it has fortunately happened of late, that few emergencies have occurred requiring an united effort of the police; still it cannot be denied this is a defective point in its organization, and if some precedency could be established in the magistracy it would tend greatly to augment the strength of the civil force, when a juncture required it, while it would not cause the smallest additional expense. The chief obstacle, we apprehend, to such an arrangement would be the *ancient rights* of the city of London, which could probably only be conciliated by giving the supremacy to the lord mayor, in preference either to the chief magistrate at Bow-street or the high steward of Westminster. It is a point, however, to which we do not attach much importance, the military being always at hand to aid any weak point in the police; and we pass on to the next and more important consideration.

The absence of uniformity, in the parochial police, is a serious and almost unaccountable defect. If any scheme of watching and patrolling can be devised, or is found, by experience, most beneficial in one parish, it is sheer folly not to extend it to every other. The property to be secured and the outrages to be prevented are the same in every district;—why, then, should not the Legislature at once, out of the various modes of parochial police, adopt that which is best, and establish an uniform and consistent police practice through the whole metropolis? There would be nothing new nor encroaching in the attempt; the city of London and every parish has already submitted to the interference of Parliament, as we have before observed, in the regulation of watchmen, patrols, and coffee-houses.

Obstructions to the police, from conflicting jurisdictions, chiefly occur in the execution of warrants directed either against the person, or to search suspected places for stolen property. The delays in executing process for these different purposes is considerable in both cases, but greater in the latter than the former. If, for example, a justice of Middlesex issues his warrant to apprehend an offender in Hertfordshire, it must be backed by a magistrate of that county; or, even if directed into the city of London, it must be backed by an alderman of the city. But the power of backing is limited by 24 Geo. II. c. 55, to *personal* warrants; a *search* warrant cannot be backed: if a person robbed go before a justice of Middlesex, the justice cannot direct a search warrant into Hertfordshire, or the city of London; the sufferer can only be referred to a magistrate of these jurisdictions, who, after hearing the details of his loss afresh, may alone issue a search warrant. The impediment to justice, by this circuitous procedure, is glaring, leaving out of consideration the inconvenience and annoyance to which individuals are subjected: by the delay, in one case, the offender may have fled; in the other, the stolen property may have been removed.

The Police Committee, of last year, suggested a simple and effective remedy in both cases, by recommending that, in future, "warrants, whether to apprehend the person, or to search the premises, be executed, in all parts of the kingdom, under the authority of the magistrate from whom they issue, who alone can and ought to be responsible for the legality of the proceedings." Report, p. 17.*

* Since the above was written, Mr. Peel has applied to the city authorities, to obtain their assent to an arrangement, by which county and city magistrates may have concurrent jurisdiction in the issue of warrants: but the court of aldermen has refused its concurrence, on the ground that it would be an abandonment of one of the ancient privileges of London. We are inclined to think this conclusion has been come to rather precipitately, and is not sanctioned by the deliberate wisdom of the corporation. In the late Police Act, (3 Geo. IV. c. 55,) and in Mr. Taylor's Act, the city submitted to legislative interference in matters of civic regulation; but the proposed alteration does not

The *second* general defect in police is the inadequacy of its numerical force through almost every grade of authority. We have magistrates, paid and unpaid, patrol, horse and foot, and watchmen and superintendents in every parish, but the number of each is disproportioned to the duty they have to perform. What can be more futile than the Bow-street day-patrol of twenty-four men, with 10,000 streets, or the city patrol of twenty-three, with 4000 streets, or the horse-patrol of sixty, with a circular area of 1200 square miles, to protect and look over? and how totally inadequate are twelve public offices to hear all complaints, quarrels, thefts, frauds, &c. occurring in a population approaching two millions? They form little more than the skeleton of what ought to constitute the conservative force of the metropolis. Except the establishment of the Thames office, the operations of which are chiefly confined to the river, there has been scarcely any augmentation in the police since 1792; while the population, houses, and property, to be

imply any sacrifice of privilege—merely an interchange of powers between neighbouring justices, by which some useless forms may be abolished, and the operations of justice facilitated. To make the privileges of the city an obstacle to public improvements is not to defend them, but to place them in jeopardy. Charters are said to be only *leases*, and grants of immunities *loans*, which the power who gave may take away, when they are indiscreetly made barriers to the general interests of the community.

Though the police of the city is better conducted than in any other division of the metropolis, it is neither pure nor perfect. According to the evidence of officer Q. R. before the Police Committee, nine out of ten of the late compromises were effected in the city. In a Report to the Common-Council, in 1827, it was stated (*Times*, Sept. 21) that the number of watchmen employed was as great as in the reign of Queen Anne, when the darkness of the streets obliged them to be stationary; the citizens of London, compared to the out-parishes, had watchmen in proportion of three and a half to one, yet the crime of burglary had increased tenfold in the last seven years.

guarded, have more than doubled. Eight of the public offices contain within their limits a population of 1,100,000. The Union-hall district alone extends over a circuit of twenty-seven miles, containing a population of 280,000 inhabitants, consisting of a miscellaneous assemblage of the depraved and destitute intermingled among the opulent and respectable.

Some idea may be formed of the inadequacy of the magisterial branch of police by comparing the number of acting magistrates in the metropolis with those in the country. In England and Wales there are 595 places at which are held divisional meetings for petty sessions of the peace;* in the metropolis there are not more than fifteen, including the liberties in which magistrates assemble in petty session. In the country are 4430 acting county magistrates, besides 183 cities and towns, having chartered justices claiming exclusive jurisdiction; in the metropolis there are not more than 80 acting magistrates, and of these there can scarcely be reckoned more than the police magistrates and aldermen of the City, who actually do duty. Yet the population of the metropolis is one-twelfth of the population of England and Wales; and, from the character, employment, and avocations of that population, is calculated in a much higher proportion to be productive of justiciary business.

That this is the fact is shown by the proportion between criminal commitments in the metropolis and in the country. In 1827 the number of persons committed for criminal offences to the gaols in the cities of London and Westminster, and the county of Middlesex, (that part of the metropolis situated in the county of Surrey not being included,) amounted to 3381;† the committals

* Parliamentary Report on Population, for 1821, page xxxiv.

† Police Report, 1828, page 289.

to the different gaols in England and Wales during the same year amounted only to 17,921.* Thus, while the proportion between the population of the metropolis and the country is one-twelfth, the criminal commitments are upwards of one-sixth, or more than double in an equal number of persons in town than in the provinces; affording very clear evidence of the excess of duty falling to the metropolitan justice.

The consequences of this redundant business are great delay, and inadequate protection and assistance to the public: complaints are not made; prosecutors, witnesses, and bail, are loth to come near a public office; and the magistrates, hurried and perplexed by the multiplicity of cases brought before them, are often compelled either to dismiss them without proper investigation, or to solicit the precarious aid of the county magistrates to lighten the pressure of their duties.

A *third* defect in the police is, the absence of classification among its officers, and a correspondent scale of remuneration and responsibility. While the metropolitan police continues in its present divided and diminutive state there is not much scope for classification; but should a more general and consolidated system be established, this would form a point of the first importance. The police constables, now attached to the different offices, have the same pay, (except one, called the chief constable,) hold the same rank, and are eligible to the same employments; no distinction being made, further than as the magistrate, according to his experience or prepossessions of fitness and ability, selects this or that officer for a particular service or undertaking. This, however, is too arbitary and capricious a discrimination to be admitted, and one founded on

* Police Report, 1828, page 275.

better criteria it would certainly be expedient to establish.

The duties of the police are of a very miscellaneous character, and confer on the officer not only different degrees of trust, but demand great diversity of talent and qualification. Any person, for instance, who can walk the streets may serve a summons; but something more is requisite to execute a warrant, and peculiar stamina is demanded to suppress a riot, or force a door to apprehend a burglar. These, however, are only the ordinary duties of police; there are others of a higher and more delicate nature: such, for example, as where a series of informations for the violation of penal statutes are to be exhibited; a nest of coiners or passers of forged notes to be traced; a brothel or low gambling-house to be verified and rooted out; a gang of swindlers, living in apparent respestability, and preying upon the industry of others, to be exposed; stolen goods to be identified; or a banker's parcel recovered :—these and many others call for peculiar talent, experience, and ability.

By a division of labour, with corresponding rewards and distinction, the officers would attain proficiency in their respective departments. It would excite emulation, the offices of greatest trust and emolument, and lightest duty, being the reward of superior ability, long and exemplary service. As it is they are all placed on the same level, there are no prizes to stimulate a class of persons of ardent minds and peculiarly susceptible of notice and distinction. Their lives are in constant peril, and the highest reward they can now look forward to, after perhaps being mutilated and worn out in the service, is the very precarious chance of being placed in constant attendance about the royal palaces, or at the Bank of England.

But the suggestion we have offered is not so much

for the sake of the officers, but to effect a substantial improvement in the police. It would tend to elicit and train up a class of men of a superior *caste* to those generally found about the public offices. We have shewn, in a former chapter, (page 9,) that there are several duties appertaining to ministerial police which, to be properly discharged, require considerable general information, legal knowledge, and gentlemanly demeanour; and nothing, we think, is more likely to draw persons so qualified into the service as a plan of graduated rank and emolument. The office of police is, in most cases, one of delegated power, in the execution of which the agent is necessarily without control or superintendence; he is frequently exposed to great temptation, and, whether he yields to it or resists, must, in great part, depend on his personal character and situation, on the inflexible notions he entertains of the duties imposed upon him, and the loss he would incur by a corrupt or inefficient discharge of them.

The *fourth* general defect in police applies to the office of parochial constable. The constables form by far the most numerous class of preventive officers, amounting, in the metropolis, to near 1100, and, according to the forms of the constitution, to them is confided almost the entire business of preventing crime and apprehending offenders. The office, however, has greatly degenerated, and is now in about the same predicament as that of metropolitan justice prior to the appointment of stipendiary magistrates; those on whom it devolves by operation of law being, for the most part, above its functions; while those who actually discharge them are unworthy of the trust.

By some oversight, the Legislature has entirely overlooked the constabulary branch of police; while the magistracy, and even watchmen and patrols, have undergone many salutary reforms, the most ancient and important class of functionaries have been left in that state of abuse to which they have naturally fallen from the lapse of centuries and changes in society. Few constables in London serve in person; they nearly all appoint deputies, to whom they pay an annual sum varying from £5 to £15. It is obvious no person in decent circumstances will act for such a paltry remuneration, and the consequence is, the office has fallen into the hands of the lowest class of retailers and costardmongers, who make up the deficient allowance of their principals by indirect sources of emolument; by winking at offences they ought to prevent; by *attorneying* for parties;* by encouraging prosecutions for the sake of obtaining their expenses; by screening the publican, pawnbroker, brothel-keeper, and receiver of stolen goods. Living in obscure courts and corners, they can seldom be found in any hazardous and unprofitable emergence requiring their assistance, while they are ready enough to start forth, and even distribute their "card" among those on whom they can levy contributions, either in money or kind. They do not, in fact, consider themselves preventive officers; they take their round of nightly duty at the watchhouse, and attend sessions and other public occasions; but they do not consider it their duty to interfere in any criminal case, unless expressly called upon so to do.

The duties of the office require that it should be discharged by a respectable and really responsible person; by one whose residence is known, and conspicuous to the whole parish; and whose evidence in criminal trials and justiciary proceedings can be implicitly relied upon by judges and magistrates. If the established

* Police Report, A.D. 1828, pp. 69, 70, 154, 156.

police be merely to undergo alteration, and not an entire change, one of the most practicable and important improvements in it would be a reform of parish constables. They form the groundwork of our preventive system; and the name and office are familiar to the ears of Englishmen. Perhaps the best mode that could be adopted would be to lessen the number and increase the efficiency and direct emolument of those retained. Over them should be placed one or more stipendiary officers (according to the size of the parish) well versed in police duties; and the whole be placed under the direction and control of the magistrates.

With a view to an improvement in the parochial constabulary, it has been suggested that the office of high constable should be re-established. This officer has nominal control over all the petty constables in the hundred over which he presides, and his bills are paid out of the county rates. Ostensibly, he has no salary, and his remuneration is supposed to arise either from balances of the county-rates, which he collects, or from advantages in his private trade, derived from the influence of his office.* The chief objection to the revival of this office is that it would, perhaps, be an unnecessary multiplication of officers and expense: every parish, in our opinion, should have at least one paid and efficient police officer, having under his control the constables, patrol, and the watch; and if over this stipendiary should be placed a salaried high constable, it would be creating, unnecessarily, a superfluous intermediate officer between the parochial-chief constable and magistrate.

This, however, is a point we shall advert to again, and shall now consider the *fifth* general defect in police,

* Some high constables are coal-merchants, and, of course, supply the publicans.

arising from the local division of the metropolis into parishes.

Owing to the unequal size of parishes, as originally fixed, and subsequent changes in society, a parish presents no definite idea either as to extent, wealth, or population. Several of the city parishes do not contain above a dozen families; one has disappeared on the site of the New Post Office, and another has been nearly swallowed up by St. Katharine's Docks. The population of the out-parishes, and those without the bills of mortality, is extremely unequal, varying from 3000 to 96,000 inhabitants. Yet these different allotments of territory and population have all nearly the same permanent staff of a minister, churchwarden, constable, overseer, vestry-clerk, beadle, &c. and are subject to a similar form of parochial government, through which alone (the city excepted) any new plan of police could be introduced; but it is obvious no general system could be founded on the present parochial divisions, a scale of establishment adapted to one parish being too large or too small for another. It would be necessary, therefore, in forming any general plan of police for the whole metropolis, either to found it on the present division of parishes, having a separate and differently constituted establishment of police for each parish, according to its magnitude; or to disregard parochial divisions altogether, and form new and equal police-districts, with an establishment to each, according to the amount of property and number of inhabitants to be protected.

The *sixth* and last defect in police we shall remark, is the absence of preliminary information in the subordinate functionaries, and the want of agreement and consistency in the general principles of watching and patrolling.

The ludicrous mistakes frequently committed by watchmen, constables, and patrols, from ignorance of their most ordinary duties is familiar to every one, and cannot form a subject of surprise, when it is considered these functionaries are chiefly taken from the more laborious and illiterate classes, and that they mostly receive their appointment without previous inquiry or instruction in the knowledge of their official duties. A somewhat different system is adopted with respect to the Bow-street patrol, who have printed instructions, which are read over to them every month by their conductors. A similar plan ought to be adopted in respect of the parochial police: we would have drawn up in a clear and simple form the powers and duties of constables, watchmen, and patrols; and every candidate for these offices should be examined previous to their appointment, and, unless sufficiently versed therein, rejected.

Next, as to the absence of agreement and consistency in watching and patrolling; it seems most extraordinary that scarcely two parishes agree in these points: if one parish adopts any good scheme of protection, its benefits are often neutralized by the want of similar arrangements in the neighbouring districts. There must, however, be some plan which is best, and it ought to be generally enforced. It must be advisable or not to have a double watch in the winter season, to call the hour, to have watch-boxes, to have lanterns, as well as to have a general uniformity in dress, equipment, and rate of wages. The parish of St. James, Westminster, presents an example of a well-regulated watch, and the suggestions in the report of the watch-committee of the city of London (mentioned page 49) are well deserving attention.

CHAPTER V.

GENERAL PLAN OF POLICE.

*Report of the late Police Committee.—General Plan of Police.—One head Officer of Police preferable to a Board of Magistrates.—A District Officer of Police might be attached to each Public Office.—Subdivision of the Bow-street Foot-Patrol.—Advantages of the Consolidated System:—*1. *Fixes Responsibility;* 2. *Would admit of an uniform Code of Regulations and Discipline;* 3. *Affords scope for Classification of Officers and interchange of Districts;* 4. *Supersedes the Parochial Constabulary;* 5. *Increased Vigilance and Energy;* 6. *And last, would diminish the Expense of Preventive Justice.—Concluding Observations on the Prejudices and Interests likely to be hostile to the Establishment of the New System.*

THE more general and prominent defects in police developed in the last chapter were the following:—

I.—Want of co-operation and dependence between the several bodies of police in the Metropolis, resulting from the different jurisdictions into which its civil government is divided, and which produced,—1st. A want of union and subordination in public emergencies requiring a concentrated force; 2d. An absence of uniformity and consistency in the police and preventive regulations of parishes and districts; and, 3d. The existence of obstacles to the prompt execution of legal process in districts without the magistrate's immediate jurisdiction.

II.—The inadequate number of the police in the several grades of magistrates, constables, patrols, and watchmen.

III.—Want of classification and division of employment among police officers, with corresponding remuneration, rank, and responsibility.

IV.—Defects in the Parochial Constabulary.

V.—Obstacles arising out of parochial districts and authorities.

VI.—Constables, Watchmen, and Patrols, without preliminary instruction in their duties, and no general principles established on the best mode of watching and patrolling.

Remedies for these several defects were shortly adverted to, chiefly on the supposition that an entire change in the metropolitan police would not be attempted; but our own opinion is decidedly in favour of the latter alternative, and we feel convinced that all efforts to improve the existing system will prove abortive, and that nothing short of one uniform, consolidated, and responsible establishment for the whole metropolis and environs will afford adequate protection to persons and property. Before, however, developing any specific plan for this purpose, it will be proper to refer to the important suggestions in the Report of the Select Committee of the House of Commons, appointed during the session of 1828, "to inquire into the cause of the increase in the number of criminal commitments and convictions in London and Middlesex, and into the state of the Police of the Metropolis, and of the districts adjoining thereto."

The frequency of these parliamentary investigations show at once the inadequacy of the existing system, and the necessity of attempting a substantial improvement. The subject had been previously almost exhausted, and the inquiries of the late Committee were much more limited than those of their predecessors; they referred chiefly to the state of the parochial police in the metropolis and environs, and to the commission of certain specific crimes, in which it had been justly charged that the police themselves had been guilty either of culpable negligence or of actual participation. After investigating these points at great length, after considering the recommendation of former committees, for the improvement of metropolitan police, and after dwelling on the present disjointed and inefficient system which there was no hope of materially improving with the apparatus now in use, the Committee came to the determination to recommend an entire change in the constitution and organization of the police of the metropolis. This change, in brief, is no less than to convert the whole parochial police into one homogeneous government police, having one head, and being disciplined, officered, and distributed through the whole of the metropolis and environs, to the distance of eight or ten miles.

Before enlarging on the advantages of a consolidated police, it will be proper to give the reader a correct idea of the form and course it would assume. The Police Committee have not put forth any detailed plan of police; they have simply recommended the establishment of a board of magistrates, having the entire control of the police of the metropolis, (the city of London excepted,) and whose duties shall be confined entirely to that department. This is not a new suggestion; precisely the same thing had been strongly recommended by Dr. Colquhoun, and indeed it is the first measure that suggests itself to any one who bestows attention on the subject. The paragraphs in the Report containing the outlines of the Committee's plan are the following:—

That there should be constituted an office of police, acting under the immediate directions of the Secretary of State for the Home Department, upon which should be devolved the general control over the whole of the establishments of police of every denomination, including the nightly watch.

That the immediate superintendence of this department should extend over a circumference comprising the whole of that thickly inhabited district which may be considered to include the metropolis and its environs.

That the magistrates attached to this office should be relieved from the discharge of those ordinary duties which necessarily occupy so much of the time of the present police magistrates; and that they should be the centre of an intimate and constant communication with the other police offices on all matters relating to the disturbance of the public peace, and to the commission of all offences of a serious character.

That the entire control over the nightly watch should be assumed by this department, not immediately and simultaneously, but gradually; and that the powers which are now exercised with respect to the nightly watch, either by parish vestries or by commissioners or trustees appointed by local acts, should continue to be exercised until an efficient substitute in each case shall have been provided, subject to such modifications as may be thought advisable.

That authority should be given to the department of police to direct the discontinuance of the parochial watch in any parish, on certifying to the proper authorities of that parish that arrangements have been made for the due performance of the duties theretofore assigned to the watch. Your Committee are of opinion that the public funds ought to continue to be charged with the amount of the expense not less than that to which they are at present subject, on account of the police establishment of the metropolis, and that the charge which will be incurred by the increase of that establishment, at least as far it can be considered as contributing to local protection, ought to be a local charge, to be defrayed, according to certain principles, to be hereafter determined, by the parishes or districts included within the superintendence of the new police.

With respect to the parishes which have at present an efficient watch, the amount of the contribution to which they will be subject will probably not exceed the amount of the rate which they now pay.

With respect to those parishes in which there is either an imperfect provision for a watch establishment, or no provision at all, it is right that they should contribute proportionably to the maintenance of an establishment by which they will materially benefit.

The present system which prevails in many parishes, of defraying the expense of the watch by partial subscriptions, is manifestly unfair. It throws the burden exclusively on those who are willing to subscribe, while the advantage is common to all parties who are interested in the security of property, whether they subscribe or not.

Your Committee will abstain from entering into a consideration of the detailed regulations which should be formed for the constitution and management of the new police establishment.

Precise rules ought to be laid down in respect to the qualifications of candidates, with reference to their age, previous occupations and character.

There will be a manifest advantage in considering the whole force, of whatever denomination it may consist, as one united establishment, in introducing an efficient system of control and inspection through a regular gradation of intermediate authorities, and in holding out every inducement to good conduct, by giving promotion as much as possible to the deserving officers.—pp. 30–2.

The Committee had not sufficiently matured the details of their plan to bring them forward, but the following appear some of the leading points they will probably embrace.

First, we apprehend, it will be necessary to adopt a new division of the metropolis into local districts of police, without regard to parochial boundaries. This course was pursued on the establishment of the public offices in 1792, and is rendered necessary from the unequal size and irregular manner the parishes intermingle with each other, rendering them an inconvenient basis for a local distribution of police force.

Secondly, to each police district should be assigned nearly an equal number of day and night police, consisting of a chief constable, constables, superintendents, patrols, and watchmen. It is indispensable the first two, at least, should reside in the district, in order to become well acquainted with the character of its inhabitants, to watch over the conduct of publicans and the movements of all suspected persons and places.

Over a certain number of districts should be placed the high constable, or other equivalent officer, whose duty would consist in a general superintendence of the districts forming his division, and in communicating with the board or head office of police. Fewer the number of intermediate officers and subdivisions of power, and smaller will be the expense and more defined the responsibility. If, therefore, each police district could be made complete in itself, and communicate, by its chief constable, with the board, it would probably conduce to the simplicity, economy, and efficiency, of the establishment. But this is a point which will be best determined after considering the functions of the head office of police.

The Committee propose a board of magistrates. Boards are not remarkable for efficiency, and are of vague and undefined accountability. We have only one responsible secretary of state for the entire home affairs of the United Kingdom, and, therefore, we should think one responsible secretary, as head officer of police, assisted by subordinate functionaries, would be sufficient. It would concentrate in *one* person the responsibility of the police department, and as it is intended to render the police board strictly ministerial and not a judicial office, a plural number is not essential to the business of justiciary proceedings.

In order to aid the head officer of police, or board, and next to it in rank, it would be expedient to attach to each of the public police offices a person who should have the entire control of the several bodies of district police within the limits of the jurisdiction of the public office to which he belonged. The duties of this officer might be made to supersede those of the high constable. He would form a medium of communication between the chief constable of districts and the head office of police. His duty would be to attend, during certain hours, in his own room or apartment in the public office, to receive the reports, every morning, of the chief constable of districts, to hear all complaints on the conduct of superintendents, patrols, or watchmen; in minor cases to punish, in more serious ones to bring them under the cognizance of the head office; to receive all communications from individuals respecting crimes committed or to be prevented, and in particular cases to collect evidence, institute, and conduct the prosecution of offenders; occasionally to inspect the police of the several districts within the limits of the public office; and, finally, to have daily communications and act in concert with the police magistrates.

An intermediate centre of communication and action between the police board and district or parochial police (if that local division be retained) seems indispensable. The head office, or board, would, in many cases, be too remote for applications; whereas, the public offices, by their situation in different parts of the metropolis, do at once present the focus at which may be converged all the *materiel* necessary for the detection, prevention, and adjudication of crime.*

As it is intended to place the entire metropolitan police under the control of the police board, a new disposition will probably be made of the Bow-street foot-patrol. At present it is under the exclusive direction of

* If one of the three magistrates now attached to each public office could be spared to assume exclusively the duties prescribed to the intermediate officers, it would render unnecessary the creation of an additional functionary. The police magistrates have certainly enough to do during their present limited hours of attendance; but there appears no reason why the hours of duty might not be extended. The regular attendance of each magistrate is only two whole days and two half days weekly (*Evidence of Mr. Swabey, Police Report*, 1828, *p.* 145); the whole day's duty from eleven till three, and again an hour in the evening; the half day's duty from twelve till three in the afternoon. Thus there are two whole days in the week, besides Sunday, a magistrate does not attend at all; and the second business on the half days is not unfrequently done by the country magistrates, who, in a friendly way, drop in for a little gossip or to read the newspapers. Two days' holiday for each magistrate weekly makes the six spare days required for the duties of the officer we have proposed to attach to each public office. The chief magistrate of Bow-street, in addition to his ordinary magisterial duties, has daily to communicate with the Home-office, and has the general superintendence of the patrol; and there appears no reason why similar additional duties should not be discharged by one of the magistrates belonging to the other offices.

the chief magistrate at Bow-street, to whom the reports of its conductors are made, and the magistrates of the other offices have no control over it, nor receive communications from it, though its rounds extend through their districts. This has been frequently a subject of complaint at Union-hall and the other offices, and it would, doubtless, be a great advantage, under the new organization, to divide the foot-patrol in certain quotas among the public offices, or be incorporated with the district police.

The gradation and general organization of the police, as above described, would then be as follows:—1. Would be the board, or head officer of police, having the entire control of the police of the metropolis, subordinate only to the Secretary of State for the home department. Next to the board, is the intermediate officer attached to each public-office, having the inspection and control of the several bodies of police within the limits of the public-office. Then follow the chief constable, constables, superintendents, patrols, and watchmen composing the district police, and which is intended to supersede the parochial establishments.

Whether this mode of organizing the police be adopted, or only some approximation to it, is not very important. The great advantages of the new system will consist in its forming a separate, responsible, and co-operating department.

Constituting, as the police would under the new arrangement, an extensive and important branch of the public service, it is proper that the members thereof, like servants in other public departments, the excise, the customs, the post-office, the army, and navy, be subject to legislative regulations and discipline: persons and property being entrusted to their protection, it is reasonable the public should have security the trust will not be betrayed, or negligently executed. One of the chief causes of the inefficiency of the present police is the absence of all punishment for dereliction of duty. Dismission from the employment is not enough, when a police-constable or patrol is found corrupt or unfaithful; or where a watchman is found neglecting his duty, by sleeping on his post, or associating with improper characters; fine or imprisonment, or something still more penal, ought to be superadded.

One important consideration, connected with the new system, has not yet been adverted to, namely, the expense—by whom paid, and how levied. If the new organization should be extended through the whole metropolis, one general and uniform police-rate, collected in the manner of the county-rate, seems the best mode of regulating the fiscal department. On the other hand, if it has only a partial operation, the police funds will be raised, probably, as they now are, by the respective local and parochial authorities of the parishes to which the new establishments are extended.

Advantages of a General and Consolidated Police.

It has been justly observed, that "one of the most effectual among the indirect expedients for insuring good government is to assign a clear and well-defined class of duties to every distinct set of public functionaries. It is by this means much more readily and much more strongly perceived when the business is done well and when it-is done ill. The honour is raised to a much higher pitch which is bestowed upon good conduct, and the infamy to a much higher pitch which falls upon bad conduct.* This is one of the advantages which would result from consolidating the police under one depart-

* Edinburgh Review, vol. xv. page 95.

ment; the business of preventive justice being in the hands of one class of persons, and each of these having specific duties to perform, faults in execution and the stages in which they occur will be apparent. Moreover, such divisions of employment will tend to elicit improvements, by the minds of the officers being concentered on one particular occupation, and by their receiving the reward and distinction to which superior talent and activity will be entitled. Under the present system, an ill-defined mass of duties are attached to the police, which creates a temptation to negligence, and holds up a screen for misconduct. The attention of the police-magistrate is divided between his ministerial and judicial duties; the police-constable contests the jurisdiction, and objects to the duty of the parish-constable. From this confusion of functions and the absence of anything like an *esprit du corps* must be ascribed the few improvements that have originated in the police themselves; each has been content with discharging his own routine of business without feeling any pride in the character and general success of the body to which he belonged; and the improvements introduced have chiefly resulted from parliamentary inquiry and discussion.

The *next* important advantage will consist in establishing an uniform and consistent code of regulations and discipline through the whole police department. One of the greatest defects in the existing system is the absence of union and conformity of discipline in the police; not only is there considerable jealousy between the government and parochial police, but also between the several bodies of parochial police. The latter conceive their duty strictly limited to their respective parishes; a watchman, going down one side of a street, does not feel himself obliged to cross over to check a delinquency on the other side, provided it is in another parish or ward. This want of concert is aggravated by the police of neighbouring parishes being perhaps under a different system of regulation and superintendence. But all these separate interests would disappear under a consolidated system; the whole would be placed under one general head; the mode of watching, the hours of duty, the dress and equipments, which experience showed to be best, would be made general through the whole body.

A *third* advantage would consist in the facilities it would afford for checking the conduct of officers by removing them periodically, or otherwise, from one district to another. This system has been adopted in the excise, and might be advantageously extended to the metropolitan police. It is obvious that the long residence of a watchman, patrol, constable, or even magistrate, in one district, may give rise to connexions with publicans, hotel-keepers, keepers of infamous houses, and abandoned characters, which may end in a compromise of public duty. An effective check on these *liaisons* would be in a partial exchange of the police of districts, and for which there would be an opportunity, if the whole police of the metropolis was brought under one government, and not forming, as it now does, so many separate independent establishments.

A *fourth* advantage would consist in the classification of the police with corresponding remuneration and responsibility, and multiplying the objects of their jurisdiction. We have before remarked on the miscellaneous duties of a well-organized preventive establishment, consisting not merely in the prevention of crime and apprehension of offenders, but in watching over the execution of penal statutes, and protecting the community generally against all fraud, annoyance, injury, and adulteration. These duties are now imperfectly discharged by parish beadles, inspectors of nuisances, court leets, annoyance juries, and ward inquests; or they are left to the unprincipled informer, who converts an important duty into an engine of extortion and partial oppression. Impartial justice requires, and it is the obvious interest of individuals, that such duties be discharged by competent and responsible agents. The head office having under its observation the entire body of police, it would be able to select and organize classes of persons best qualified for the several functions enumerated, and the public would more readily submit to their inquisition, knowing they proceeded without fear or favour—that they acted for the common good—and that they were responsible to a higher power for the just exercise of their authority.

A *fifth* advantage we anticipate from the establishment of a general and consolidated police is, the entire abolition of the *parochial constabulary*. We should esteem the new system extremely imperfect, unless an effective substitute be found for this decayed remnant of an antiquated institution. When an office comes to be almost universally executed by deputy, it affords indubitable proof the original mode of appointment has ceased to be adapted to the existing state of society. Such is the case with parish constables; they are nearly all deputies drawn from the lowest class of retailers and journeymen, who have a mortal aversion to habits of honest and patient industry: and what is more extraordinary, these night Dogberrys, these petty magistrates, are empowered, by a recent statute, to take or refuse bail for the appearance of offenders! Respectable parishioners, we are sure, would hail this as a most salutary reform, and would deem the sacrifice of any little parochial patronage the new system would demand, amply compensated in being relieved from a troublesome and expensive duty.

A *sixth* advantage would consist in a wonderful increase in energy and vigilance in all the subordinate retainers of police. It must have been remarked by most people that there is a singular feebleness and indifference evinced by watchmen and patrols in the discharge of their duty, even in the best regulated parishes. Their object is only to get through the night; they would sooner wink at, than incur personal risk by the apprehension of thieves, and as for touching any well-dressed rogue, they are afraid, lest he turn out to be their daily employer, or a parishioner who has some power in removing them from their situation. There would be no hesitation of this kind in a body of men deriving their appointment from Government, and they would evince as much superiority over their predecessors as is shown by regular troops over a militia or volunteer force. The men would be instructed in their duty, they would know they were placed under a vigilant superintendence, that they would be protected in the proper discharge of their functions, and infallibly punished for abuse or neglect. Parliamentary power is proverbially omnipotent, and any measure derived from thence, whether it is for the collection of a tax, or the establishment of a preventive force, carries with it a weight and energy that can never be infused by parochial legislation; and in respect of an establishment for the general security, it would be doubly advantageous, by striking terror into the depredator, and arming the officer with augmented confidence and authority.

A *seventh* and last advantage resulting from a general police would consist in diminishing the expense of preventive justice. We do not mean that the charge of a general police would be less than the parochial: that we think is improbable; 1st. because one of the improvements suggested has been an increase in numerical force as well as remuneration; and 2d. that additional protection should be afforded the public by enlarging the objects of police jurisdiction. Should, however, the *direct* charge of the police be greater, the community would be more than compensated in the augmented security of persons and property, in the decrease of depredations, and diminution of the expense of criminal prosecutions, so that a real saving would accrue to the public. The costs of criminal prosecutions in London and Middlesex alone have been shown to amount to £55,883 per annum, and the loss of property from depredations to several millions, (see page 65.) Under an improved system of police we feel confident both these enormous sacrifices would diminish; while the feelings of humanity would not be outraged, nor the national character disgraced by the number and frequency of criminal punishments. Experience proves that in every parish where a better police has been attempted, it has been followed by a decrease in crime, and no doubt if a more vigilant and energetic system be generally established in the metropolis, it will be followed by a similar result.

We have now laid before the reader the plan of an effective police, and one that would obviate the principal defects which, in a preceding chapter, have been shewn to pervade the existing establishment. Superior as the new system would ultimately prove, we foresee many obstacles to its adoption, in the interests of some and the honest prejudice of others, who are always apprehensive at the least appearance of government interference. The idea of regimenting a body of two or three thousand watchmen and patrols—of having them officered and paid by government—of making such an enormous addition to the standing *military* force (such is the language that will be employed) of the country—and of placing a sort of preventive man, with a glazed hat or other distinguishing symbol, in every street, will not only excite attention, but even some degree of alarm both in the metropolis and in the country. Startling, however, as this project is on the first presentment, we are convinced, after deeply considering its tendency, that the dangers with which it is apparently accompanied, are purely illusive; and that it is the only one that offers a remedy commensurate with the evils of an overgrown, luxurious, and delinquent capital. It is merely a supplement to the police reform of 1792, when the corrupt volunteer justices of the metropolis were converted into a responsible and efficient stipendiary magistracy. If the new system did not perform well at first, practice would soon make it perfect; and we have no doubt it would speedily be found as much superior to the old parochial machinery, as the steam and iron pipes of the New River Company are to the wooden troughs and creeking wheels of the late London Bridge water-works. Still, without the concurrence and even support of those who are to be benefited by the change, it is not likely to succeed nor even be attempted; and it is in order to anticipate some of the more formidable objections that can be urged against it, we have placed it before the reader under the most unfavourable aspect it can be represented.

The great obstacle to an effective reform of the police is the subdivision of its powers, and the first question that occurs is—whether it shall be parochial or general—whether it shall be a poor frittered, disjointed, imbecile thing, without union, organization, or concert: or it shall be one united, energetic establishment, acting for a common purpose, and under real responsibility for the lives and property of two millions of persons. To this consideration we have concentrated our attention, and we can safely affirm that it is only by the parish authorities surrendering, for the common good, the little powers they now exercise in matters of police, and the whole being consolidated and organized afresh, that a preventive system, at all deserving the name, can be established. Any attempt to patch up the present *disjecta membra* will assuredly fail of success ; for there is no foundation either to repair or build on, and recourse must at last be had to an entirely new constitution of the civil force, sanctioned and carried into effect by Government. Even this might not at first answer expectation ; great difficulties will have to be surmounted in arranging the fiscal details of the new system, in the transfer of authorities, and in selecting proper instruments to carry them into execution. Still the elements of improvement will be constantly at work, and we have no doubt that there will soon be occasion for surprise that the old machinery had been so long tolerated after its defects were apparent, and improvement so easy.

The only way to give the new orginazation a fair trial is to make it general at once, and not limit its operation to a few parishes. It is only upon a large scale that a plan of police, like that we have described, can be economically or advantageously administered. It is the first duty of Government to protect the persons and properties of the people, and it seems preposterous to have any hesitation about trusting them with the necessary power for the accomplishment of these objects. A vast deal of jobbing will be endangered by the new system, and watch committees, vestries, and local trusts will probably raise a loud clamour, as they did against the appointment of the metropolitan road commissioners ; but such personal interests can never be allowed to stand in the way of a great public improvement, the utility of which is evinced by the success of every similar experiment. Some honest people may feel alarmed on account of the additional patronage thrown into the hands of Government; but on this ground we see no cause for apprehension. The dissolution of the yeomanry corps, the reduction of the militia staff, and the measures in contemplation for the curtailment of the "*dead weight,*" sufficiently evince that Ministers are not at all tenacious of influence when in competition with the public interest; and certainly such reductions call for reciprocal confidence on the part of the people. If, however, the question of influence be a paramount consideration, a sacrifice equivalent to the increase of influence under the new system had better be made in some other department, by the reduction of a regiment of guards, or the conversion of them, or a portion of the half-pay, into metropolitan police;—at all events, the citizens of a great capital ought to be made secure in their beds, and their daily and nightly vocations.

CHAPTER VI.

CRIMES IN THE METROPOLIS.

General Causes influencing the Character of Crime in England.—Exposition of Offences against Trade and the Public Economy.—Gaming in London—Number of Gaming-houses—Illustration of Games of Chance—Sums lost by gaming, and enormous Expense of the first-rate Houses.—Laws to repress Gambling.—Intoxication of the pursuit to Military Men and others. — Regulations for Gaming-houses, a Tax on them unobjectionable—Low Gaming ought to be suppressed.—Bankruptcy, Insolvency, and Imprisonment for Debt—Recent Taint on the Mercantile Character—Number of Bankrupts and Insolvents during late Years, and Amount of their Dividends.—Anecdote of Major Semple.—Vast Source of Emolument to the Legal Profession.—Injuries to the Fair Trader from the Practices of Fraudulent Debtors.—Compromises and Trusts for the Benefit of Creditors.—Consequences of Imprisonment for Debt.—Persons arrested on Mesne Process in London, Middlesex, and Surrey.—Number of Persons in the Metropolitan Prisons for Debt, and Amount of Sums.—Credit too extensive, and its injurious Effects on Buyer and Seller.—Thraldom of Housekeepers in London to the Retailers.—Society for the Relief of Small Debtors.—Suggestions for the gradual Reform of the Debtor Law System.—Utility of abolishing all Remedy for the Recovery of Small Debts.

THE proportional excess of crime in England over other European countries forms a difficult problem which has not yet obtained satisfactory solution. Distinguished by superior wealth and intelligence, it seems extraordinary we should also be pre-eminent in that which is usually presumed to result from the absence of the advantages we enjoy. Great as is this anomaly, we think it admits of explanation, and that both the magnitude and complexion of our criminal calendar may be traced to certain obvious peculiarities in the pursuits and character of the population.

England is pre-eminently a commercial community, abounding in manufactories, shipping, and well-stocked warehouses; combined with these, commodities are constantly being conveyed and transferred from one to another, which affords opportunities, and enlarges the field for depredation. Commerce requires much individual confidence, and clerks, factors, and agents cannot always resist temptation. It is productive of luxury, and leads to the assembling of people together in large towns, to the creation of credit and paper money—the intoxicating and illusive stimulants to adventure and fruitful source of offences. It leads to sudden vicissitudes in men's fortunes, creates extreme inequality of condition, avidity of gain, and contempt for poverty; in short, makes the acquisition of wealth the ruling passion, and offences connected therewith the distinguishing trait of the community. Where there is little chattel property there cannot be much theft, either from the person, the dwelling, the warehouse, or in transfer; where there is little agency breaches of trust must seldom occur; and where men, as in agricultural countries, are in a fixed grade, without the chance of being either much better or worse, they are exempt from allurements to which sudden wealth or raging poverty is exposed. Hence, we apprehend, may be traced the general causes of the predominance of crimes against property in this country. We are peculiarly an enterprising, industrious, and emulative people; the field of depredation among us is more extensive, the necessities of individuals are greater, and the uncertainties in men's fortunes beget a recklessness and excitement which make them less scrupulous in the means employed to better their condition, or repair the reverses they have sustained.

On the other hand we are an enlightened people, and this seems to account for the second trait in our criminal character in the comparative fewness of offences against the person. Crimes accompanied with personal violence and indicating great depravity of heart are fewer in England than in other countries. We are, in fact, too calculating a people to give way to the unprofitable impulses of mere passion, and hence crimes originating in revenge, jealousy, lust, or mere atrocity, do not frequently occur. Our offences are *mercantile*, like our pursuits; even highway robbery is nearly extinct among us, and the depredations now chiefly pursued are forgery, coining, swindling, smuggling, pocket-picking, house-breaking, and intercepting bankers' parcels. They indicate no particular hostility to mankind, and form only a culpable and indirect pursuit of those objects which are in universal request, and form the chief basis of favour and distinction.

These appear to be the general causes of the number and description of criminal offences in England. Minor causes may be found in the state of the police, and in the imperfections of our criminal code; but these seem to refer rather to the *increase* of crime than its character, and will be more properly adverted to in a subsequent chapter. What has been said on the country generally applies strictly to the capital. The metropolis represents, on a large scale, the prevailing pursuits of the whole community, in being the great mart of commerce, the resort of shipping and navigation, the site of extensive manufactures, and in a large proportion of its population being actively engaged in the vicissitudes and speculations of trade: and hence its criminal character is the same, exhibiting the same excess of crimes against property and similar paucity of personal injuries.

In contrasting the manners and delinquencies of the metropolis, sixty or seventy years since, with those now prevalent, there is, certainly, no reason to think society has deteriorated in the interval. This opinion was held by the oldest officers and magistrates examined by the Parliamentary Committees on Police in 1816, 1817, and 1818; and we observe the same opinion was maintained last year. The crimes and vices now most rife in London are gaming among the higher and more opulent classes—theft, swindling, and fraud, among the middle classes—drinking among the lower classes, chiefly labourers. We shall, however, proceed to give a separate account of the more predominant delinquencies, beginning with those of a more venial character, and ascending to the higher and more atrocious crimes.

GAMING-HOUSES.

Gaming is a fruitful source of demoralization and crime, by forming only bad habits and destroying good ones. No one expects exemplary private virtues nor public spirit in a professed gambler, knowing that the excitement, selfishness, and anxiety engendered by the pursuit is destructive of every generous feeling. Whether a gambler is successful or unfortunate the influence on individual character is alike pernicious: in the former case the sudden acquisition of wealth usually leads to vicious indulgence and ostentatious insolence; in the latter, recourse is often had to criminal acts to retrieve losses, and enable the infatuated votary to resume his destructive vocation. From a propensity to this fatal vice has chiefly originated, as from a nursery or hot-bed, the vast host of cheats, sharpers, swindlers, forgers, and passers of counterfeit coin, with which the metropolis is infested.

Gaming rapidly extended in this country after the French Revolution, many novel games being introduced by the emigrants; prior to this event, according to Colquhoun,* there were not more than four or five gaming-houses in London, exclusive of those established by subscription. The chief site of them at present is at the West End, in Bury-street, Pall-Mall, King-street, Piccadilly, St. James's Street, and Leicester-place. Attempts have been made to locate them in the City, but to the credit of the authorities there, they have always shewn much jealousy against their establishment, as well as against houses of ill-fame and temples of atheism. The chief houses, or "hells," as they are significantly termed, are open only during a period when the town is filled with the idle, the opulent, and luxurious. Some of them are supported by subscription, others are partnership concerns, consisting of ruined gamblers, pettifogging attorneys, and unprincipled tradesmen.† In 1821, there were no fewer than twenty-two gaming-

* Treatise on the Police of the Metropolis, p. 140, seventh edition.

† Ascot races form the *champ de mai* of sporting men, and last year the ground was covered with gamblers. Being broad-day we had a favourable opportunity for observing, accurately, some of the labourers in the vineyard, and we amused ourselves in endeavouring to discover some facial lines or other traces by which the fraternity might be generally known and described. But, we confess, they baffled our attempts at classification; in dress and manner they all appeared *civil* and *plausible*, and, doubtless, it was only from more intimate acquaintance that any thing hurtful would have been experienced. Some would have passed very well for first-rate merchants or bankers; others looked really like local preachers,—

"Just with ROGER's head of hair on,
"ROGER's look and pious smile;"

while others again had clothes of such ante-diluvian cut, that they ap-

houses, at which play was continued with little interruption, at one or other, from one o'clock at noon throughout the night. They are now reduced in number, by consolidation, into larger establishments. The games mostly in vogue, are French—*rouge et noir*, *un deux cinque*, *roulette*, *and hazard*, at all of which a bank is put down proportioned to the means of the parties played against, the limitation of stakes varying according to its amount. Thus some play 1*s*. to £5, others 2*s*. 6*d*. to £10, and 5*s*. to £20, £50, and £200,—the bank amounting, generally, to twenty times the highest limits. The banks have certain points in their favour, which are deemed a *fair profit* for the capital embarked in the concern, and an equitable contribution by the players towards rent, refreshments, attendance, and other expenses of the establishment.

It is on the number of points in favour of the bank that the fairness of the game depends, and which determines the average loss or gain of the players. In a perfectly fair game of chance, wholly independent of skill, and in which no points are reserved, it is obvious that nothing could be ultimately won or lost by continued play, but the parties would leave off as they began. If, however, one point is reserved, it is clear the players have not only to contend against the equal chance of loss, but the recurrence of the event or point in which they cannot possibly win, and the effect of this must be to render the loss the greater the longer they play; and if they play long enough, the whole of their money, whatever its amount, must be swallowed up by the losing chance of the game.

peared much more like *flats* than *sharps*, and of an age long anterior to the devices of *thimble-rig*. No doubt the object of all was to appear respectable, inoffensive, and undesigning—the very reverse of what they were.

To put this in a simple form, we will suppose fifteen white and fifteen black balls put promiscuously into a bag, and that stakes of a sovereign are put down on each, and that the game is the white or black balls shall win according as a white or black ball is first drawn. This would be a fair game of chance, in which the chance of winning or losing is equal. But suppose a red ball is put into the bag, making the number thirty-one, and it is agreed when the red ball is drawn the stakes on both sides shall be forfeited, in consideration of the friction of the balls in playing, the wear of the bag, and the trouble of holding it by the proprietor. Now, as all the balls have an equal chance of coming up, the red ball will take its turn among the rest, and, agreeably to the law of chances, will be drawn on an average once in thirty-one times playing, and that £30 will be thus obtained for profit and expenses. If a ball is drawn every minute, the stakes would be swept away twice every hour by the bag-holder ; and, supposing play to continue five hours, he would clear £300, which inflicts an average loss of £10 on each player, exclusive of losses they sustain by the equal chances among themselves.

This is a correct illustration of the tendency of *rouge-et-noir*, *roulette*, *hazard*, and every game of chance in which points, or bars, are reserved to the proprietor of the bank, or gaming-table. Crockford, or whoever else puts down the bank, is the *bag-holder*, and takes his $\frac{1}{31}$ chance of winning, without risk of losing. Greater is the amount of stakes and quicker the recurrence of the reserved event, and larger will be the profits of the gaming-house-keeper.

The proportional points in favour of the bank vary in different games. At *French hazard*, which is played with a backgammon box and dice, it is calculated that, out of every eighteen events, the bank has a chance of winning once, without risk of loss ; which carries off a stake, whether of 5*s*. or £200, every hour from the player, without a chance of gain. At *rouge-et-noir*, played with cards and dice, the points come up two in sixty-eight events dealt in one hour, which is 1½ per cent. per stake, or 102 per cent. per stake per hour against the player. *Un deux cinque* is played with a large ivory ball, and gives six out of forty-eight events in favour of the bank. *Roulette* is played with a small ivory ball in a cylinder, and gives two in thirty-eight events rolled in half an hour, 3 per cent. per stake, 200 per cent. per hour against the player. These are the points against the player, provided the games are played according to admitted principles, but this is frequently not the case. Novices are often inveigled into the houses when the double ball is planted against them, or the cramped box, false or loaded dice, or packed cards, are employed for their destruction.

A writer in *The Times*, July 26, 1824, estimated the gain of the several banks, by points alone, at £234,000 per annum, from 1814 to 1824, making a total gain, in ten years, of £2,340,000. This was exclusive of what had been got, by cheating, upon the equal chances, and by attending races, fairs, fights, pigeon-shooting, and other gambling matches. The profits of one season at a well known pandæmonium, in St. James's, are supposed to have amounted to £150,000, over and above expenses. In one night a million of money is said to have been turned over at this place, and that £10,000 was occasionally down upon single events !*

* All attempts to estimate the plunder of the gaming-houses can, at best, be only approximations. There are, however, certain external circumstances, known to all the world, which sufficiently indicate the immense wealth accumulated. Most of the proprietors were originally in indigent circumstances ; one of them, T——v, who not long previously had taken the benefit of the insolvent act, was estimated, years ago, to be worth £150,000, and A—t, £70,000 ; both partners with Crock-

The most sure test is afforded of the wealth realized by the gaming-houses in the number of individuals

ford, when he opened a house in Piccadilly, where they cleared £200,000, in one season, at French hazard. The late P. Holdsworth had a mansion in Clarges-street, fitted up in a style of Eastern magnificence, where he wallowed in luxury and profusion. A noted hellite, in Leicester-place, is known to have spent £7 in cherries, at Christmas, a moment after he had refused a poor Major he had ruined a sovereign for charity. The celebrated Crockford—the great archangel of gamblers—is described, in the Court Guide, as having two residences in the most fashionable parts of the town, and another in the country. Most of them have their carriages, mistresses, and servants, vying with the aristocracy in costly magnificence.

The houses are generally fitted up in a very splendid style, and their expenses are very great. Those of the highest are said to be not less than £1000 a week.—(Crockford's; or, Life in the West, vol. ii. p. 93.) The next in eminence, £150 a week; and the minor ones of all vary from £40 to £80. The inspectors, or overlookers, are paid from £6 to £8 a week each; the *croupiers*, or dealers, £3 to £6; the waiters and porters £2; there are also bonuses to police-officers and watchmen. At the close of the season, in 1824, at Crockford's, £1000 was given to be divided among the waiters, and the head servant had half that sum presented to him as a new year's gift.—(*The Times*, October 9, 1824.) To these outgoings must be added the cost of refreshments of the choicest quality. At the high houses are tea, coffee, fruit, confectionary, wine, supper, &c.; at the low hells, tea, biscuits, and liqueurs.—See "Crockford's; or, Life in the West;"—a book which, among some extraneous nonsense, contains a good account of the gaming-houses.

The late Dr. Colquhoun estimated the amount of sums won and lost by gaming, in the course of a year, at £7,225,000. In his *Treatise on the Police of the Metropolis, seventh edition, p.* 143, he gives the following classification and summary of the gaming-houses in London, twenty years ago:—

	Persons attached.	Money played for nightly. £	Yearly aggregate lost and won. £
7 Subscription-houses, open one-third of the year, or 100 nights ....(*suppose*)	1000	2000	1,400,000
15 Houses of a superior class, one-third of the year, or 100 nights	3000	2000	3,000,000
15 Houses of an inferior class, one-half the year, or 150 nights..................	3000	1000	2,225,000
6 Ladies' gaming-houses, open 50 nights ..	1000	2000	600,000
			£7,225,000

known to have been reduced to poverty and crime by frequenting them, and the sums expended to compromise prosecutions instituted by their infatuated victims. We have seen a list of eight who, in a short time, committed suicide in consequence of losses in gaming; several have been transported for embezzlement; others have been hanged, under assumed names, for forgery and other capital offences. The history of Captain D——, of the King's Yeomen of the Guard, who escaped from the Giltspur-street Compter, disguised as a porter, having been apprehended for forgeries committed to meet his loss at the tables, must be still fresh in public recollection.

The sums expended in compromising prosecutions instituted by the infatuated victims of play are also considerable. In 1824, a series of actions and indictments were commenced against the keepers of a noted gaming-house in King-street, St. James's; but the proceedings came to nothing: the ruined men who instigated them were quieted by a gift of money, and the application of the same specific kept back the witnesses. The settling of these cost under £2000, which, it was boastingly said, was more than three times repaid to the defendants by the first throw of the dice on the night following.* Some prosecutions instituted two years preceding were more successful, when seven or eight keepers of gaming-houses, out of forty-five or fifty, were indicted and convicted. They were sentenced to certain terms of imprisonment, and to fines amounting to near fifteen thousand pounds.

The Doctor also makes it appear that £3,135,000 was annually won and lost by fraudulent insurances in the lottery. Thanks to the wisdom of the Legislature, this whirlpool has been closed!

* Morning Herald, December 28, 1824.

There is certainly law enough to restrain gambling, and punish the keepers of gaming-houses. By 33 Hen. VIII. c. 9, no apprentice, servant, or artificer shall play at tennis, bowls, cards, dice, quoits, or other unlawful sport, except at Christmas, and then in their master's houses; and justices and other head officers may enter houses suspected of unlawful games. By 9 Ann, c. 14, all bonds and other securities given for money won at play, or for money lost at play, are void. Persons losing £10 at play may recover it back from the winner; if the loser do not sue within three months, any other person may sue the winner for treble the sum so lost, one half to himself, the other to the poor. By several statutes of George II. all games at *hazard*, *roulette*, and other games with dice (backgammon excepted) are prohibited, under a penalty of £200 to the keeper of the tables, and £50 to the player. Persons losing £10 at one time, or £20 in twenty-four hours, may be indicted, and fined five times the amount. By 3 Geo. IV. c. 114, the keeping a common gaming-house subjects to imprisonment and hard labour in addition to or in lieu of any other punishment. Lastly, by 5 Geo. IV. c. 83, all persons playing or betting in any *open* or *public place*, with any table or instrument of gaming, at any game or pretended game of chance, may be treated as VAGRANTS, and committed, by a justice, to the house of correction for three months.

Thus, it appears, the Legislature has laboured hard to abate this destructive nuisance, but, somehow, with little success. One cause of failure may be ascribed to the mode of proceeding. Actions for recovering back sums lost at play must be brought within *three months*, which is too short a period for the victim of play to recover from his intoxication, to wean him from old connexions, and set him in array against them. Two years are allowed for *qui tam* actions for the penalties, which is a period as much too long as the other is too short. The exact amount of the sums lost, or the date, is often forgotten in the interval; and if the action cannot be turned by these means, recourse may be had to motions for new trial or writs of error, which effectually exhaust the funds or patience of the plaintiff. Proceedings by information before a magistrate, or indictment at the sessions, are generally frustrated by appeal, or by putting in bail, which is forfeited, the defendants paying the amount. But the most usual mode of evasion is in threats of arrest or of counter-persecution, or recourse is had to buying off prosecutors and witnesses. The last rarely fails of success: the parties being mostly ruined or rival gamblers, with whom money exerts a sovereign influence.

The vice is one of high antiquity, is sanctioned by imposing names, and we fear, despite of the pernicious influence it exerts on the character, it is not one that can be repressed or even greatly curtailed. Frequenters of gaming-houses are well aware of the frightful odds against them; and that the wealth of the Indies must inevitably be absorbed by perseverance in play: yet such is the effect of example, the fascinations of the scene, and the love of excitement, that they prefer certain ruin rather than forego the flutter of hope and of fear which the rattling of the dice-box creates. To the military and naval officer, in time of peace, the chances of the tables serve in lieu of the vicissitudes and stimulus of actual warfare. To the nobility, gentry, and great moneyed classes, it forms a species of traffic or barter; their incomes vastly exceed their wants, and staking the surplus on the cast of a die, even if lost, is mere child's play with counters, which deprives them only of that for which they had no indispensable use, neither abridging their comforts nor luxuries, nor incapacitating them for the discharge of the few duties society has left them to perform.

Unfortunately, the passion does not stop here ; it has extended through every grade and class in the community; is found not only at every watering-place, but at every inn, publican's, and almost every private house in the metropolis, and seems the natural offspring or accompaniment of immense wealth and luxury. Commerce, of late years, has become little more than a vast arena for gambling. Merchants have bought and speculated, not on previous information of scarcity or probable rise in prices, but solely from the superfluity of resources, a vague chance of increased demand, or that prices could be forced by the manœuvres of mere capital and combination. The funds have formed another great field for gambling, in which hundreds of persons are daily engaged, and in which the chances of loss are more certain than at the gaming-houses. Here the bank to be played against consists of the national dividends of thirty or forty millions per annum ; the differences to be paid at the closing of the accounts form the stakes ; and the brokers hold the reserved points of the game—they are, in fact, the *bag-holders*, whose gains are sure, whatever accrues to the adventurers.

Such being the extent of gaming, and the various shapes it has assumed, any attempt to subdue it altogether must prove hopeless, and perhaps unprofitable. But a vice that cannot be repressed may be regulated and rendered less hurtful to individuals, and perhaps even profitable to the State. From what has been said, it is obvious the gaming-houses are a source of immense profit to the keepers, and that there are a number of individuals in this opulent community, possessed of a redundancy of means, which they are bent on dissipating in their own peculiar way, and to their own personal injury. Such being the case, we apprehend the wealth that now flows into the coffers of the Abbotts, the Crockfords, the Taylors, and others of that description, might as well be diverted into those of the State, either as an augmentation to its resources, or for the relief of the public burdens.

What we would suggest on the subject is,—

1. That gaming-houses, including billiard-rooms and subscription houses for the purposes of playing games of chance, should be licensed.

2. That they should be placed under the control and occasional inspection of the police.

3. That all gaming in taverns, inns, public-houses, and coffee-houses should be rigorously interdicted.

The advantages of the *first* would be fourfold: 1. It would enable the magistrates, or other authority to whom the power of licensing was conceded, to locate them in such parts of the metropolis as was deemed most convenient and eligible. 2. It would empower them to close such as were improperly conducted, or had become a nuisance or annoyance to the neighbourhood. 3. Gaming-houses being licensed and tolerated, all games might be confined to them, and not allowed in public houses and other places of entertainment. 4. It would enable the Legislature to subject them to such amount and mode of taxation as might be deemed expedient. Raising a revenue from gaming-houses would not be liable to the objections which were justly urged against state lotteries. The last encouraged a vice productive of the worst consequences among the working classes; the former would have no tendency to render gaming more prevalent, even among the opulent, while it gleaned from their improvidence a portion of the redundant wealth which now only tends to swell the fortunes of profligate men.

With respect to the duty of inspection, by the police, it would require to be exercised under suitable control. It would be a vexatious annoyance if a common police officer could at any time intrude into the gaming-houses; his duty would be merely to observe how they are conducted, and report such as are disorderly, or managed upon nefarious principles; and these powers ought never to be exercised without the express permission of a magistrate. Subscription-houses might be exempt even from this surveillance, or might be subjected to the visitation of a magistrate only. It is inconsistent with all principles of police that many of the gaming-houses should be tolerated, as they now are, with a triple line of iron doors, bolted, and defended by fighting-men, which bid defiance to the entrance of an officer, whatever may be the pretext or occasion. Notwithstanding the full toleration conceded to religious sects, they are not yet allowed to celebrate their rites, even in the day time, with closed doors, and still less ought such a privilege be conceded to the midnight orgies of the gaming-house.

The suppression of low gaming, at taverns, public-houses, &c. would be an unmixed benefit to the community, and would be merely confining them to the purposes of their establishment, as places of refreshment, not of play. There are few public-houses in which the law is not violated in this respect, and at which may not be found, nearly at all hours, mechanics and tradesmen engaged at cards, dice, or other unlawful games. This is productive of the most injurious effects. Habits of drinking, late hours, and neglect of business and families are formed, that totally unfit them for the pursuits in which their social duties and individual happiness are identified.

BANKRUPTCY, INSOLVENCY, IMPRISONMENT FOR DEBT, AND PRIVATE CREDIT.

Commerce, of late years, has been little better than desperate gambling, and the mercantile character has undergone a serious depreciation. Under perilous circumstances, men are liable to become more selfish and unprincipled; and if, during the convulsions of 1825, the commercial classes had shown less honour and disinterestedness, it might have been ascribed to the overwhelming embarrassments with which they were suddenly visited; but the moral blight originated in causes operating long anterior to that period. Much of it, no doubt, may be ascribed to the avidity of gain, to the loose principles engendered by gambling in the funds, and a thirst for the distinctions wealth confers; but a great deal more to the operation of the debtor and creditor laws. The property lost by the industrious and confiding, from mere theft and robbery, forms only a drop in the sea compared with the immense sums drawn from them by the fraudulent debtor. It is not our intention to enter largely into this subject, but merely to concentrate a few observations and facts which will develope the tendency of the existing system, and its connexion with the growth of immorality and crime. Next to gambling there is not a more prolific hotbed of sharpers, swindlers, and rogues of all kinds than bankruptcies, insolvencies, compositions, bills of exchange, credit, and debtors' gaols.

Two principal observations may be made on the general tendency of the debtor-laws; one applies to their inutility in favour of the creditor; the other to their unjust and injurious operation on the debtor. All the laws of bankruptcy, insolvency, arrest, and imprisonment, are intended either to indemnify the creditor or to punish the debtor. As respects the interests of the former, they usually fail to give anything like an equivalent for his loss, and the chief advantages result to those whom the law never intended to benefit by their operation. As regards the latter, they are pernicious by the undefined power it gives the creditor to punish for immorality, which is no crime or even misfortune. Under the Insolvent Act, this power is limited to the first imprisonment of the debtor, and subsequently opposing his discharge on examination; in bankruptcy, the creditor may refuse the certificate without reason assigned; but, in arrest on *mesne process*, and in execution, the power is direct, arbitrary, and unlimited.

From 1790 to 1825 inclusive, there had issued, in England, 49,754 commissions of bankruptcy, making at least 100,000 bankrupts. It would be curious to ascertain the amount of debts and the average dividends paid on this mass of commercial ruin. But we are not aware there exist any authentic returns upon which such a statement could be founded. Of 16,202 bankrupts, between the years 1786 and 1805, there were 6597 who did not obtain their certificates.* If the dividends paid by bankrupts bear any proportion to those paid by debtors who take the benefit of the Insolvent Act, they are hardly worth the creditors' acceptance. The following is an authentic return on the subject:—

Insolvent Debtors discharged........15,249
Gross amount of their debts................£10,979,943 2 9¾
Gross amount of property got in by the assignees ..£60,084 1 2¼†

This leaves about *one penny farthing* in the pound to the creditor, without deducting court-fees, &c.

* Report on the Bankrupt Laws, Parl. Papers, 1818, vol. vi. p. 97.
† Parl. Paper, No. 311, vol. xvii. 1819.

I 2

The facilities afforded, under the Insolvent Act, for escaping from pecuniary obligation, have tended, yearly, to swell the number of persons who have availed themselves of the benefit of the statute till the number averages nearly 5,000 per annum, upwards of one-half of whom are passed by the court in London, the remainder by the commissioners on circuit. The following statement exhibits the number yearly discharged since the passing of the 53 Geo. III. abstracted from Parl. Paper, No. 42, Sess. 1828:—

Years.	Insolvents Discharged.	Years.	Insolvents Discharged.
1813	61	1821	5290
1814	1893	1822	4955
1815	2886	1823	4241
1816	3263	1824	3593
1817	3548	1825	3665
1818	3484	1826	4681
1819	3352	1827 to June 12	2199
1820	4012		

All these bankruptcies and insolvencies must have tended enormously to the emolument of the legal profession, and have rendered them by far the richest class in the community.*

* The gleanings of the gentlemen of the long robe, from this fertile field, have been well touched upon in the *Morning Herald:* —

"In most bankrupt cases the solicitors, the bar, the commissioners, the accountants, and auctioneers divide the assets. Very few estates pay anything worth a man's while going after. Under the present bankrupt law, a man has nothing to do but to get into credit to as large an amount as possible—buy goods in every quarter—turn merchant—ship off such goods to every quarter of the world—fly kites in every possible way—keep no books, or those so confusedly that no man, called in by the name of an accountant, could make head or tail of them—carry this system of buying, and exporting, and kite-flying to its utmost extent—purchase goods on credit at any price, and for the greatest length of time—declare his insolvency—go into the *Gazette;* the solicitors, the bar, the commissioners, the accountants, the auctioneers, &c. &c. &c. would set to work; the larger the amount of the

Professional men, however, are not the only devourers of the estate: it is notorious a large portion of bankruptcies are concerted—that is, conspiracies of the bankrupt and a few personal friends, for their common benefit, at the expense of the creditors. This mode of acquiring property has been the most common of mercantile speculations, and the routine is so well known, that description is almost superfluous. The preliminary step is the establishment of an extended credit by ostentatious appearances, by accommodation paper, by artful introductions and false representations of wealth and connexion. Next come the preparations for the *catastrophe*—the mistifying of the books, the creation of a mass of fictitious debts, and the sale for cash of stock bought at high prices and for long credit; the creditors of the bankrupt who have acted as decoys in raising the concern, are got out of it by prompt payment, or are retained under imaginary claims to be chosen assignees; in which capacity they assist the bankrupt through his examinations, and smooth the way for the certificate, by softening the asperity of creditors, with artful representations of the bankrupt's character and extraordinary misfortunes; or, as has been frequently the case lately, the friendly assignee *buy in*, at an insignificant price, a large part of the estate, by the aid of a third person, either for himself or the bankrupt, having first depreciated its value to co-assignees and others, by the disadvanta-

man's debts so much the better for the legal, accounting, and auctioneering agents. In such case, the legal men call it "*a good fat bankruptcy*;" and if they can get it into Chancery, so much the better; and, in general, it is contrived that "*a good fat bankruptcy*" shall get into Chancery. The result, in general, is—ten or twelve years' meetings of commissioners, actions, bills in Chancery; and at length, when the legal men have the assets, they tire, and the creditors are told, "Here, gentlemen, are the accounts."

geous form in which it is presented in advertisements and catalogues to the public.

One of the greatest abuses in trade has its chief origin in the forced sales of the incipient bankrupt and insolvent: they buy goods at any price, knowing that the terms will prove merely *nominal,* and that the seller will at most receive only a trifling per centage in payment; these goods are re-sold under prime cost, to houses commanding ready money, and who are thus enabled to monopolize the trade, to undersell the regular dealer, and defy competition.*

* If the averments of a daily paper may be credited, still more objectionable practices are resorted to by some houses, to enable them to accommodate bargain hunters with a cheap article. "There are, in London," says the writer, "several extensive shops, out of which occasionally a few poor countermen are hanged or transported, who, provided they be cheap, will buy every description of goods offered them. Stolen goods—goods received from pawnbrokers—goods, the real owners of which are unknown—silk shawls, purloined by servants—ribbons, cut from the loom by thieves—bales abstracted from warehouses and waggons, are, at the marts to which we allude, sold cheap to our loving countrywomen."—*Morning Journal,* November 16, 1828.

This is slashing work, and can apply only to a small portion of the trade in the metropolis: it must be received with some grains of allowance, like the affirmation of the same editor, December 2d, when, in observing on Hunton's case, he said, "Forgery is, or has been, committed by *half the traders* in London." Large capital, a quick return, and a judicious and economical management, will always enable some houses to sell cheaper than others. What follows is deserving more attention, it being partly corroborated by a return made to parliament last session of the amount of seizures for frauds on the revenue:—

"There are several wholesale and retail warehouses in the metropolis, whose joint stocks of French manufactures, chiefly silks, cannot be estimated at less than a million sterling. Two-thirds of this stock consist of smuggled goods—of goods which ought to pay nearly forty per cent. *ad valorem,* but which have not contributed one single sol to the revenue. They have paid some duty, we admit, but this has been in the shape of hush-money to certain officers, and to certain commis-

It is not surprising that highway robbery and the more hazardous enterprises have decreased, since so much easier an access to plunder has been discovered; and this appears to have been found out by the more notorious depredators. Alderman Waithman relates that Major Semple, in conversation, once said, "Why, sir, I have been a fool all my life-time; I have not known how to go to work; I have been running the risk of my life for little trifling things; but if I were to begin my life again, I would open shop as trader or merchant, and become a bankrupt, and make my fortune at once."

There is an instance of one person in London having been bankrupt four times during the last fifteen years, and once taken the benefit of the insolvent act. In short, the observation of Foote, in one of his farces, has been found no joke, when he said, "The king had not a better thing in his gift than a commission of bankruptcy."

Compromises and trusts for the benefit of creditors are also frequent, and answer like purposes, and are conducted to similar issues, as bankruptcies and insolvencies. In these, however, the lawyer and attornies do not profit so largely: their functions have been partly superseded by the accountant, who has lately become an important agent in these affairs, and forms a new species of bird of prey. He is mostly applied to by the debtor to look over and *prepare the*

sion agents. The men who continue this traffic, who are the originators of it, and who pocket the profits of it, are generally esteemed wealthy. They keep their carriages, they are the patrons of education; their names adorn the lists of our charitable subscriptions; they aspire to offices of honour and dignity; and yet they thus launch into a trade which is the parent of every kind of vice, leads to flagrant breaches of the law, corrupts public morals, makes our seamen the accessories of crime, and consign to penury and helplessnes the families of our industrious artizans.—*Morning Journal*, November 31st, 1828.

books: to go round to the creditors, making such representations as are most likely to bring them to terms, usually unexampled and unavoidable losses; or, perhaps, he proceeds on an opposite tack—expatiates on the spendthrift character of the insolvent; that something certain is better than nothing; and that half a crown in the pound is preferable to encountering the costs of bankruptcy, the making up of the schedule in the Insolvent Court, or the dissipation of a gaol.

But what is the utility of dwelling on topics which are familiar to most people of the least experience in the mercantile world? We have said enough to show how little the creditor profits by bankruptcy and insolvency, as now managed; while the practices they foster familiarize the mind to all kinds of fraud and swindling, and open the way and are the prelude to the highest crimes. In modern commercial practice, an honest creditor may be likened to an animal whose name we have forgotten, which is thriving in itself, but so void of art and offence that it is the common prey of every other.

Bankruptcy and insolvency have been chiefly considered in their tendency to benefit the creditor: we shall now offer a few remarks on the tendency of *arrest and imprisonment for debt;* from these the creditor derives still less pecuniary benefit than the former; but we shall chiefly view them in their operation on the debtor.

Whether it is politic in a commercial country to allow imprisonment of the person for debt, either on mesne process or in execution, forms a question which could not be fully discussed in this place; and, therefore, is one we shall not presume to determine. Non-payment of debt, if a crime at all, is a crime against property only; and, perhaps, it would be enough to allow property to answer for it: and there is this peculiarity between it and other crimes against property that it is committed with the mutual consent of the parties. Goods sold on credit are mostly charged extra; this extra charge is the premium exacted by the creditor on account of the risk of repayment; and, having thus fixed the equivalent for his chance of loss, it seems supererogatory in the law to grant him, in addition, the power of *ex post facto* punishment, the amount of which he is the sole judge, merely because he has failed in a voluntary adventure, into which he had been tempted to embark, from the prospect of reaping a greater profit than is charged by the ready money tradesman. This is certainly not treating the two classes of dealers fairly; it is encouraging one at the expense of the other, and that, too, in a course inconsistent with the true interests of the country.

A host of eminent writers have signified their hostility to the power of arrest; among them, BURKE and JOHNSON, by declaring "That the end of all civil regulations, which is to secure private happiness from private malignity, is apparently violated when a man, irritated with loss, is allowed to be the judge of his own cause, and to assign the punishment of his own pain." Lord ELDON said, "the law of arrest is a permission to commit acts of greater oppression and inhumanity than are to be met with in slavery itself, and that redressing such a grievance would not be attended with any fatal consequences to the country."

In practice, the power of arrest is often perverted to purposes foreign to its ostensible object. It has been resorted to as a means not of recovering a just claim, but to prevent a just claim being preferred; and the same artifice of a false allegation of debt has been frequently employed to remove a person out of the way who happened to be troublesome, or that some criminal intention might be effected during his incarceration.

Creditors rarely derive any advantage from imprisonment beyond the indulgence of vindictive feeling, which it is inconsistent with the true ends of public law to encourage. Those who do benefit by it are usually the most unfair and ungenerous, who, by a sudden arrest, often embarrass and prejudice all the other parties interested. To the debtor, the consequences are peculiarly hurtful—personal degradation,—augmented incapacity and diminished inclination to satisfy his prosecutor,—and the contraction of habits inconsistent with future integrity and industry.

Those who chiefly profit, as in bankruptcy and insolvency, are lawyers and attorneys. From returns of affidavits of debts it appears in two years and a half 70,000 persons were arrested in and about London, the law expenses of which could not be less than £500,000.* In the year 1827, in the metropolis and two adjoining counties, 23,515 warrants to arrest were granted, and 11,317 bailable processes executed. The following is an abstract of the parliamentary return of last session, No. 149:—

	Warrants granted.	Baleable Processes executed.
Secondary's office, London	3,979	2,362
Sheriffs of London, in Middlesex	16,258	7,264
Ditto of Surrey	3,278	1,691
Total	23,515	11,317

More than eleven thousand persons deprived of their liberty, on the mere declarations of others, before any trial or proof that they owed a farthing! So gainful is the trade to attorneys, that they frequently buy up small bills, for the purpose of suing the endorsers and bring nine or ten actions on each. One house alone has brought 500 actions in this way, and most of them for sums under £20.

* Mr. Hume, House of Commons, February 19, 1827.

The legal expenses, no doubt, far exceed the amount of the sums sought to be recovered. In 1827, in London and Middlesex, 2318 executions were issued against the *person* for sums amounting to £178,427; against the *goods* 2,088 executions for sums amounting to £380,707: total, 4408 executions, for £559,134.*

But it is not the pecuniary bearings of the question which are so important as the moral and criminal consequences; and it is fortunate for society the opinion is daily becoming more prevalent of the hurtful tendencies of imprisonment. The debtor laws in France by no means present an example for imitation, but in some respects they are superior to the practice in this country. Under the *Code Napoleon* (articles 2065 and 2067,) the arrest of persons aged seventy is prohibited; nor can any person be arrested unless judgment has been pronounced. Some further improvements in the law are in contemplation: it is proposed to restrict the power of personal arrest to sums exceeding 500 francs, and to exempt every one from arrest for debt, not actually in trade, even though the debt be acknowledged by a bill of exchange.† The principle upon which these ameliorations have been introduced is the necessity of diminishing the number of credit transactions in cases where the interests of trade do not require an indulgence of this nature; and thus reducing, at the same time, the risk of the trader and the improvidence of the buyer.

In England, the sum on which arrest is allowed has been gradually augmented to £20, but this sum is too small, and the consequence is the prisons are crowded with debtors for the most paltry amounts. The number of persons committed to the five principal prisons of the

* Parliamentary Paper, No. 192, Sess. 1828.

† Examiner, January 4, 1829.

metropolis, exclusive of crown debtors, and those imprisoned for contempt, averages 6000 per annum. Of these more than one-third are for sums under £20. In the years 1826–7, the Court of Requests for the city of London imprisoned 753 persons for various terms, from 20 to 100 days, for sums under £5. In the same year the Court of Requests for Southwark ordered 9758 executions, and 1893 persons were actually imprisoned for debts amounting only to £16,442.*

The state of the great debtor prisons, in January, 1828, will appear from the following return to parliament.

Number of Persons committed for Debt to the several Prisons of the Metropolis in the Year 1827, *and the Sums for which they were committed.*—Parliamentary Paper, No. 76, Sess. 1828.

	For sums above £100.	For sums between £50 & £100.	For sums between £50 & £20.	For sums under £20.	Total.	In custody Jan. 1, 1828.
King's Bench Prison	474	354	550	213	1591	674
Fleet Prison	206	141	223	113	683	253
Whitecross-street Prison	206	273	816	600	1893	378
Marshalsea Prison	20	30	166	414	630	102
Horsemonger-lane Prison	57	58	134	923	1172	105
Total	963	856	1889	2263	5969	1512

Some of these prisons, especially the Fleet, the Marshalsea, and the great city prison in Whitecross-street, are known to be perfect hells, in which deeds of the most revolting nature are of ordinary occurrence. The last of these receptacles of crime and calamity is a living picture of the ancient Alsatia, described in the "Fortunes of Nigel," in which the most abominable oppression and personal annoyance are perpetrated with impunity. There is no classification, except of men from women, and London prisoners from Middlesex prisoners. In the very confined space of Middlesex yard are

* Parl. Paper, No. 487, Sess. 1828.

frequently congregated from three to four hundred persons, presenting a motley assemblage of those called "gentlemen"—of poor tradesmen, who owe their incarceration to unavoidable misfortune—of cheats, swindlers, litigants, and squabblers, of whom it may be said it is for the good of the community they should be here, were their confinement perpetual, in lieu of a temporary seclusion, that enables them to hold a congress in which to concoct future schemes of fraud and depredation.

Having brought together the chief facts connected with the operation of the debtor-laws, it only remains to offer a few concluding observations.

Our first observation is, that these laws have failed in attaining the chief object for which they were intended. The bankrupt and insolvent laws were framed for the benefit of trade, and the operation of the first limited to traders only; still it appears, owing to the expenses, fraud, and collusion, attending their execution, that traders—honest traders, at least—derive little advantage from them, and that the chief advantages result to those whom the law never intended to benefit by their operation.

Notwithstanding the failure of these laws, they have become in some measure indispensable, from the *system of credit* established amongst us. Credit is an excellent auxiliary to infant states, abounding in dormant resources, demanding the quickening power of individual confidence, and an artificial circulation, to bring them into activity. It has formed the ladder of England's prosperity, which has unfortunately been retained after her own stature had become sufficiently matured to stand on the level ground of real property. Hence it has latterly been an agent of evil, and in the shape of bank-notes and private paper has contributed to the disastrous vicissitudes which have recently marked our commercial history. The lowness of interest and the readiness with which funds can be obtained for any project of improvement or speculation, sufficiently indicate the abundance of ready money for the legitimate purposes of commerce, and that credit to the extent to which it has been recently carried can only tend to national impoverishment, by augmenting the mass of unemployed capital, and forcing the wealth of the country into disastrous channels of employment, into foreign loans, mines, and the other improvident speculations that distinguished a period still fresh in public recollection.

But if credit has become less necessary in the higher pursuits of commerce, the excuse is still feebler for its prevalence in all the transactions of private life. In foreign commerce and in the long unbalanced accounts necessarily subsisting between merchant and merchant, mutual confidence is unavoidable; but the same plea does not exist for the retail dealings of every class of society. In no other country is this system so diffused; in England, it has been justly observed, credit is the rule; abroad it is the exception. None but men of known good character are trusted any where but in England, and they but for a short period; few in England are compelled to pay money except those against whom some ground of suspicion exists, and credit for the unsuspected has scarcely any limit. It is this facile confidence which chiefly contributes to engender the swarm of bankrupts and unprincipled insolvents, and to nurture those schemes for swindling traders out of their goods by worthless bills, by plausible references to colleagues in fraud, living in apparent respectability, and who are placed in reserve to support the out-door accomplices, who, with the easy air and equipage of persons of fortune, lounge into the shops of upholsterers, jewellers, and other tradesfolk, exchanging "sleek promises for solid wares." Such a system is an offence against public morals and economy, by encouraging extortion in the seller, waste in the buyer, and fraud and crime in profligate adventurers. "See (says *The Times*, Sept. 6, in concluding an able article on this subject) what an encouragement it affords to improvidence in the sanguine and to dishonesty in the cunning! See to what risk it exposes the tradesman who might be of himself inclined to deal for money, but who must do like other tradesmen, or be left altogether without customers! Again, is it not obvious that the danger of incurring bad debts must compel the tradesman to balance his frequent losses by enhancing his general prices, so as to make the upright and prudent customer pay for the rogue or extravagant defaulter? Hence the cost of numerous articles made and sold in England above all calculation of reasonable profit, if *bad debts* were not to be invariably taken in as an important item in the estimate."

Flagrant as is the evil described, it is one for which there is no law, nor could any be framed with advantage to the community. Trade is said to be "universal cheating by mutual consent," and, certainly, to root out the tares therein might endanger the whole produce, and bring man back to his primæval resources. But though the Legislature could not interfere by positive enactment, it might withhold the encouragement present laws afford to a system injurious to individuals and hostile to the progress of national wealth. The bankrupt and insolvent laws and the the power of imprisonment for debt are direct promotives of the credit system; though in great part illusive and unprofitable to the trader, he deems them his great auxiliaries to compel restitution or inflict punishment. Without these credit would be sufficiently abridged;

it would not be refused or abolished entirely—that would not be requisite; but it would be granted under such circumspection that at least the industrious, frugal, and honest would not have, as is now the case, to pay for the knavish, idle, and luxurious.

It is only by gradually approximating to such a change that one of the greatest abuses in domestic trade can be abated. No single tradesman, as remarked above, can safely deviate from the existing system; he would merely ruin himself without achieving the least general good, and his fate would operate rather as a warning than an example. The Legislature can alone afford adequate aid by removing the ancillary resources on which creditors falsely rely, and thus compel a simultaneous change in existing practice.

And even an alteration attempted by public authority would require to be slowly introduced; the interests of a numerous profession are bound up in the administration of the debtor-laws; and many not interested think that any great amelioration in them would be inconsistent with commercial policy. The *first* and easiest step, perhaps, would be to augment, considerably, the sum on which arrest on mesne process could be made, and to abolish it entirely on bills and notes: these have tended, far more than bank-paper, to effect sudden changes in the volume of circulation, and thus lead to disastrous vicissitudes: moreover, the business of discounting and accepting them is often perverted to the vilest purposes of fraud and swindling.

The *next* step in reform would be to augment the amount of the petitioning creditor's debt in bankruptcy; to render the execution of the bankrupt-laws more economical; and the checks against fraud and evasion more effective. Bankruptcy is the least objectionable part of the debtor system; for nothing appears more equitable when a tradesman becomes embarrassed, either from loss or mismanagement, than that he should surrender up the whole of his property for the common benefit of himself and creditors. If this *cessio bonorum* could be more economically administered, and rendered more productive to the creditor, and measures could be framed to compel an insolvent to a more prompt surrender of his effects, before they have been in great part prodigally expended, or indirectly disposed of, in contemplation of such an event, some of the strongest objections against the utility of the bankrupt-laws would be obviated. But, after witnessing the unsuccessful attempts of the legislature to improve these laws, and after considering the evidence of persons of the greatest experience in these matters, of Messrs. Waithman, Bainbridge, Kemble, Montagu, Barclay, and others, we confess there appears little prospect of such improvements ever being devised.

The Insolvent Debtors' Act seems to have degenerated into little more than a series of forms and ceremonies; the getting-up the schedule is such that rarely any thing accrues to the creditor from the assets; and the short imprisonment of the debtor scarcely operates either as disgrace or punishment. It certainly empties the gaols; but if this be an advantage, it would be an improvement upon it never to fill them, rather than resort to a preventive which does not correct the defaulter, and only renders him a worse social member.*

* Offers of compromise from debtors are said not to be so frequent, in consequence of the Insolvent Act; and Sir Peter Laurie stated to a parliamentary committee, that tradesmen charge ten per cent. more for their commodities, on account of the facilities it afforded to the escape of debtors. (*Report on Insolvent Debtors' Act*, 1816, Parl. Paper, No. 472, page 21.) This is a pretty heavy tax upon the *paying* part of the community, tending greatly to lessen consumption, and, consequently, the returns and profits of vendors. Tradesmen are

The last and most important reform would consist in the abolition of all process, and of all courts instituted solely for the recovery of debts below a certain sum—£10 or £20. This, in our opinion, would be the most feasible change of all, and productive of incalculable advantages. No prudent man ever thinks it for his interest to sue for a debt below £15;* the expenses in prosecuting for a small debt being equal to a large one, owing to the proceedings being the same and the pleadings as voluminous for the recovery of a few shillings as £100. Attempts have been made to remedy this evil by establishing courts of conscience; and it has even been proposed to restore the efficiency of county courts for the recovery of debts. But these measures appear to proceed on a mistaken principle; they promote a disease which a sounder legislation would altogether prevent. Increasing the facilities for the recovery of small debts only multiplies their number, and thus encourages credit transaction among classes where it is most pernicious, and where there is no pretext of public utility for its existence.

Upwards of one-third of the persons incarcerated in the metropolitan gaols are for debts under £20, and most of these have been contracted by clerks, curates, mechanics, labourers, half-pay officers, small annuitants, and others, with the butcher, baker, hatter, shoemaker,

mostly inclined to severer laws towards debtors; they appear to have no idea that all laws would become unnecessary by a simultaneous decline in the custom of credit. That credit can be avoided entirely, even in retail trade, we do not believe; this is the opinion of the best-informed merchants and tradesmen of the metropolis; persons of the greatest respectability often taking the longest credit, to the great profit of their domestics: but what we reprobate is its indiscriminate indulgence to all classes—its not being the exception, but the rule of trade.

* Report on Small Debts, Parl. Papers, 1823, vol. iv. page 1.

victualler, and coal-merchant, and who, having a weekly or other periodical income, depending on no contingency, ought never to be suffered to be involved in any debt whatever. It is obvious, however, that the temptation to incur debt by such persons is irresistible, and will never be refrained from unless firmly resisted by the retailers, who, as they cannot singly adopt this course, ought to be compelled to act simultaneously, by the law withholding from them all power to punish or compel payment. This would bring credit within wholesome limits; it would compel the dealer to discriminate among his customers, and exclude from his books those whom he knew, from the nature of their incomes, if they did not pay, according to the proverb "upon the peck bottom," would have no additional means of paying an accumulating account. It would also be advantageous to the buyers, by making them more economical, keeping their expenditure within their income, and relieving them from the thraldom to which they are now subjected by the shopkeepers. Most housekeepers are in a state of degrading vassalage to the retailers; they live under a species of *soke*, and are obliged, from having incautiously got into their books, to deal with them, whatever be the price or quality of their goods.

It is astonishing to what an extent this trumpery system is carried in the metropolis: from the inquiries of a Parliamentary Committee* it appears hatters and shoemakers have often £4000 and upwards on their books in debts below £10, and that five-sixths of their book-debts are below that sum. Half of these debts are, probably, lost, and, as all these traders do not go into the *Gazette*, the loss is averaged, and the "good made to pay for the bad."

* Report on Small Debts, 1823, Parl. Paper, vol. iv. page 3.

The anxiety, loss of time, and expense incurred in suits for small sums, is another reason why all pretext for instituting them should be avoided. Whether an action is begun in a superior court, or in one of the numerous local courts in the metropolis, the costs are enormous, and which the debtor, not unfrequently, by availing himself of the insolvent-act, throws upon the creditor. In the King's Bench, Westminster, the expenses of recovering a debt under £5, even if no defence is made and judgment goes by default, is not less than £15; if defendant appear, and, as is not uncommonly the case, puts in a dilatory plea, they are increased to £20; and, by taking out a writ of error, they are still further augmented. By a series of proceedings, which every debtor in confinement is promptly made acquainted with, it is well known the defendant may put the plaintiff to an expense of upwards of £300, while his own is less than £25. In the minor courts the costs are something less, but even here they form a tax of at least 25 per cent. or upwards, payable either by creditor or debtor. A debt can seldom be recovered in the Marshalsea or Palace Court for less than £8, even if no resistance is offered; in the several courts of request for the city of London, Middlesex, Westminster, and the Borough, the expenses of recovering a debt of 40*s*. or under, is at least 11*s*.; above that sum, twice as much. Such a system can be no advantage to the tradesman or shopkeeper; it can only tend to his own ruin or that of his customers.

A society instituted for the "Discharge and Relief of Small Debtors" has for many years been in beneficial operation, and contributed, as far as its funds would admit, to abate the mischief of the imprisonment-law for debt. As the bankrupt and insolvent acts are chiefly applicable to the relief of the higher class of debtors, this Society limits its efforts to the minor objects, and never advances more than a composition of £20 for debts of any amount. Restricted to this sum, the number of persons relieved is astonishing, chiefly artizans, seamen, and servants, who, to the great benefit of their parishes and themselves, have been restored to their families and employment. From the last report of the Society we collect that 44,710 debtors have been discharged, of whom 28,651 had wives, with 79,614 children, making a total of 152,975 persons benefited by an expenditure of £133,983, averaging £2 : 19 : 10½ each debtor, or 18*s*. 8*d*¾. each individual. This is certainly creditable to the society, and shows how much may be effected at a little charge; but, as prevention is better than cure, an act of the Legislature, which should deprive the creditor of the power of injuring himself and others, would be a still greater boon. The liberties of Englishmen are, certainly, not so high priced, when 44,710, most of them family men too, can be deprived of personal freedom, merely because they cannot raise 18*s*. 8¾*d*. per head!

The last advantage we shall notice as likely to result from abolishing all process for small debts, is, that it would be a great relief to the superior courts. It is well known that one cause of the pressure of business before those tribunals is the number of actions for small sums, which often compels suits of greater importance to be postponed, compromised, or abandoned, from despair of getting them brought forward.

We have thus endeavoured to convey to the reader some idea of the operation of the debtor-laws, and the consequences of indiscriminate credit. The reforms we have ventured to suggest are not such as impose additional restrictions on individual freedom; our object has not been to recommend new laws, but to repeal old ones that have become pernicious, to compel individuals to abandon a system injurious to themselves and the public, and to rely more on their own prudence and less on coercive legislation. It may be asked—What has this to do with the police of the metropolis? Debt, it is true, is only a civil injury, and simply in that light is unconnected with police; but, in its consequences, it is a prolific source of crime, and, as such, is within the sphere of preventive justice. Bankruptcy, insolvency, and imprisonment are great demoralizers, and the nursery of fraud, swindling, perjury, and embezzlement. They are the first steps in the delinquent's progress, and leave an indelible stain on the mercantile character. No one passes through any of these without feeling himself a different person, and he is so thought by others. Imprisonment is as fatal to the virtue of a man as the loss of chastity to a woman. Such are the defective provisions in some parts of the Metropolis, that debtors, committed by local courts for a few shillings, are actually sent to the house of correction,* and thus are treated in all respects as criminals, though not even suspected of crime. What can be expected from such insult and contamination? One witness examined by the Police Committee (Mr. Pearson) ascribed the increase of juvenile offenders to parents being dragged from their families to jails for paltry debts. The same person ascribed many depredations to information given by prodigal persons of family confined in prisons to low attorneys, fences, and other hangers-on, of such places. But we have already detained the reader too long on this subject, and shall conclude with expressing a hope that the Legislature will shortly see the wisdom of cutting off at least one-third of the evil resulting from the existing system.

* Report on the Police of the Metropolis, 1828, page 96.

CHAPTER VII.

MENDICITY—FEMALE PROSTITUTION—JUVENILE DELINQUENCY—THIEVES AND RECEIVERS.

Mendicity without Excuse in England.—Causes of Mendicity in the Metropolis.—Culpable Conduct of Metropolitan Police.—Measures to prevent Begging in Paris.—Exposition of the Frauds and Artifices of Beggars.—Parliamentary Report on Mendicity.—Irish Emigrants, their Cost to Parishes.—Society for the Suppression of Mendicity.—Almsgiving.—FEMALE PROSTITUTION.—*General Character of Metropolitan Females.—Prostitution in London and the Country.—Partnership for vending obscene Books and Pictures.—In the Arts of Beggars and Prostitutes no Improvement for Centuries.—Number of Prostitutes.—Brothels chiefly kept by Jews.—Magdalen Hospital and London Female Penitentiary.—On the Interference of the Police for the Suppression of Brothels.*—JUVENILE DELINQUENCY, *its Origin and general Character.—Painful Dilemma of Magistrates from the present State of the Law.—Children on board the Hulks.—Suggestion for the Disposal of Juvenile Delinquents.*—FENCES, *or* RECEIVERS, *Thieves' Attorneys, Family-Men, Negotiating Police Officers and Flash-House-Keepers.—Robbery of Bankers.—Dangerous System of Compromising.—Share of Police Officers in these Transactions.—Magistrates not exempt from Blame.—Conduct of a well-known Solicitor.—Laws affecting Compositions, and Suggestions for their Improvement.*

WHERE there is no public provision for the relief of indigence and misfortune, it would be extreme inhumanity to refuse to the wretched the liberty of soliciting alms from their more fortunate fellow-creatures. The conservation of society demands that neither ignorance of the laws nor the pressure of want can justify their violation, and no man, however urgent his necessities, shall, with impunity, seize on the property of another; but it would be a great stretch of this principle, unwarranted by the same social interests, to interdict to distress the bare permission to ask for what charity may be freely and voluntarily disposed to bestow. One is a crime of the deepest dye, the other, in its own nature, scarcely appears a crime at all, and can only be so construed from the extraneous evils it tends to induce. Unless distress be allowed openly to manifest itself, neither its intensity nor extent can be known; measures of alleviation will not be adopted—its origin investigated; nor can those salutary reflections be excited in the beholder, tending to warn him from errors, by which the calamities of others have been produced.

All these reasons, however, for the open toleration of MENDICITY, in countries where there is no provision for the destitute, can have no place in England. Here the institution of the poor-laws dispenses with all the pretexts for begging for subsistence. Every Englishman has his parish, and every parish is bound to find work for those unable to get employment; to bring up to useful trades the children of the destitute; and to provide for the lame, impotent, blind, and others, being poor and unable to provide for themselves.

Under these humane provisions the rich and poor are bound up in a common fate and reciprocal ties of obligation; neither prosperity nor adversity can visit one without operating a corresponding influence on the other; the rich have an interest paramount to the poor themselves in every circumstance influencing their condition, and with their number, employment, education, improvidence, and vices, they are necessitated to feel a concern, and apply to their consideration, in order to the permanent security of their own enjoyments, whatever superior knowledge or foresight they possess.

An Englishman does not need the public exhibition of distress to be apprised of its existence; he knows it from the amount of his poor-assessment; but, owing to an imperfect police, the preventive wisdom of the legislature has in part proved unavailing, and the industrious householder is not only impoverished by the relief of indigence, but he is everywhere pestered with its clamours, and his feelings lacerated by the spectacle of real or fictitious suffering, which ought ever to be excluded from his sight.

But, though there is a compulsory provision for the indigent, yet every parish being bound only to maintain its own poor, there are various causes, especially in a great metropolis, tending to accumulate a mass of destitute objects, of variable amount, who have no claim to relief in the place where they happen to dwell. Of the causes which multiply objects of this description, in London, the first is the influx of strangers from every part of the United Kingdom, from the Colonies and foreign parts. Some have fled hither to avoid the penalties of their crimes; many come to seek employment, and supply the waste of population; others for the purpose of trade: disappointed in their hopes, or afflicted by disease, and without claim anywhere for succour, many resort, as a temporary expedient from starvation, either to charity or crime.

The number of persons who, with their families, find their way to the metropolis from the remote parts of Great Britain and Ireland, in hopes of finding employment, is inconceivable. They are subject to all vicissitudes in the demand for labour, as well as to uncertainties in health and strength, even when they procure employment. In case of failure, their parochial settlements are either at a great distance, or, as natives of Scotland or Ireland, they are without this resource. Having incurred the expense and fatigue of the journey, and entertaining hopes, probably, of a change in circumstances, they are loth to apply to the parishes where accident has fixed them, and thereby subject themselves to forcible removal. In this dilemma they often linger till all they possess in the world is sold or pledged, and then falling into utter destitution, the females not unfrequently resort to prostitution, the feeble-spirited among the males to begging, those of more profligate principles to petty thefts or more atrocious offences, contributing to swell the general mass of delinquency.

Another cause of mendicity is found in the ignorance of many of their places of settlement. It seems extraordinary that any one should be uninformed of the place of his birth, or such other important fact in his personal history, as entitles him to parochial relief. Yet such is the case. Exclusive of those having country-settlements, there are many who beg in London who belong even to the metropolitan parishes, yet are so little acquainted with themselves, as to be unable, though willing, to establish their claim to parish aid.

A number of females lose the benefit of their settlement by marriage. During coverture a wife can have no settlement separate from the husband. Hence, if an Englishwoman marry a native of Scotland or Ireland, and he desert her, as is not unfrequent, she has no claim to parochial relief in England, and, in the event of being chargeable, may be removed to the country where the husband was born.* This often brings a destitute woman and her children into the streets.

* Rex v. Leeds, 4 Barn. and Ald.

These are the general causes of mendicity, originating in what may be termed the *casual* or *unavoidable* poor; but by far the most numerous, obstinate, and disgusting class of mendicants, who torment the passenger, infest the shops of tradesmen and the dwellings of the opulent, are those resulting from the arts of the idle and profligate. Ninety-nine out of every hundred of London beggars consist of this class of impostors, whose craft we shall shortly more particularly expose. Whether, however, mendicity originates in fraud or indigence, there seems no pretext for its toleration. The law has made a provision for all *legal* distress, and having so provided, it has made it a crime to annoy the public with the solicitation of alms, and formerly it was an offence to bestow alms on those able to work.* If an Englishman falls into distress he ought to apply to his parish; if not resident in his own parish, the parish where he happens to dwell is bound to take charge of him. If from accident or disease he is not in a state to be removed, he is entitled to temporary aid on the spot, or he is eligible to be admitted into one of the numerous hospitals and charitable institutions, founded and supported by private benevolence. Natives of Scotland or Ireland have no claim to parochial relief in England, but the law has provided for their removal to the country of their birth. Foreigners cannot be justified in begging; they are immigrants into a country where mendicity is a crime; and, having voluntarily submitted to its laws, cannot complain if their penalties be enforced.

The reason why these laws and provisions are not made available, is the inadequate and defective state of the metropolitan police. The stipendiary or government police do not consider it part of their duty to

* Giving alms to a beggar able to work is prohibited by 23 Edward III. c. 7 & 117.

apply themselves to the investigation and prevention of mendicity. With regard to parochial authorities, all the concern they take is to keep the evil as much as possible without their respective boundaries; hence there are perpetual efforts to force or frighten mendicants into each others limits; by which means a flux and reflux of mendicity is kept up in the different districts of the metropolis, and the beggars driven to and fro like a weaver's shuttle. All this would obviously disappear under a general and consolidated police, whose business it would be to decompose and investigate the mass of wretchedness that now infests our streets and squares; —to punish imposture;—and direct the really distressed to those sources of relief which the law or benevolence has provided.

For a long period mendicity displayed itself at Paris in its most hideous and afflicting characteristics. Beggars in great numbers followed persons in the streets, entered the houses, imposed on tradesmen, and exhibited to public view the painful spectacle of wounds and diseases, either true or pretended, presenting the afflicting contrast of abject wretchedness in the midst of opulence, and of idleness in the midst of industry. Under judicious regulations and a vigilant police this pest of a great city has been subdued; the entire mass of misery has been analysed;—the stranger beggar sent to his own department;—the criminal, concealed under the disguise of a mendicant, detected;—the sick, whose real infirmities rendered them fit objects to be admitted, have been sent to the hospitals;—impostors have been punished; —and those willing and fit for work, but unable to get employment, have been placed at Viller Cotterets.*

* Report presented by M. De Belleyme, prefect of Police of Paris, to the Royal Society of Prisons, Jan. 6th, 1829.

It is by similar policy mendicity in London ought to be assailed and extirpated, as one of the most pregnant sources of annoyance, immorality, and crime. From the inquiries of a Parliamentary Committee, in 1815, it was ascertained, beyond all doubt, that gross and monstrous frauds are practised by mendicants in the metropolis and neighbourhood; the success of which affords a direct encouragement to vice, idleness, and profligacy, as much more is gained by importunate solicitations in the streets for charity, than is earned by the sober and most industrious artizans, by their utmost application to the work in which they are employed. As the number of beggars has certainly not since decreased, and their craft is carried on upon nearly the same principles, we shall insert a digest of the results of the Committee's inquiries, from the "Report on the State of Mendicity in the Metropolis, 1816." (Parl. Pap. No. 396.)

Beggars on being searched when brought before the magistrates, a great deal of money has been found about them, in their pockets and in their clothes.

Beggars make great profits by various practices, such as changing their clothes two or three times a day, and getting money intended for others. Clear proof that a blind man, with a dog, got 30s. in one day. Another man got 5s. a-day; he could, with ease, go through sixty streets in a day. Another got 6s. a-day.

Two houses in the parish of St. Giles, frequented by from 200 to 300 beggars; receipts from 3s. to 5s. a-day; they could not be supposed to spend less than 2s. 6d. at night, and pay 6d. for their bed.

A negro beggar retired to the West Indies with a fortune, it was supposed, of £1,500.

Beggars gain 3s. or 4s. a-day by begging shoes.

A woman alleged that she could go through sixty streets in a day, and that it was a bad street that did not yield a penny.

A beggar would spend 50s. a-week for his board.

Children are made use of to excite compassion.

Beggars are furnished with children at houses in Whitechapel and Shoreditch; some, who look like twins, frequently carried on their backs Children frequently sent out to beg and not to return with less than 6d

A girl of twelve years of age had been six years engaged in begging; on some days got 3s. or 4s.; sometimes more, usually 18d. or 1s.; on Christmas day, 4s. 6d.

One man will collect three, four, or five children from different parts, paying 6d. or 9d. each, to go begging with them.

A woman with twins, who never grew older, sat for ten years. Not once in a hundred twins are the children of beggars.

A little boy and girl earned 8s. a day.

A night school kept by an old woman for instructing children in the street-language.

1 Edward IV. c. 3, notices the practice of employing children by vagrants in begging.

Beggars are most numerous in the outskirts of the town: thirty or forty sleep in a large round bed.

In the neighbourhood of St. Giles's thirty or forty houses, apparently crowded, in which are not less than 2000 people, one-half of whom live by prostitution and beggary: the remainder Irish labouring people. The rector of St. Clement Danes describes them as living very well: especially if they are pretty well *maimed*, *blind*, or if they have *children*.

From 200 to 300 beggars frequent two public houses in St. Giles's, divided into companies and subdivided into walks; they have hot suppers and live luxuriously at night. They eat no broken victuals, but have ham and beef. The *walks are sold*.

Forty or fifty sleep in a house, and are locked in lest they should carry any thing away, and are let out in the morning all at once.

At some of the houses the knives and forks are chained to the tables, and other articles chained to the walls.

Worthy persons, however distressed, will not have recourse to begging. Street-beggars, with very few exceptions, are utterly worthless and incorrigible. Beggars evade the Vagrant-Act by carrying matches and articles of little intrinsic value for sale. Out of 400 beggars, in St. Giles's, 350 are capable of earning their own living.

In course of these inquiries, the Committee found that, in almost all the City parishes, and in some of those of the neighbourhood, the poor were farmed. One person, at Hoxton, farmed the poor of 40 parishes, all within the City; the number of paupers 300, many of whom begged. In another house, at Hoxton, the poor of 17 parishes were farmed; in some parishes there were no poor. At Mile-End was a house where the poor of nearly 40 parishes were farmed; at Old-Ford, 150 paupers were farmed. The persons farming them did not *admit they begged, to their knowledge;* they had not, however, always distinguishing dresses, and, as they got out two days in the week, there was no check upon them. A practice of "slating" prevailed in some of these houses, in which 2½d. was allowed in lieu of a dinner. The situation of paupers, in the houses of these contractors, is described as very wretched. What follows refers to *begging-letters:*—

Some thousand *(by letters)* applications are made to noblemen, gentlemen, and ladies; 2000, on an average, were within the knowledge of one gentleman. Some were from persons receiving pensions as soldiers and sailors, or from public companies.

Several persons subsist by writing letters; one woman profits by the practice who receives a guinea a week as a legacy from a relation, and has £200 in the funds. Letters have been written, by the same person, in five or six different hands. A Greenwich pensioner, with £7 a-year, gets from 5s. to 10s. a-day by writing these letters. A man, who keeps a school, writes them for 2d. each. A person, who has been an attorney's clerk, is much employed in writing these letters and petitions, which often obtain money.

In the begging-letter and every other branch of mendicity there has been a great augmentation since the Report of the Parliamentary Committee, and we are convinced, from our own observation and inquiries, the metropolis was never more infested with beggars, presenting a painful contrast to the recent numerous and magnificent works of public improvement. In the City, the vigilance of the officers renders the evil less visible; but, in the suburbs, one has to run the gauntlet through files of squalid objects, whose cunning and pertinacity keep pace with their numbers: they do not, as formerly, disgust the beholder with the spectacle of wounds and deformities; nor do they, from the same salutary dread of the Vagrant Act, always venture to solicit alms, but they fill up, in silence, the doorways, courts, and pavement, and, provided with a mockery show of famishing looks, miserable children, matches, brooms, and tracts, they raise a *chevaux de frise* round the passenger, presenting to view scenes of apparent want and suffering not less annoying and afflicting. We do not think these sights evidence of general distress ; indeed, the increase of the public revenue and the proof it affords of national consumption shows there can be no general distress at present; they rather evince the increasing luxury and mistaken benevolence of the public, and demonstrate the mass of idleness, imposture, and dep avity in the community, originating, chiefly, in the inertness and inefficiency of metropolitan police.

Attempts have been made to estimate the number of beggars in London. Mr. Martin, thirty years since, calculated them at 15,000, of whom 3500 were Irish.* They must now be double or treble that number. The number of persons who presented themselves, last year, to the " Society for the Suppression of Mendicity in the Metropolis," amounted, including their families, to nearly *forty thousand*.† Out of this immense number of objects, only 806 could be selected whose cases were *plausible* enough even to merit investigation, and, among the e 806 it was ascertained 397 were gross impostors and confirmed vagrants, and of the remainder seventeen refused parochial relief on condition of admission into the workhouse, and 155 either refused to return to their homes or absconded from work provided by the Society. In short, of the whole 806 only 237 merited and received relief, and of these fifty-four were placed upon their parishes in London, and thirty-five upon their parishes in the country.

* Parliamentary Report on Mendicity in the Metropolis, 1816, p. 5.
† Tenth Report of Society for Suppression of Mendicity, p. 11.

The alleged causes of distress are mostly want of employment, want of tools and implements of work, sickness and accidents, loss of friends by death, desertion, or imprisonment, failure in business, suspension of pension, pay, or prize-money, and shipwreck. Some allege they are foreigners, wanting means to return home. How few of them are inclined to honest industry is evinced by the results of the Society's wharf, at which able-bodied applicants are employed in breaking stones, for which they receive adequate remuneration. Of the number of persons qualified for work and sent to the wharf, not more than *one in thirty* have been found willing to avail themselves of it, the rest having absconded!

This useful Society, since its formation, in 1818, has apprehended, by means of the constables it employs, 7,050 vagrants: 3,407 of whom were convicted. Last year the Society apprehended 778 vagrants, being an increase of 262 above the number apprehended in the preceding year. In the *begging letter* department, for the last year, 2,968 letters were received for investigation, of which 1,680 were from new applicants.

Half the mendicity and vagrancy in London originates in the vast influx of lower Irish, who not only depress the English labourer in competing with him for employment, but, from their half-civilized habits, effect a complete debasement in his manners and character. Unless the Legislature can frame some measure to regulate the admission of these immigrants, no police will be strong enough, nor prisons large enough, to contend with mendicity and vagrancy. Of 11,741, registered and non-registered, cases brought before the Mendicity Society last year, 4,708 were Irish. The cost of Irish paupers to the metropolitan parishes is enormous: and, contrary to all principles of equity, the natives of both Ireland and Scotland obtain that relief from the parishes which is denied them in their own country. For want of a better system of passing, the removal of an Irish pauper from London to Liverpool costs, for conveyance alone, £4 : 11 : 3 ; while the charge for an inside passage in the mail is only £4 : 4.* Many of the Irish, who burden the parishes and impose on the charitable, are able to support themselves, but artfully conceal their property. Those who apply for money to pay their passage from Liverpool, appearing utterly destitute, have been found, on examination, to have several pounds sewed up in their waistcoats and trowsers.† The late Lord Dillon used to receive sums from his poor tenants in London, for which he gave them orders upon his agent in Ireland, for payment in Roscommon and Sligo. Mr. Powell contiuues to receive small sums from labourers and others, to be remitted to Ireland for the payment of their rents.

The pressure of the Irish upon the English population, and its deleterious effects, are not evils of yesterday ; they have been gradually augmenting for centuries, till lately they appear to have attained almost their maximum. Early in the reign of Charles I. 1629, a proclamation was issued, that proves the existence of the calamity now complained of: it begins—"*Whereas, this realm hath of late been pestered with great number of* IRISHE BEGGARS, *who live here idly and dangerously, and are of ill-example to the natives of this kingdom.*"

Mendicity, whether Irish or English, is an obstinate disease, requiring the most vigorous and persevering applications ; for any thing short of these only subdues the disorder for a time, leaving it to break out afresh with augmented violence. Upwards of 13,000 beggars are annually conveyed out of the Metropolis by the

* Report on Irish and Scotch Vagrants, Parl. Pap. Session 1828, No. 513, p. 4.

† Ibid, p. 7.

parishes; many of them return repeatedly; those passed to their parishes usually return, and most of them escape and disperse after the first stage. The efforts of the Mendicity Society are laudable, considering its whole expenditure is under £3000 per annum; but the state of the streets attests the inadequacy of its power. Nothing less than a *general and consolidated police for the whole of the Metropolis*, which would act in concert and uniformity—be present everywhere—and have authority to question, apprehend, and disperse—would be competent to grapple with and subue the evil. Prior to this, provision ought to be made for the relief of *casual* distress, originating in ignorance, want of settlement, changes in the seasons, sudden bereavements, illness, and accidents; which even prudence cannot always avert, and to which it would be cruel and unchristian to deny permission to solicit alms without first establishing a tribunal to which they could resort for advice, direction, or temporary aid. Having done this, the horde of impostors, of which the vast majority of London beggars consists, might be assailed without remorse, and a fruitful source of demoralization and crime extirpated; and that without inhumanity, without complaint, without new laws, and comparatively little additional charge.

FEMALE PROSTITUTION.

Next to the highest crime against human nature, female prostitution is almost the earliest depravity recorded in Holy Writ: nearly in all places and at all periods of time it has been found more or less prevalent, and its universal existence seems to imply it is an evil inseparable from the social state. The most rigid moralist that we are acquainted with has never contemplated its entire extinction, and the Legislature has seldom sought more than to repress its pruriences, and keep it within the bounds of general decorum. It is, indeed, one of those private vices, the consequences of which are chiefly personal to the offender, and, consequently, does not fall properly within the cognizance of public law. With the exception of a short period, during the ascendancy of Puritanism, it has been always so treated in England; and efforts have never been made to repress lewdness, unless it became *open and notorious*, and such as was a source of annoyance to others, of riot and disorder.

It is generally admitted, by the oldest residents in the metropolis, and those who have had the best opportunities for observation, that there is a decided improvement in external manners and behaviour. The public tea-gardens, the minor assemblies and concerts in public houses, and even Vauxhall, exhibit none of those scenes of gross licentiousness which abounded in their former prototypes, the Dog and Duck, Apollo's garden, and Ranelagh. The eye is not so frequently offended by the exhibition of obscene prints and pictures; and we are confident, from our own observance, that the behaviour of unfortunate females in the streets is more orderly and decorous than prevailed among the same class sixteen or eighteen years since. In the language of society and external presentment of vice, the improvement in manners over what prevailed at the commencement of the late reign, has been frequently remarked: the dialogue in the comedies of Congreve, of Vanbrugh, and Cibber would be quite revolting to modern ears, and we do not think there are above three or four living examples of the grossness in expression and conduct recorded in the scandalous chronicle of Lord *Orford's Reminiscences*. The scenes in the *Adventures of a Guinea*, though highly-coloured by Johnstone, are generally considered not to exhibit a very exaggerated picture of living manners, for the period in which they were written; but in the public men of the present day, or in private individuals, we should be at a loss to point out any corresponding examples of turpitude and profligacy. Though not more moral than our grandfathers, yet such is the taste of the age, as Sir Walter Scott has remarked, that "modern vice pays tax to appearances, and is contented to wear a mask of decorum."*

There are none of the factitious allurements to vice which disgraced a former period; we have no *Bon Ton Magazines*, nor trash of that description; the periodical literature is totally free from impurity, and the whole newspaper press, with the exception of one or two weekly papers addicted to personal libel, cannot be charged with grossness or indecency.

About twenty years ago, a very extensive traffic was carried on, in the metropolis, in obscene books, prints, drawings, and toys. Several persons of apparent respectability were united together in partnership, for the principal and almost exclusive purpose of vending this description of merchandize. Their agents, mostly Italians, under the assumed character of itinerant hawkers, established a systematic trade throughout a great part of the United Kingdom. These itinerants, after providing themselves with a considerable stock, were accustomed to disperse themselves in parties of two or three, visiting Birmingham, Leeds, Liverpool, Manchester, and all the principal places in the country, and when their wares were exhausted, their confederates in London furnished them additional supplies by the coaches and waggons. The principal vent for the commodities was in schools, and these chiefly for females, into which they would

* Miscellaneous Prose Works, vol. iii. page 516.

contrive to introduce them by means of servants. Women also were employed as agents in the deleterious trade, who would gain admission into houses under the pretence of purchasing cast-off clothes from the domestics. The number of persons employed in this business, as principals, artists, agents, and hawkers, were supposed to amount to six hundred.*

We believe there are few remains of this abomination now in London; there are, we think, not above two or three shops regularly devoted to the sale of obscene books and prints, and the penury and wretchedness of the owners of these are such as sufficiently shows how little their miserable calling accords with the prevailing taste of the times. To the credit of young men of the present day, they have not much appetite for absolute grossness, and this improvement in manners must certainly be ascribed to the diffusion of knowledge and more general cultivation of the productions of art and literature.

But, though the age has improved in appearances, there is none, we fear, in *sentiment*. In number, female prostitution has certainly not diminished, and we verily believe there are fewer conscientious scruples entertained respecting sexual intercourse than at any former period. There is a laxity of manners among the females of London generally, which strikingly contrasts with the behaviour of the same sex in the country. Before marriage, the shrewdness and superior tact of the London women superinduce a greater strictness and reserve for which they often indemnify themselves afterwards, by a license that would be quite startling in a provincial town. Indelicacies in conversation, however, are never tolerated, and an inuendo which would pass in a country circle as a mere *plaisanterie*, would give serious offence in London.

* Second Report on the Police of the Metropolis, 1817, page 479.

But though not in words so pure, the country dames, we suspect, are more chaste in deeds, and examples of infidelity, and illicit intercourse of rarer occurrence. While, however, the metropolitan ladies are, on the average, less exemplary in practice, it cannot be denied their manners are more fascinating and agreeable; and perhaps it is to this greater attractive power their more serious failing may be attributed. That grace and refinement in demeanour, which the poet Burns remarked only in the "high-born dames" of Edinburgh, he would have met with in almost every female denizen of this great metropolis.*

It is something gained to virtue even when the external exhibition of vice is subdued, since it lessens temptation, and the corruptive influence of example. Though the behaviour of abandoned women in the streets is less outrageous, and the passenger is not so frequently accosted and disgusted with obscene language, we fear this is the only improvement we can remark in their condition. While every other pursuit has been improving, the arts of mendicity and prostitution appear to have been stationary; exhibiting starving children, soap-eating, mock fits, creating wounds, and maiming arms and

* It is well known that *faux pas* and kept mistresses are considered in the country among the phenomena of nature, and that female prostitution is scarcely known in towns of the third or fourth rate. To this cause may be probably ascribed the greater number of illegitimate children in county parishes than in the Metropolis. Two or three years ago we made a tour through several of the provincial towns, and, among other objects of interest, had the curiosity to inquire into the general conduct of females. We learnt that such a thing as a *common prostitute* was rarely to be found in towns not containing more than 6 or 10,000 inhabitants; which, we believe, is the amount of population necessary to support a weekly newspaper. Matters, we have heard, are still more exemplary in Scotland, but not having been there, we can affirm nothing of our own knowledge.

legs, were the ordinary tricks of beggars before the Reformation; and the modern brothel has not improved a jot over the stews abolished by Henry VIII. Most of these infamous houses are now farmed by Jews, and such is the ignorant and grasping avarice of the race, that they are blind to improvements, which would even conduce to their own interests. Crimes of the most dreadful nature are known to be often perpetrated in these dens of iniquity, and if the dread of these has not been sufficient to destroy the trade, and if men are found hardy enough not only to brave the loss of life or limb, but even the risk of that more terrible mutilation after death, which the law has only awarded to the most atrocious crime, it shows how inseparable an evil female prostitution is from great capitals, and that its extinction would be productive of still greater calamities.

Dr. Colquhoun has subjected himself to some ridicule in attempting to estimate the number of female prostitutes in London, which he made amount to 50,000, divided into the following classes:—

Of the class of well-educated women	2000
Of persons above the rank of menial servants	3000
Of persons who have been employed as menial servants, and seduced in early life	20000
Of those in different ranks in society, who live partly by prostitution, including the number of females who cohabit with labourers without matrimony	25000
	50000*

By including women unmarried, who cohabit with labourers and others, and of which the number is very great in the metropolis, we do not think that Dr. Colquhoun's estimate is greatly beyond the truth. The

* Treatise on the Police of the Metropolis, page 340, 7th edition.

number of prostitutes in some parishes, especially those in the vicinity of the docks and river, is almost incredible; while, again, some of the out-parishes, as Islington and others, are comparatively exempt, and abound as little in female prostitution as any country parish of equal extent and population.

From a statement laid before a Parliamentary Committee, in 1817, it appears that, in the parishes of St. Botolph-without-Aldgate, St. Leonard, Shoreditch, and St. Paul, Shadwell, containing, together, only 9924 houses, and 59,050 inhabitants, there were 360 brothels, and 2000 common prostitutes.*

It is painful to think of the tender age at which poor creatures are exposed to prostitution in the streets and brothels of London, and to which they are compelled to resort, either by the keepers of infamous houses, or their idle and abandoned parents. Some of these wretched children are under ten years of age, and, consequently, are below that period of life, during which it is a capital crime, under any circumstances, in any, to have carnal intercourse with them.

When the *Guardian Society* visited the City Bridewell there were 111 wretched women, the ages of whom varied from 14 to 54; the largest proportion appeared to be of the ages from 18 to 22. There were,—

1 of 14	12 of 19	1 of 24	4 of 28	2 of 33
1 of 16	10 of 21	3 of 25	6 of 29	5 of 35
1 of 17	13 of 22	10 of 26	7 of 30	3 of 36
11 of 18	6 of 23	9 of 27	5 of 32	1 of 54

Out of these, 85 had been in a state of prostitution from two months to two years; and the largest proportion of these from two to three years. The unfortunate creatures had been repeatedly committed to prison; and

* Second Report on the Police of the Metropolis, 1817, page 459.

instances occurred where they had been committed from eighteen to thirty times.*

The situation of these unhappy women is a subject not unworthy serious attention; they form a numerous class in society, and, however fallen and degraded, it cannot be forgotten that they not only constitute a part of our species, but, also, that part of it which it is the pride of an enlightened age to treat with indulgence and honour. Many of them were born and educated to better hopes; others have doubtless resorted to their degraded course merely to eat the bread of idleness; but the greater number, we apprehend, have been the unsuspecting victims of their good looks and too confiding dispositions. Among the varied wretchedness which afflicts humanity, there are none whose lot is fraught with acuter anguish or more certain and hopeless misery. From the theatres to the streets, and from thence to some miserable lodging—the workhouse—or an hospital—their career is short and fleeting. Of the multitude of unfortunate females, elegant in their persons and gay in their attire, who have fluttered in the saloons and other places of amusement during the last twenty years, what has become of them? Could their progress be traced, and their ultimate situations and exit from this world disclosed, it would lay open scenes of suffering and remorse far beyond any fancied descriptions in *Anastatius*, or what the imagination of a Maturin could conceive.

But this is a subject on which it would be superfluous to enlarge; the miseries of prostitution are too often obtruded on the eye of the passenger, in London, to need description. While, however, we are disposed to view the situation of women of the town with some

* Third Report on the Police of the Metropolis, 1818, page 30.

sympathy, it affords us pleasure to notice the asylums instituted for the reception of those disposed to forsake their abandoned course. For those bent on continuing their mode of life we have nothing to ask; but to those inclined to reform we would throw open the door of repentance as wide as individual benevolence would admit, and afford them every facility for regaining their lost station in society.

The chief asylums for repentant women are the *Magdalen Hospital*, in Great Surrey-street, and the *Female Penitentiary*, in the New Road, Pentonville: the former was established in 1758, the latter twenty-two years ago; they are chiefly supported by donations, legacies, collections, and subscriptions; and the funds of both, we believe, are barely adequate to the purposes of their institution.

During a period of sixty years, there were admitted into the Magdalen Hospital 4594 persons, of whom 3012 were restored to their friends, or placed in respectable service; 912 were discharged at their own request; 556 for improper behaviour; and 85 died while in the hospital. Of 264 who were discharged in the last four years, of every description, 157 had reformed; 74 had relapsed; 4 were insane; 1 died; and of 10 the situation was not known: so that it may be estimated that two-thirds of the women who enter the Society are permanently reclaimed: the average age of the females is from seventeen to eighteen. They apply very young, some few even at thirteen or fourteen, but generally from fifteen to twenty-five; some have been admitted there at twelve years of age.*

The London Female Penitentiary contains 100 persons, at an average expense, per head, of £23. Dur-

* Second Report on the Police of the Metropolis, 1817, page 332.

ing the first ten years of its establishment, 2000 females petitioned to be admitted, but only 565 could be received, of whom 265 were reconciled to their friends, and placed out to service; 18 married; 87 were discharged from various causes; 17 relapsed; 66 left the house at their own request; and 14 died.

It cannot be concealed that the women reclaimed by the penitentiaries, indirectly tend to the injury of more virtuous females by their entering into competition with them for employment in domestic service. Perhaps it would be an improvement if a more enlarged system were adopted, and the condition of protection to consist in removal from the country to some of the Colonies, where the paucity of females would render them a valuable acquisition.

Various plans have been suggested for subjecting female prostitution to magisterial controul, by which inexperienced youth might be less exposed to its allurements, the public eye guarded from scenes of lewdness and indecorum, and the chastity of females protected from the inroads of violence. Holland, under the government of the Stadholder, has been cited as an example of a better system. In Italy prostitutes are *licensed;* and in India female chastity is preserved by rearing up a certain class of females, who are under the conduct of matrons in every town and village, and with whom, under certain circumstances, an indiscriminate intercourse is permitted. Every thing of this kind, however, would be inconsistent with English feelings, and we believe the only improvements the practice is likely to receive in this country, are such as result from the prudence and selfishness of the individuals who pursue the vocation.

The chief legitimate object of legislation is, to prevent it becoming a nuisance to the more virtuous portion of the community, and this seems well attained by the existing laws. Under the 3 Geo. IV. c. 114, the keeping a *common bawdy-house* subjects to imprisonment and hard labour. And under the 5 Geo. IV. c. 83, every common prostitute wandering in the public streets, or public highways, or in *any place* of public resort, and behaving in a *riotous* or *indecent manner*, is deemed an idle and disorderly person, who, on the evidence of one witness before a magistrate, may be committed to the House of Correction, to hard labour, for one calendar month.

For facilitating the prosecution and suppression of any *common bawdy-house*, the 25 Geo. II. c. 36, provides that if two inhabitants of any parish, paying scot and lot, give notice, in writing, to the constable, of any person keeping a bawdy-house, the constable shall go with them to a justice, and, upon their making oath that they believe the notice to be true, and entering into a recognizance in £20 each to produce evidence, the constable shall enter into recognizance in the sum of £30, to prosecute the same with effect at the next sessions or assizes. Provision is made for the payment of the constable's expenses in the prosecution, and also of £10 to each of the inhabitants, by the overseer of the parish. The party accused may be then bound over to appear, and the magistrate may also take security for their good behaviour in the mean time.

Houses of ill-fame, however, if they once get established in a neighbourhood, are very difficult to root out. It is not easy to obtain the evidence necessary to prove a house to be a common bawdy-house; a female entering with three or four strange men daily is generally deemed enough; but this is for the discretion of a jury. In short, the act of Geo. II. affords, in practice, little encouragement to prosecute: the costs of proceeding by indictment, and the impediments thrown in the way of discovering the real name of the occupier often deter parish officers from interfering; and when a verdict has been obtained, the same conduct has been frequently carried on in the same house under a new name. The vulgar exhibition of *burning out* is still often resorted to, in order to get rid of such troublesome inmates, and this winter we observed a street in which a lantern was suspended at almost every door; but this practice, like the ancient custom in the City of *carting* fornicators through the streets, back to back, is almost as great a nuisance as that sought to be suppressed, and gives notoriety to an offence which ought, as much as possible, to be concealed from the view and knowledge of the public When a house has become a nuisance in a neighbourhood a more summary jurisdiction ought to be given to magistrates, by two justices being empowered upon information, on oath of two respectable householders, to summon the accused, and hear and determine the case, and, upon conviction, have power to punish by fine or imprisonment.

JUVENILE DELINQUENCY.

Though we are strangers to the institution of *castes,* yet children, in the ordinary course, mostly follow the vocation of their parents. This is observable in the legal profession, in the army and navy, as well as among players and show-people, mendicants, gypsies, and other vagrants. In like manner there can be little doubt that the stock of thieves is chiefly kept up by propagation among themselves, and that most of those engaged in the trade are only following the path of their progenitors.

Sir Richard Birnie was asked by the late Police Committee, " Are the thieves in general low artizans employed in any trade or business, or are they a class distinct by themselves, who do nothing but thieve?—Generally speaking, I think they are trained up from what I may call juvenile delinquents; they go on, step by step, and have no trade at all; certainly a great portion of them have had trades, and very likely by their own fault they are out of employ."—Report, page 45.—This, no doubt, is the true generation of the majority of thieves; they are born such, and it is their inheritance: they form a *caste* of themselves, having their peculiar slang, mode of thinking, habits, and arts of living. Indeed, it is obvious that picking pockets, picking locks, *starring* windows, and breaking into houses, are not such easy operations that any uninitiated from the ranks of honesty could pursue them with advantage without much previous training, example, and discipline.

There are, probably, 70,000 persons in the metropolis who regularly live by theft and fraud; most of these have women, with whom they cohabit, and their offspring, as a matter of course, follow the example of their parents, and recruit the general mass of mendicancy, prostitution, and delinquency. This is the chief source of juvenile delinquents, who are also augmented by children, abandoned by the profligate among the working classes, by those of poor debtors confined, of paupers without settlement, and by a few wayward spirits from reputable families, who leave their homes without cause, either from the neglect or misfortune of their natural protectors. Children of this description are found in every part of the metropolis, especially in the vicinity of the theatres, the market-places, the parks, fields, and outskirts of the town.* Many of them belong to organized gangs of depredators, and are in the regular

* Police Report, 1828, pages 38, 46, 48, 54, 57, and 81.

employ and training of older thieves; others obtain a precarious subsistence by begging, running errands, selling play-bills, picking pockets, and pilfering from shops and stalls. Some of them never knew what it is to be in a bed, taking refuge in sheds, under stalls, piazzas, and about brick-kilns; they have no homes; others have homes, either with their parents, or in obscure lodging-houses, but to which they cannot return unless the day's industry or crime has produced a stipulated sum.

It is from the thousands of children so situated that the chief mass of criminals is derived, who fill our prisons, the hulks, and convict-settlements. It is a most extraordinary fact, that half the number of persons convicted of crime have not attained the age of discretion. During the last seven years, out of 16,427 commitments in the county of Surrey, 7292 were under twenty years of age, and 370 under twelve years of age, and several of these not more than eight or ten years of age.*

Now, the origin of criminality being ascertained, it is afflictive to humanity, and a reproach to preventive justice, that more effective measures are not employed to assail the evil at the source. In the present state of the law, the magistrates have little power, and the punishments that are inflicted mostly tend to harden the offenders and return them upon society with additional aptitude for mischief.

We are constantly reading in the newspapers of the painful situation in which the civil authorities are placed by this part of their duty; crowds of destitute beings are brought before them, by the officers, from eight to fourteen years of age; they have been found gambling, sleeping in the open air, or committing some other

* Report to the Magistrates of the County of Surrey, 1828, page 5.

act of vagrancy; they are known to be in the first stages of delinquency, obtaining a livelihood dishonestly, yet the magistrate has no means of disposing of them in such way as may break up their guilty connexions, and prevent them being returned on society to complete their career of crime.

In the *Morning Chronicle*, September 27, 1828, it is stated, that 120 miserable creatures were brought up at one of the public offices; they had been found sleeping in a brick-field, and twenty-eight were sent to the *House of Correction.* In the same journal, September 17, is the following occurrence:—

Middlesex Sessions.—John Murray, a little hungry looking boy, about twelve years of age, was indicted for stealing two buns and eight biscuits. The Chairman, in passing sentence, said "That it was a melancholy thing to see the crowd of children then in the dock. Here are nearly twenty children, all of them, I fear, belonging to organized gangs, in which every member has a peculiar department. The only effectual mode of putting down this system is, to send every one of them out of the country for life. Whipping used to make some impression upon them, but now they quite disregard it. However, I'll give these boys another chance—let them be confined for *three months, and be twice well whipped.*"

Now, this mode of proceeding is both cruel and absurd. It is certain these poor creatures, at the expiration of their punishment, will and must return to their old courses; they have no other means of living, and perhaps have never been taught any other; the punishment awarded is a gratuitous aggravation of the hardships of their lot, and neither reforms them nor benefits society. Even boys sentenced for a short period to transportation, or to confinement on board the hulks, mostly return to their old courses. Mr. Capper stated to the Police Committee that eight out of ten so returned.* And this must always be the case till such

* Report on the Police of the Metropolis, 1828, page 105.

provision is made as shall for ever remove them from the scene of old habits, connexions, and associates.

It might be thought these juvenile delinquents consisted of boys without education, or parents to take care of them, but it is not the fact. Mr. Wontner, the keeper of Newgate, informed the Police Committee* that four out of five of the boys committed to him could read, and three-fifths of them could read and write. Mr. Rawlinson,† one of the magistrates at Mary-le-bone office, also stated that nineteen-twentieths of the boys had been taught reading and writing.

In the evidence of Mr. Capper we have a good account of the previous character and condition of this class of offenders. Out of 4000 convicts on board the hulks, 300 boys under sixteen years of age were taken and placed on board the *Euryalus*, at Chatham. Of these boys,

199 had fathers living.
66 had only mothers living.
35 had neither fathers nor mothers.
133 had been in custody more than once.
66 could read and write on their arrival.
64 could read only.
170 could neither read nor write.
2 were eight years of age.
5 were nine years of age.
13 ten years of age.
23 eleven years of age.
59 twelve years of age.
69 thirteen years of age.
82 fourteen years of age.
42 fifteen years of age.
5 sixteen years of age.

All the suggestions of modern philanthropy for the reform of these offenders have been adopted on board the hulks; they are separated from older criminals, the

* Report on the Police of the Metropolis, 1828, p. 54. † Ibid. p. 57.

ignorant are instructed, useful trades are taught them, and they have nothing before them but examples of industry, sobriety, and religion. Yet such is the force of early impressions, that they no sooner return to their native element, as it may be termed, in the purlieus of Covent-garden, Tothill-fields, Bethnal-green, or Saffron-hill, than, like ducks at the sight of water, or a wild Indian who has been temporarily clothed in the habiliments of civilization, they rush into their former scenes of iniquity and crime.

The methods now employed to dispose of delinquent children failing either to reform them or relieve society from their presence, it is certainly expedient a new experiment should be tried. Crimes which mostly bring this class of offenders before the tribunals, are either acts of vagrancy, or petty thefts; in the former case they may be imprisoned and whipped, in the latter transported for a limited term. Neither of these punishments serve any salutary end, and, when applied, the magistrates generally take occasion to remark, at the time, that they have resorted to them merely because they have no other way of disposing of the objects before them.

Under an act of Anne, a magistrate is authorized, with the consent of the churchwardens of the parish, where the delinquent is found, who either begs or his parents beg, who cannot give a proper account of himself, to bind that boy to the sea service. This, in time of war, afforded a convenient outlet for profligate youths, but now it is with great difficulty persons can be found to take them, as is proved by the experience of the Marine Society. On shore, as at sea, the market is overstocked, and boys, if willing, cannot always find employment, as errand-boys, pot-boys, stable-boys, &c.

But the difficulty of dealing with the destitute children of the Metropolis consists not so much in providing a suitable punishment for the actually delinquent as in disposing of the multitudes against whom no offence can be proved. However much their waywardness and wretchedness may be deplored, and however strongly their incipient guilt be suspected, still, having committed no offence known to the law, they are not within cognizance of the civil power. Now it appears to us that it would be real humanity towards these unfortunate creatures to subject them to compulsory and perpetual exile from England. Experience proves that terminable punishment rarely effects a permanent reform in older criminals, if suffered to revisit former scenes of guilt, and the same inveteracy of habit predominates in the juvenile offender.* Abroad, in New South Wales, they often become prosperous and useful citizens; but, at home, they seem incapable of resisting the temptations presented by a luxurious and refined community.

Under a sentence of banishment, we do not mean that children who have committed merely an act of vagrancy, or even larceny, should be perpetually subject to convict treatment in a penal settlement. Our idea, as before explained, (page 21,) is, that the punishment should be of a mixed nature; if a serious crime had been committed, limited probationary treatment, as a convict, should be awarded; afterwards, the offender to become a free settler, subject only to a certain degree of sur-

* We know no better illustration of the incorrigible nature of a London thief than is exhibited in the " Memoirs of James Hardy Vaux," in Hunt and Clarke's Autobiography, and which were sent to this country, for publication, by Baron Field. In spite of better resolves, Vaux could never keep his long fingers from " picking and stealing," and, in fulfilment of his destiny, is now suffering the penalty of a *second* visit to New South Wales, where he has narrowly escaped a more ignominious fate from a sudden eruption of the old distemper.

veillance and the perpetual law of exile from the mother country. In cases of mere vagrancy and destitution, exile, under the protection of the State, without any preliminary punishment, might be inflicted.

In order to carry into execution this plan, little alteration in the existing law is required; the act of Anne and the Vagrant Act are sufficiently comprehensive to bring within their provisions every object it would be desirable to embrace; the only amendment requisite is that, in lieu of the unprofitable and unfeeling punishments now provided, compulsory emigration should be substituted, with the addition of preliminary convict treatment, where serious offences had been perpetrated.

Society would thus be relieved of a very distressing evil in a way most likely to benefit young offenders, and least painful to humanity. Unfortunately, population is so redundant, that boys of good dispositions cannot always find employment, they are almost compelled to be criminal; but, in acting on the suggestion we have ventured to recommend, they would be provided for, and the best chance afforded them of escaping a criminal life and ignominious death. Compulsory exile to them would scarcely be a hardship; they are less connected in life than older persons, have the world almost to begin, and removal to a new scene would snatch them from temptations they could not resist, the wiles of more hardened offenders, and the corrupting example of vicious parents.

FENCES, OR RECEIVERS—THIEVES' ATTORNEYS—FAMILY-MEN—PUTTERS-UP—NEGOTIATING POLICE-OFFICERS, AND FLASH-HOUSE-KEEPERS.

It has always formed a difficult task, in police, to prevent a criminal connexion between those appointed to guard the community from depredation and those by whom depredations are committed. Security is an obvious inducement, to the latter, to seek an amnesty, and the former may be drawn into the unnatural union, from the temptation of greater emolument arising from the betrayal than faithful execution of their duty. An abuse of this nature is of old standing in the metropolitan police, as we learn from two pamphlets, published at the beginning and middle of last century; one entitled "*A True Discovery of the Conduct of Thieves and Thief-takers, in and about London. By Hitchin, one of the City-Marshals, A.D.* 1718." The other, "*A faithful Narrative of the most wicked, bloody-minded Gang of Thief-takers,* alias *Thief-makers, Macdonil, Berry, Salmon, and Gahagan, A.D.* 1756. Another offence, very rife about this period, was that of taking a reward under pretence of helping the owner to his stolen goods. "This was a contrivance," says Blackstone, "carried to a great length of villany in the beginning of the reign of George I., the confederates of the felons thus disposing of stolen goods, at a cheap rate, to the owners themselves, and thereby stifling all further inquiry. The famous Jonathan Wild had under him a well-disciplined corps of thieves, who brought in all their spoils to him, and he kept a sort of public office for restoring them to the owners at half-price." To prevent this audacious practice, a statute passed, under which Wild, still continuing his old course, was convicted and executed.

The practices of this veteran offender have been lately revived, with improvements adapted to the discoveries of modern science. An organized system of depredation has been carried on under a regular subdivision of employment among putters-up, operative thieves, receivers, negotiating attorneys, and police-officers. Robbery, in the opinion of this fraternity, appears to have been deemed little more than a harmless pastime, a game at hide and seek, or an exercise of Spartan dexterity, in which a person might very innocently have his property abstracted, and then restored to him, on condition of allowing them a part, as a reward for superior finesse and adroitness. Anything more hostile to preventive justice cannot be imagined; and, therefore, the system of compromising and negotiating for the restitution of stolen property formed a prominent subject of inquiry by the late Police Committee. From an examination of persons actually participant in these nefarious transactions, they found such compromises had been negotiated with an unchecked frequency, and under an organized system far beyond what had been supposed to exist. The negotiators were mostly "thieves' attorneys,"—so called from their practice being chiefly in the defence of culprits,—or police-officers, who, on a stipulated sum being paid by the party robbed, managed the business with the plotter, or "putter-up," of the robbery, and the "fences," or receivers.

"A great majority of these cases (Report, pp. 9, 10) have taken place where large depredations have been committed upon country bankers. Two banks, that had severally been robbed of notes to the amount of £4000, recovered them on payment of £1000 each. In another case, £2200 was restored, out of £3200 stolen, for £230 or £240. This bank having called in their old circulation and issued fresh notes immediately after the robbery, the difficulty thus occasioned was the cause of not much above £10 per cent. being demanded. In another case, Spanish bonds, nominally worth £2000, were given back on payment of £100. A sum, not quite amounting to £20,000, was, in one case, restored for £1000. In another, where bills had been stolen of £16,000 or £17,000 value, but which were not easily negotiable by the thieves, restitution of £6000 was offered for £300. The bank, in this case, applied to the Home Office for a free pardon for an informer, but declined advertising a reward of £1000, and giving a bond not to compound, as the conditions of such grant. In another case, £3000 seems to have been restored for £19 per cent. In another case, where the robbery was to the amount of £7000, and the supposed robbers (most notorious "putters-up," and "fences") had been apprehended, and remanded by the magistrate for examination, the prosecution was suddenly desisted from, and the property subsequently restored for a sum not ascertained by your committee. In the case of another bank, the sum stolen being not less than £20,000, is stated to have been bought of the thieves, by a receiver, for £200, and £2800 taken of the legal owners, as the price of restitution. The Committee does not think it necessary to detail all the cases which have been disclosed to them; but, though it is evident they have not been informed of any thing like all the transactions that must have occurred under so general a system, they have proof of more than sixteen banks having sought, by these means, to indemnify themselves for their losses, and that property of various sorts, to a value above £200,000, has, within a few years, been the subject of negotiation or compromise. They have found it difficult, for many reasons, to ascertain, in several of the cases they have examined, the actual payments made to the thieves or receivers, but they have proof of nearly £12,000 having been paid to them by bankers only, accompanied with a clearance from every risk, and perfect impunity to their crimes."

A very erroneous opinion appears to have been entertained on the pernicious tendency of these compositions, and the bankers tolerated a reprehensible practice, in order to protect themselves from the repeated heavy losses to which they were subject. A society, called "The Committee of Bankers," instituted for prosecuting, at the common expense, frauds and forgeries, allowed their solicitor, under the specious pretext of furthering these objects, to seek an intercourse with "*family-men*" and "*fences*." In consequence of knowledge thus acquired of thieves and their haunts, he was generally employed by the country bankers upon the loss of parcels, and information obtained from him as to the robbery of coaches, a species of depredation not among the professed objects of prosecution by the society, but which has been so common that a banker's parcel is known by the cant name of "a child." Through this agent a regular channel was opened, offers were made, and terms negotiated for the restitution of the stolen property of bankers. Acting on this short-sighted policy, any effort to detect and punish the delinquents was lost sight of, and public justice was made the 'scape-goat of private disasters. The owners of stolen property thus purchased indemnity for present losses by strengthening and continuing a system which re-acted upon themselves and the community in reiterated depredations committed with almost certain success and impunity.

The Parliamentary Committee chiefly limits its exposition to compromises for bankers' parcels; but it may be collected from the Minutes of Evidence, *not published* by the Committee, that a medium exists in the metropolis for recovering, by the negotiation of police officers, or solicitors, every other description of property, down to a gold watch or diamond pin. In some instances, the Committee think the officers were not induced to undertake these negotiations from a dishonest or corrupt motive; it does not appear, they say, " that any one of them stipulated for a reward before-hand; nor connived at the escape of a thief; nor negotiated a compromise when he possessed a clue that might lead to the detection of the guilty.* Suspicion, however, arose, in one case, that £800 more was received by the officer who negotiated than the thieves *asked or received;* and, in another, £50 was paid to procure restitution of £500, and neither the £500 nor the £50 was ever restored.

It is obvious the least toleration of such a system as this must be destructive of all police, by making it the interest of officers that robberies should not be prevented; and the long practice of compromising has established a gang of putters-up and fences, with means of evading, if not defying, the arm of the law, who are wealthy enough, if large rewards are offered for their detection, of doubling them for their impunity, and who would,

* Report on the Police of the Metropolis, 1828, page 12.

in one case, have given £1000 to get rid of a single witness.* The wealth of these persons is astonishing, and is far from holding out encouragement to the pursuits of the honest and industrious. Saunders, who was tried for the Greenock Bank robbery, was able to expend £700 in his defence, and was acquitted. Of the circumstances and character of the principal putters-up and fences the Committee give the following account:—

"Some of these persons ostensibly carry on a trade; one, who had been tried formerly for robbing a coach, afterwards carried on business as a Smithfield drover, and died worth, it is believed, £15,000. Your Committee could not ascertain how many of these persons there are at present, but four of the principal have been pointed out. One was lately the farmer of one of the greatest turnpike-trusts in the metropolis. He was formerly tried for receiving the contents of a stolen letter, and as a receiver of tolls, employed by him, was also tried for stealing that very letter, being then a postman, it is not too much to infer that the possession of these turnpikes is not unserviceable for the purposes of depredation. Another has, it is said, been a surgeon in the army. The two others of the four have no trade, but live like men of property; and one of these, who appears to be the chief of the whole set, is well known on the turf, and is stated, on good grounds, to be worth £30,000. Three of these notorious depredators were let out of custody, as before stated, when there was a fair prospect of identifying and convicting them. It is alarming to have observed how long these persons have successfully carried on their plans of plunder; themselves living in affluence and apparent respectability, bribing confidential servants to betray the transactions of their employers, possessing accurate information as to the means and precautions by which valuable parcels are transmitted; then corrupting others to perpetrate the robberies planned in consequence, and finally receiving, by means of these compromises, a large emolument, with secure impunity to themselves and their accomplices. It is scarcely necessary to point out the difficulties which must obstruct these persons, even after they may have amassed a fortune, in betaking to any honest pursuit. This, your Committee have evidence, is deeply felt by themselves, and the fear of being betrayed by their confederates, should they desert them, and of becoming objects

* Report on the Police of the Metropolis, 1828, page 14.

for sacrifice by the police, to whom they, at present, consider themselves of use, leaves little hope of any stop to their career but by detection and justice."—Report, pages 14, 15.

Every age is marked by some prominent characteristic, and one of the novelties of the present is in the undisturbed career of a class of persons who have acquired wealth and importance by the regular commission of one of the highest crimes against public justice. Were the system to continue, we might expect some of the receivers to find their way into the House of Commons, and the interests of the "family" be supported on the benches of the Legislature, either in person or by their dependents. A well-known character, alluded to by the Committee, is described by one witness as already in familiar intercourse with persons of the highest rank, and noblemen and gentlemen ready to "jump down the throat" of C——, a most notorious fence!

The conduct of some of the police appears to have been highly reprehensible, and a sort of lax morality, tolerated both at Bow-street and in the City, in which the duty of the officers and the safety of the public were compromised. Under the specious pretext of becoming acquainted with thieves and aiding the discovery of stolen property, officers were allowed to frequent flash houses and cultivate a personal acquaintance with known offenders. Those employed in this delicate service were, doubtless, intended to act as spies in the enemy's camp, but it is a probable supposition, from the company they kept, that they were occasionally seduced from their duty, and, instead of communicating the plans of the enemy, betrayed the councils of their employers. From evidence before the Police Committee, it is clear both officers and solicitors in London have been in the regular commission of an offence of the same enormity as that for which Jonathan Wild was ignominiously executed.

In the case of the robbery of the Bath mail, a well-known solicitor applied to an officer for the recovery of a parcel, which was got by means of C—— and D——, the solicitor receiving £100 and the officer £100 for their share in this transaction. A watch, stolen from Lord ——, was recovered by officer A. A. through the means of a tailor who works for thieves. An officer, designated Q. R. in the unpublished Minutes of Evidence, got back a box of jewellery, stolen from the Chester mail, through the medium of Ikey Solomons. Bills, bonds, a chronometer, and box of insects, were restored on £220 being paid to two fences, C—— and H——; in this case an appointment was made at a certain place, to which the property was brought by a woman in a hackney-coach. A banker was robbed of £30,000, which was restored on the payment of between 4 and £5000; officers Q. R. and C. C. were employed in this negotiation, and received £50.

The receivers affect only to be negotiators in these transactions, but it is more reasonable to suppose they pursue their trade on the same principles as other chapmen, and buy as cheap, and sell as dear as possible. At a robbery of some hundred pounds of small notes they had the conscience to ask eighty per cent. for their restitution.*

It would appear the magistrates were unacquainted with the practices of their officers, or, at most, had only some obscure suspicions of their existence. So far as pecuniary participation is concerned, not the slightest imputation exists against them, but it would seem the negotiation for the restitution of the £2000 Spanish bonds, mentioned above, was entered into by officer B. B. with the concurrence of a magistrate, and the affair con-

* Testimony of Solicitor C. in the unpublished Minutes of Evidence before the late Police Committee.

cealed from the knowledge of the Home-office at a time when that department was engaged in making extensive inquiries into the existence of similar transactions. Indeed, it is only true to observe that both at the principal police-office and in the City, a departure from general principles has been tolerated, in order to gain a transitory advantage; and the consequences of this sacrifice to expediency have been such as usually attend deviations from a direct course—greater ultimate loss and the organization of a system subversive of police and dangerous to the security of all property. Had a negotiation with thieves in any case been allowable, police-officers were the last persons in the world to whom it ought to have been entrusted; between these and criminals of all kinds, the ends of public justice require a spirit of perpetual hostility and watchfulness should be maintained.

In the conduct of a well-known Solicitor, we have an instance how far the moral degeneracy had crept over very shrewd and acute minds. This gentleman is probably better acquainted with criminal character than any living individual, and his extended intercourse among offenders of all classes peculiarly qualifies him for the office of future historian of metropolitan delinquency. So long ago as 1819, he had numbered among his clients at least 2000 capital convicts. He is one of those to whom allusion has been made as being engaged in the laudable practice of helping owners, for a valuable consideration, to the recovery of lost property. Against his general character we never heard any imputation; but he seems to have suffered the common fate ascribed, by the Author of Waverley, to legal practitioners, whom he compares to funnels, which cannot help contracting an impure interior, from being the constant medium of deleterious communications. To this cause may be attributed the apparent gaiety and self-complacence with which he related the following anecdote to the Police Committee :—" Regretting," as he says, " to a chief officer of police, the increase of crime in the metropolis, the said officer jocosely remarked, ' Well, master, you and I have no reason to find fault, because, with us, you know, the more the merrier.' " This is quite as good as any scene in the *Beggars' Opera*, and strikingly exemplifies, too, the conviction felt by some of the police of their interest in the increase rather than the prevention of crime.*

In considering the exposition of the Committee, one is surprised that none of the parties engaged in these criminal transactions have been brought to justice; and, also, that some of them who hold respectable stations in society should expose themselves to the severe punishment the law has provided. By 4 Geo. I. c. 11, it is enacted that " whoever shall take a reward, under the pretence of helping any one to stolen goods, shall suffer as the felon who stole them; unless he causes such

* The person to whom we have been alluding made the following sensible observations on criminal punishments to a Committee of the House of Commons:—" The present numerous enactments to take away life appear to me wholly ineffectual: but there are punishments, I am convinced, a thief would dread,—namely, a course of discipline totally reversing his former habits: idleness is one of the prominent characteristics of a professed thief—put him to labour; debauchery is another quality, abstinence is its opposite—apply it; company they indulge in, therefore they ought to experience solitude; they are accustomed to uncontrolled liberty of action, I would impose restraint and decorum: were these, my suggestions, adopted, I have no doubt we should find a considerable reduction in the number of offenders."—Report on Criminal Commitments, 1819, vol. viii. of Parliamentary Papers.—The same gentleman tendered some useful advice to the late Police Committee, though it appears something like *approving* against his quondam associates.

principal felon to be apprehended and brought to trial, and also gives evidence against him." The provisions of this statute were re-enacted by 7 and 8 Geo. IV. c. 29, s. 58; but which makes the offence no longer capital, and limits the punishment to transportation for life, or not less than seven years, or imprisonment for four years. The 6 Geo. I. c. 23, s. 9, (still unrepealed,) gives a reward of £40 to the person prosecuting such offender to conviction. While these severe penalties have been in force, the offence of compromising a felony, or theftbote, to perfect which there must be an actual agreement not to prosecute, still continues a misdemeanor, punishable only by fine and imprisonment. The statute of Geo. I. has been very ineffectual, arising, perhaps, from the difficulty of detecting such offences, to which Sir Richard Birnie seems to impute it; as he says, "I believe there is law enough against compounding a felony, but the great thing is to get a discovery." The severity of the punishment, too, may have discouraged prosecutions; or the decision that "money or bank-notes" were not within the meaning of the act. This latter omission has been remedied by the statute of Mr. Peel, and, from the evidence before the Committee, it would seem the change has had a salutary restraint both on negotiators and receivers.

For the amendment of the existing law, the Committee suggest that it would be advisable to make it at least a misdemeanor in the party *paying a reward* for the restitution of stolen goods, as well as punishing the party receiving it. The advertising a reward for stolen goods, "no questions asked," subjects to a penalty of £50, under 7 and 8 Geo. IV. c. 29, and certainly there would be no injustice in making the payment of that reward a substantive crime, the published offer of which has long been an offence. The Committee also submit that the gradation of crime would be better observed by making the compounding of felony a higher offence than paying or taking a reward for the return of stolen goods, and that this might be effected either by mitigating the punishment for the latter offence, or augmenting it for the former.

Compounding is an offence very difficult to deal with, because it is only from the parties implicated that a discovery can be made, and these have obvious motives for not communicating the business. But greater the difficulties of detection and severer the punishment ought to be, and rigorously enforced against the guilty. Making the *payment of a reward* an offence might augment these difficulties, by involving giver and receiver in a common delinquency, and give them additional motives for caution and concealment. But, if to this alteration another were added, it might be effective, namely, to grant a free pardon and reward to the original thief, or receiver, who should discover any one who offered or paid a reward or negotiated for the restitution of stolen goods. Under this law, the fear of being betrayed, and the probability such would be the case from the character of the parties, would prevent any person, who valued his personal security, from engaging in compromises. Still further to cut up the abominable system, we would grant a reward and pardon to the thief who discovered a receiver, or gave such information as led to his conviction.

The law, subjecting to a penalty for advertising for the recovery of stolen goods, with "no questions asked," is easily evaded. Persons, desirous of recovering their property in this way, advertise it as "LOST," offering a reward to whoever has found it.

The whole law, as regards compromises, theftbote, and advertizing for stolen property, appears to have become nugatory, and, as they are all offences tending to defeat public justice, it is necessary they should undergo such improvement as will render them efficient. Whatever changes are introduced, it is of the first importance that such enactments should be made as will effectually deter officers of police from being implicated in such affairs; for in them it is a double crime—a crime against the public, and a breach of their official engagements. In the Post-office, the Customs, and Excise departments severe and peculiar laws are made to punish officers guilty of any act in contravention of their public duty, and there appears no reason why similar special legislation should not be extended to the retainers of the police. A more abused and defective state of police cannot be imagined than when those who are paid and appointed solely to protect the community from fraud and depredation are found leagued with receivers and thieves. It is the most unnatural of coalitions, being nothing less than an union of the shepherds and wolves at the expense of the flock. No matter under what plausible pretexts this connexion may be palliated, it obviously destroys, at the source, all preventive justice, and revives, under new appearances, the ancient extortion of *blackmail*, by which persons were wont to pay a certain sum to robbers, to be exempt from plunder and devastation.

Flash-house keepers form a link in the same criminal connexion of fences, negotiating officers, attorneys, and thieves. They are most of them sporting characters, who keep houses of entertainment for the other worthies mentioned, and the *flat-traps* for the victims of debauchery and crime. These sinks of profligacy and dissipation are found in every part of the town, and are the resort of notorious thieves, of professed gamblers, of idle and dissolute persons of both sexes: they are frequently kept without license, and never in conformity to the provisions enacted by law; from the penalties of which the keepers become secured by annual contributions to common informers, and by the negligence or connivance of the public and parochial authorities. Some of these flash-houses are open during the whole night, under the pretext of being supper-houses for play-goers, or early houses of call for carters and market-gardeners. One of the most noted, in Brydges-street, is only for the sale of wine and shell-fish, but, after the theatres are closed, is the resort of the profligate of both sexes. Two other celebrated night-houses, the Saloon and the "*Finish*," are now ostensibly kept by free vintners, and, as such, are exempt from the necessity of a magistrate's license. Police officers are in the habit of resorting to these places under the specious pretext that their object is to see and to become acquainted with the persons of depredators, in order that they may the more readily counteract them when in the pursuit of plunder, and secure their persons when become amenable to law. It appears, from evidence before the Police Committee, that some of the officers at Bow-street are in the habit even of receiving tickets to the annual dinners at these houses, where are assembled all the noted prize-fighters, black-legs, and other dubious characters in the metropolis. Such practices are wholly indefensible, and so much good fellowship between the locusts who prey upon the public and those who ought to be the guardians of that abstract personage, accounts, in some measure, for the late prosperity of crime. An important reform, in police, would consist in dissolving this unnatural communion, and in magistrates taking effectual steps to suppress the long-endured nuisance of flash-houses, by the prosecution of every unlicensed victualler, and by compelling those that are licensed to observe such rule and order as can alone warrant the renewal of their license. Motives of equity towards the regular publican, as well as sound policy towards the community, demand this exertion of magisterial authority.

CHAPTER VIII.

COUNTERFEITING THE COIN AND FORGERY.—BURGLARY, HOUSEBREAKING, AND STREET ROBBERIES.—RESURRECTION-MEN.

*Consequences to the Mercantile and Working Classes, from an Adulteration of Coin.—Amount of Metallic Currency in Circulation.—Improvements in the Coinage.—Different Sorts of Counterfeits, and Practices of Coiners.—Number of Prosecutions for Coining and Forgery.—Coinage Laws and their Defects.—Parliamentary Rewards.—Forgery Laws.—*BURGLARY *and Housebreaking—Causes of these Crimes.—Burglaries in the Metropolis and Environs.—Suggestions for their Prevention.—Cautions as to Servants.—Conduct of Savary, the French Minister of Police.—*STREET ROBBERIES.*—Three notorious Fences, C—, G—, and H—.—Robbery at Ludgate-hill.—Ostensible Trades of Burglars, Housebreakers, and Street-Robbers.—Family Men.—*RESURRECTION-MEN*—Their Number and desperate Character.—Number of Anatomical Subjects wanted in the Metropolis, and Means proposed for obtaining a Supply by a Parliamentary Committee.—Nothing ought to be done tending to lessen Respect for the Dead—Its probable Consequences.—Great Caution in Anatomical Legislation requisite.—Sale of Bodies ought to be strictly interdicted.—Suggestions offered.*

ONE of the first objects of the social state is the protection of property; and the currency being intended to represent that property, to protect it from debasement is of paramount importance. In one respect a criminal invasion of property is less hurtful to the community than a fraudulent adulteration of the coin: in wrongfully depriving an individual of a chattel, the injury is specific and definite,—it does not depreciate the value of those untouched; but in putting a single base coin into circulation an inroad is made on the whole amount of specie of that denomination, and suspicion excited as to its value and genuineness: it is like a shot discharged at random into a crowd, which, though it is uncertain whom it may strike, yet, as some must necessarily suffer, fear is generated in all. In consequence, every civilized country has endeavoured to protect, by severe laws, the integrity of its representative medium; the issue of it has been mostly restricted to the head of the state, his impress given to it, and the invasion of his prerogative, or even any interference with it, ranked among the highest crimes.

In a country like England, whose prosperity greatly depends upon her commerce, and whose exchanges and mercantile transactions are so multifarious, the preservation of the coin is an object of the utmost importance: it is one that interests all classes, especially those engaged in trade and industry—the merchant, shopkeeper, artizan, and labourer. Ten sovereigns, of which one, upon an average, is known to be counterfeit, will not buy the same quantity of goods as an equal number known to be genuine. Hence, an issue of base coin, by lessening its average intrinsic value, enhances prices, thereby diminishing trade and consumption, the amount of profits, and rate of wages. These are the indirect effects, the ultimate and direct consequences fall still more exclusively on the mercantile and industrious orders. It is obvious a progressive adulteration must gradually force out of circulation the genuine specie, and finally the whole become so vitiated, that it ceases to be a representative of value, and, consequently, must be called in by the State. But the loss will then fall upon the holders, and, as these will be chiefly the classes mentioned, it will fall upon them; and this, independently of the daily loss they had previously sustained by the base coin which was constantly passing through their hands, being worn out and detected, so as to be unfit for further circulation.

If the gold coin has been counterfeited, the loss falls chiefly upon the merchant, shopkeeper, and retailer; if it be the silver and copper coin that has suffered, the loss will be chiefly felt by those who live on wages, among whom must be many, that the taking of a single unpayable half-crown, shilling, or even sixpence, would cause serious distress and inconvenience. But the pecuniary loss does not measure the extent of the evil. A knowledge that counterfeits have got into circulation excites general suspicion and watchfulness; time is spent in examining every piece of money offered for payment; disputes arise, and a general spirit of fraud, overreaching, ill-will, and contention is generated through the community.

From these observations it is clear who are the classes most interested in the execution of the laws for protecting the national currency. Merchants, tradesmen, artizans, mechanics, and labourers, are the principal sufferers from adulteration; it is by their vigilance alone its purity can be maintained; however numerous and active the police, they cannot be behind every counter, nor in every counting-house, shop, and market-place; they must rely on information communicated by private individuals, who are directly interested in watching over and giving prompt intimation to the civil power, of every one suspected to be engaged in the making or uttering of base money.

The immense amount of our metallic currency renders these precautions doubly incumbent on individuals. Government for years has been silently, but steadily, making efforts to improve the national coin, and by the withdrawal of the small notes this great undertaking will be nearly consummated. Much of the money recently issued exhibits a specimen of the most beautiful workmanship; the sovereigns and shillings especially of 1826-7 defy all competition; and as far transcend former attempts as a lady at Almack's an Indian squaw. The quantity issued, too, appears, from a return to Parliament last session, to have been very great; in the last ten years the gold monies coined—double sovereigns, sovereigns, and half sovereigns, amounted, in value, to £39,369,770; the value of the silver monies coined during the same period, was £9,035,874, making a total addition of £48,405,644 to the precious metals previously in circulation. Having reached such a favourable juncture in the national currency, it is to be hoped the watchfulness, public spirit, and interest of individuals, combined with the exertions of the police, will be sufficient to preserve to us, against all the devices of fraud, one of the greatest blessings in a mercantile community—a beautiful, pure, and solid standard of value.

Notwithstanding the admirable workmanship applied to the present coinage, it is not placed beyond the wiles of the unprincipled counterfeitor. Whatever the skill of one artist may devise, the ingenuity of another can imitate; and hence, all attempts to fabricate an inimitable bank-note, or piece of coin, are perfectly illusive. Gold coin is in the least danger of imitation; requiring greater skill and ingenuity, larger apparatus and capital, than most coiners are able to command. Many counterfeit guineas, half-guineas, and even seven-shilling pieces, had, however, been got out before these denominations were generally withdrawn from circulation; they were fabricated of a certain proportion of pure gold with an alloy of base metal of the full weight, and of such perfect workmanship as to elude discovery, except by persons of skill; their intrinsic value was not more than one-half the legal coin. Attempts have been made to counterfeit the sovereign, but we do not believe they have yet succeeded to any considerable extent.

The great object of attack by the coiners is the silver monies, the counterfeits of which, like the forgeries of one-pound notes, offering the greatest facilities for being got into circulation. Before the introduction of the new system of coinage, the amount of base silver issued was enormous, consisting of at least five different sorts. First, the *flats*, so denominated from being cut out of flatted plates, composed of a mixture of about one-third silver, and the residue blanched copper. The artizans who stamped or coined these blanks into spurious money, were employed by the large dealer or capitalist, who paid them at the rate of eight per cent. for the coinage. The operation consists of first turning the blanks in a lathe; then stamping them, by means of a press, with dies of the exact impression of the coin to be imitated: they are afterwards rubbed with sandpaper and cork; put into aquafortis to attract the silver to the surface; rubbed with common salt, and next with cream of tartar; warmed in a shovel or similar machine before the fire; and, last of all, rubbed with blacking, to give the money the appearance of having been in circulation. All these operations are so quickly performed, that two persons can completely finish to the nominal amount of twenty-five pounds a day in shillings and half-crowns, which are sold to the utterers or *smashers*, as they are vulgarly termed, at from 28*s*. to 40*s*. for a sovereign.

The *second* sort of counterfeit silver was made of copper of a reduced size, and afterwards plated with silver, so extended as to form a rim round the edge. This was a more profitable counterfeit than the last, and could only be detected by ringing it on a table; but, as the fabrication of this kind of base money required a knowledge of *plating* as well as a great deal of ingenuity—it was confined to few hands. A *third* species of counterfeit was limited entirely to shillings, which were nothing more than copper blanks turned in a lathe, and afterwards silvered over by a particular operation, used in colouring metal buttons. They did not cost the makers above a halfpenny each, but as the coating quickly wore off, they were speedily detected. A *fourth* counterfeit consisted of blanch copper cast in moulds, having the impression and size of the silver monies, and being cleaned off and coated over as in making buttons. The fabricators of cast money are always more secure than where presses and dies are used; because, upon the least alarm, and before any officer can have admission, the counterfeits are thrown into the crucible, the moulds destroyed, and nothing to be found that can convict, or even criminate the offender: on this account the makers of cast money have reigned long, and are still very numerous. The *fifth* and last species of counterfeits were called FIGS; they were of very inferior workmanship, and confined entirely to an imitation of the sixpences.

The profits of coiners are very great, and were they frugal they might become rich; but prudence rarely falls to the lot of men who live by acts of criminality. Dr. Colquhoun mentions one who, after a successful career, had retired from business, having acknowledged to him that he had coined to the extent of *two hundred thousand pounds* sterling in counterfeit silver monies in a period of seven years. The decline in the metal-button trade—of which manufacture coining is an execrescence—the discovery of more expeditious tests for the detection of both gold and silver counterfeits, and improvements in the mint coinage, have tended greatly to abridge this nefarious calling. Add to these, several gangs of miscreants, who had fixed their head quarters at Greenwich, Vauxhall, and Mile-end-road, have been lately broken up, and suffered the just punishment of their crimes. Most of these were casters, and had discovered a new species of adulteration, consisting of pure tin and Britannia metal, which, when mixed, produce the best counterfeits, and, in fact, except impurity, they approach more nearly in their properties the legal coin, than any other imitation, and possess one quality that has long been a desideratum in the fraternity—namely, when chinked against any hard substance they ring with almost the clearness of a genuine shilling.*

It might have been thought the withdrawal of the small notes would have turned the forgers upon the precious metals, but it does not appear offences against the coin have multiplied during the last ten years, though the amount of the metallic currency has been so greatly augmented. No doubt the artificers in paper found some difficulty in transferring their industry to an en-

* German silver has lately been much used in the Metropolis, and plate made of it offered for sale as equal in value to the standard metal. It was recently assayed at Goldsmiths' Hall, and found to consist entirely of copper, zinc, and nichil. A German mineralogist, who came over as an adventurer during the speculating mania, once showed us some of this compound,—he said it might be applied to valuable purposes. The bubbles soon after collapsing, the projector got a mission to South America, before any attempt was made to convert it into the philosopher's stone.

tirely new branch of business; and it is not improbable they are now suffering severe privations from vicissitudes in trade. The following are the parliamentary returns on these subjects, showing the number of Mint prosecutions for offences against the coin, and the number of prosecutions for forgery at the sessions for the city of London and county of Middlesex, from the year 1818 to 1827.

Years.	Mint Prosecutions.	Prosecutions for Forgery.
1818	272	123
1819	279	100
1820	180	195
1821	174	107
1822	185	7
1823	214	6
1824	190	7
1825	221	1
1826	290	6
1827	232	10*

The laws for the protection of the coin are both numerous and defective, and will doubtless take their turn in the process of revision to which the criminal code is now being subjected. As the provincial tokens are withdrawn and the Mint coin is the only description issued, it will be easy to bring the law for the security of the national currency within a very short and intelligible compass. One of the most obvious defects in the existing statutes is the minuteness and prolixity of their descriptions of the different kinds of coin, of the implements of coining, and the processes of the coiners—all of which details multiply the chances of escape to the offender, who can obtain professional aid, (though of no avail to the innocent without such assistance,) to search out technical inconsistencies between the allegations in the indictment and the descriptions of the statute. The only end to be attained is to secure the Mint coin from being

* Parl. Papers, Nos. 352 and 509, Sess. 1828.

altered, adulterated, or counterfeited; and it appears to us, it would be most equitable to subject every person engaged in any of these operations, whether preliminary or secondary, as well as all who should utter, pay, or exchange such spurious coin, to the detriment of the legal coin of the realm, to the same punishment, namely, *transportation for life.* As the law stands, these different classes of offenders—all accomplices in the same substantive crime against the community—are subjected to various degrees of punishment, from simple imprisonment for six months to decollation as traitors. For example, the 5th of Eliz. c. 11, makes "clipping, washing, rounding, or filing the coin, for gain sake, high treason;" or by a more comprehensive statute of the same reign, it is an offence of equal magnitude, "impairing, diminishing, falsifying, scaling, and lightening" the coin. The 8th and 9th Will. III. c. 26, makes it high treason, knowingly, to make, mend, or have in possession any implements of coinage specified in the statute. But as a set-off to the severity of these enactments the law is extremely lenient to another stage of the offence, of more injurious tendency than *washing*, *filing*, or *diminishing* the coin, or mending coining tools. The sale of base money, for instance, under the value it imports, as forty bad shillings for a sovereign—an offence frequently committed in populous towns—is only punishable by a year's imprisonment; although, in point of fact, it is well known the sellers are the *employers of the coiners;* that with them the crime originates, and but for them it would not have been committed; while the actual coiners, who work for these dealers merely as journeymen, subject themselves to the punishment of death.

Another inconsistency in the Coinage Laws is the inadequate powers of the magistrate; though made a treasonable offence, no authority is directly given by any existing act, even upon the most pointed information, to search the houses or workshops of coiners in the *night time*. Hence, the difficulty of detecting the makers of cast-money by forcing open doors or windows at a time when they are most likely at work.

Prosecutions under 8 and 9 Will. III. c. 26, are limited to commence within *three* months, and it is incumbent on the prosecutor to show the prosecution was commenced within that time. Proof by *parol* that the prisoner was apprehended within the period will not be sufficient, if the indictment is after the three months, and the warrant to apprehend or commit is produced.* This tends to defeat justice, as offences committed in the country frequently cannot be tried in less than four, five, and in some cases six months.

The rewards allowed to informers under the 6th and 7th Will. III. c. 17, on the conviction of offenders are abolished by 58 Geo. III. c. 70. The mischiefs resulting to the community from debasing the coin, are such as almost to reconcile one to the system of parliamentary rewards, had not experience shewn the diabolical purposes to which such an artificial stimulus to ministerial activity may be perverted.† But as the circulation of spurious money is an offence which cannot be sufficiently guarded against without the co-operation of individuals, it would certainly be expedient to have a fund at the disposal of magistrates, or the solicitor of the Mint, to reward those who furnish information that may lead to the knowledge of offenders or their practices; such rewards to be

* Russ. and R. C. C. 369.

† The trial of Johnson, for coining, at the Old Bailey, January 19, 1829, is the most recent illustration of the tendency of the reward system. But the crime of Vaughan and Brock and the effect of the 10*s*. reward for the apprehension of vagrants had long since demonstrated its impolicy.

discretionary, and by no means depend on the conviction of the accused, but proportioned to the value of the service rendered.

Intimately connected in their object with the coinage-laws are those for preserving the paper currency. It is thought by some the punishment of death for FORGERY is too severe an infliction, and certainly so it appears in merely contemplating the act itself without adverting to its dangerous consequences. Punishments ought to be such as are likely to deter from the commission of crimes, and proportioned not only to the magnitude of the injury inflicted on society, but the intensity of the temptation they offer, and the difficulties of prevention. The security of all commercial paper and legal instruments depends on the inviolability of individual writing; and unless it is maintained the fortunes of entire families may be swept away in a moment, merely to serve the wants of profligate men. Such are often the inducements to forgery,—the number of opportunities for its commission—and the little strength of nerve it demands, that any punishment short of ignominious execution would, we fear, prove insufficient to restrain its perpetration. For the forger the ordinary palliatives cannot be urged; he is mostly an educated man, and rarely driven to crime by absolute want: both forging and coining are not limited in their effects to individuals, but directly attack the whole community, and are as baneful in their consequences as a diabolical effort to destroy the highways made for general convenience, or pull down banks erected to guard against irruptions of the sea. Happily the higher class of forgeries are seldom brought before the tribunals; the strict and impartial execution of the law, aided by the extinction of one-pound notes, has almost extirpated the offence, affording additional reason for continuing the existing penalty.

Still, if the punishment be too severe in public estimation, it will be incumbent on the Legislature to alleviate it. The people are the virtual administrators of criminal law, and without their concurrence it cannot be executed. We have heard of many persons declining to prosecute, (or perhaps preferring to *compromise*, would be a more correct description,) rather than be instrumental in the death of an offender, guilty of forgery. Should this be the prevailing sentiment, it will be necessary to try transportation, or other secondary punishment; though we feel pretty well convinced, from the bearings of the crime, and however we may deplore the occasion, that experience will demonstrate the necessity of recurring to the existing law.

From the difficulty of proving a *venue*, as shown by Mr. Gates to the late Police Committee, it is almost impossible to obtain the conviction of a forger, and, in the cases that mostly occur, it is now usual to indict only for the uttering, not the forgery. For, as the law at present stands, although you can show the whole of the cheque or bill of exchange to be in the hand-writing of a certain individual, you cannot prosecute for the forgery unless you can show *where it was written*, and in nineteen cases out of twenty that is impossible; thus the person committing the forgery escapes punishment, unless he were the utterer of the instrument also, which is very seldom the case, as the bill or cheque is generally given to some porter or boy, who, for a shilling or sixpence, takes it to the banker, where, if it is discovered to be a forgery, the man is on the look-out in the neighbourhood to ascertain that fact, and immediately he finds his messenger does not return within the time by which he supposes he could get the money, he is gone, and, before any one can get out of the house, he is out of the way, by which means the greatest criminal escapes punishment.

BURGLARY, HOUSEBREAKING, AND STREET-ROBBERIES.

There is no country where burglary and housebreaking are so common as in England, and this guilty pre-eminence may probably be ascribed to the superior daring and muscular power of Englishmen, the vast amount of chattel property, and the mode of living adopted by the inhabitants. The valuable plate in the dwellings of the opulent, the stores of rich merchandize in the shops and warehouses, excite the cupidity of the criminal mind; and when it is known that all these places are left during long intervals, comparatively unprotected, it cannot be a matter of surprise they are so frequently an object of plunder. The City itself consists almost entirely of counting-houses, offices, shops, and warehouses, filled with plate, jewellery, silks, piece goods, spices, and all the choicest products of every corner of the globe; and from Saturday night till Monday morning is chiefly entrusted to the vigilance of office-keepers, servants, housekeepers, and porters, and to the observer looks more like the "City of the Plague," than the busiest mart in the universe.

These are some of the causes of depredation: but latterly there appears to have been a "march of intellect" among thieves, and in the gangs which conducted the recent bank robberies, and the more successful burglaries, there has doubtless appeared geniuses of a superior *caste*, endowed with more than ordinary Satanic power. Thieves have certainly bestowed more attention on the art of breaking into houses and warehouses than the owners have in defending them. Some of the late burglaries evince a science which would not disgrace a first-rate engineer in the attack of a fortified town. The robbery of Lund's, Cornhill, was effected by the depredators placing themselves in ambush in the adjoining church, and thence descending through the roof into the shop beneath; in Grimaldi's they took shelter in a neighbouring coffee-shop, and made their way through the back area into the premises; in Loudan's robbery they broke through the partition wall of an adjoining empty house; the robbery of government stamps at the Bull-and-Mouth inn was effected in a similar manner; and the robbery at the foot of London-bridge, and of several other silversmiths and banking-houses, have been accomplished by stratagem rather than force. Except the burglary at West Moulsey, where they entered, by escalade, at the back of the house, there have been few instances lately of forcing houses in the old-fashioned way, at the front, and taking possession by *coup de main.* Thieves now proceed on a more cautious plan, founded on careful previous reconnoissance. The first step, no doubt, when a *plant* has been made, is, to survey it carefully, internally and externally, in order to discover the weak points of approach; next follow inquiries into the number of inmates, their hours of going out and return, so as to guard against surprise, and be prepared for resistance; lastly, a provision of the needful implements, consisting mostly of the centre-bit, crow-bar, pick-locks, phosphorus-bottle, bags, or large great coat pockets, to conceal and carry off the booty, with a hackney-coach, or light cart, at a convenient distance, in reserve, to aid the flight.

With all the accomplishments, however, of London *cracksmen,* their success is a matter of astonishment, and must be imputed in a great measure to the culpable negligence of individuals. People confide too much in the power of the police, and seem to think it will take care of them, though they take no care of themselves. But it is obvious that the protection to be derived from the civil force, under any system, must be chiefly *ex-*

ternal; they cannot have the control of the fastening of areas, nor of empty houses, neither can they be acquainted with the character of domestics, and their followers, by whose agency, it has generally happened, robberies have been effected.

Most robberies of warehouses and houses are "put-up ones," either by those who are, or have been employed or domesticated there, and are never committed without the aid of persons acquainted with the premises. The utmost caution is requisite in taking servants, and in the degree they are admitted to the confidence of their employers. Perhaps a servant, after living honestly with his master, leaves his situation, contracts dissipated habits or bad company, becomes connected with thieves, and points out the way to their booty. This may not happen till years after, so that masters, without great precaution, are in danger, not only from the servants in their employ, but from those who have formerly lived in their service.

In France they are less scrupulous about the character of servants than we are, and it is not of so much importance in a country less commercial and abundant in chattel property. While SAVARY was minister of police, a curious expedient was adopted to bring domestics under the surveillance of that department. They were all registered, their abodes, last situation, and every particular connected with their personal history. A servant could not be engaged without producing a small book from the prefecture, containing these particulars, and which was returned to the police on leaving his situation, with a note, expressing the cause of his removal.*

Nothing of this kind would be either desirable or

* Memoirs of the Duke of Rovigo, vol. ii. page 263.

practicable in the metropolis, but something, we are persuaded, might be invented for rendering both houses and warehouses more secure; and it is really a reproach to this mechanical age, that nothing in the construction of locks, doors, and windows, and even in the protection of walls, and in the mode of giving alarm, can be devised, that shall frustrate any nocturnal efforts of the midnight plunderer. However much of *castles* houses may be in law, they prove weak defences when opposed to the burglar. In warfare, a dwelling-house is always deemed a good military position; and, with a little preparation, can be put in such a state of defence, as to resist, for a time, the attack of a powerful army, and we are convinced if mechanics and builders would direct their attention to the subject, such precautions might be devised as would defeat any attempt at housebreaking that could be made during the few hours afforded by the longest night.

There is one simple suggestion we would beg to recommend. It is, that all occupiers of houses and warehouses likely to become objects of attack, should have them surveyed by persons qualified for the office; their internal securities, and adjacent premises examined, and such precautions recommended as might be deemed necessary. This is a duty which we trust, under the new arrangement of the police, some of its officers, qualified for the purpose, will be appropriated to perform, on the application of individuals and the payment of a trifling gratuity.

Next to burglary and housebreaking, STREET ROBBERIES have multiplied in the metropolis to a dangerous extent, and are perpetrated in the most daring manner. Gentlemen have frequently their watches plucked out of the fob, or their pocket-book or purse snatched or cut away, in the most crowded thoroughfares. Gangs of thieves and pickpockets, exhibiting often, in their dress and exterior, the appearance of gentlemen and men of business, assemble about the theatres, the coach-offices, streets and corners adjacent to the banking-houses, Exchange, the docks, and warehouses, ready to hustle, rob, or knock down any one carrying or bearing about his person anything valuable; or at the doors of the banks, shops, and warehouses, in the evening, about the time they are locked, ready to seize loose parcels, when unperceived, or hide themselves on the premises, with a view to more extensive depredation. Many of these atrocious miscreants are, also, constantly in waiting at the inns, disguised in different ways, personating *travellers, coach-office clerks, porters, and coachmen*, for the purpose of plundering every thing that is portable; which, with the assistance of two or three associates, if necessary, is carried to a coach, called for the purpose, and immediately conveyed to the receiver.

Three of the most notorious fences, in London, C——, G——, and H——, almost began their career in this way nearly twenty years since, and are now, by the connivance of a disgraceful police, with whom they live in habits of familiar intercourse, wealthy enough to support their carriages. A coachman, named Payne, had a parcel taken out of his pocket, worth £7000, and the parties to whom we allude, being notorious and on the spot, were taken to Bow-street, and would certainly have been committed, had not all proceedings been suddenly stopped, by a compromise and restitution.

There appears no way of checking street-robberies other than by greater individual precaution and augmenting the day and night patrol. Robberies in the street are more frequent in the day-time, and in the most busy thoroughfares. Last spring we witnessed a most audacious attack of the kind, on Ludgate-hill, at midday. A gentleman descended from a stage-coach, took out his purse to pay the fare, when a well-dressed villain snatched it out of his hand, passed it to an accomplice, and instantly darted across the street up an adjoining court. He was pursued, taken, and searched, and the magistrate, at Guildhall, committed him, but we never heard he was tried.

The most adroit thieves in the several lines of business mentioned in this section are generally prize-fighters, E O table-keepers, convicts from the hulks, or returned transports, who, under pretence of some ostensible trade —while they carry on the real trade of thieving—open a chandler's, a butcher's, green-grocer's, or pamphlet-shop, get into public-houses, or keep livery-stables; one of the most notorious, named Wright, was actually a *police-officer*, and is now in Newgate, having been cast for death for breaking into a house in Long Acre. They are all in a connected chain, and truly "*family men*," nourishing, aiding, and supporting each other in every criminal enterprise and disaster.

RESURRECTION-MEN.

There has long been a set of wretches in the metropolis whose ostensible calling is the violation of the sanctuary of the grave, to obtain subjects for the advancement of anatomical science. The number of persons who regularly live by raising bodies is supposed not to exceed ten, but the number occasionally employed in the same occupation probably exceeds two hundred. Nearly the whole of these exhumators are occupied, also, in thieving, and form the most desperate and abandoned class of the community. Many of them keep a horse and cart, which they employ in carrying stolen goods, and, if out late at night, and questioned by the police, they allege they are getting subjects for the surgeons :—

scarcely a year elapses without some of them being convicted either of stealing or housebreaking. Their ferocity exceeds every thing that can be imagined of human beings. In speaking of them, Sir Astley Cooper, in his evidence before a Parliamentary Committee of last Session, says :—" They are the lowest dregs of degradation: I do not know that I can describe them better : there is no crime they would not commit; and, as to myself, if they should imagine that I would make a good subject, they really would not have the smallest scruple, if they could do the thing undiscovered, to make a subject of me." Mr. Brodie affirms, " They are as bad as the worst in society. When I consider their character, I think it a dangerous thing to the community that they should be able to get ten guineas for a body." Mr. Brooke says, " They are the most iniquitous set of villains that ever lived." These testimonials to their infamy are from gentlemen eminent in the medical world, and who have been partly indebted for their eminence to an intercourse with the miscreants they describe.

The law, in its present state, neither tolerates the practices of resurrectionists nor anatomists. In the Court of King's Bench, *Rex* v. *Lynn*, A. D. 1788, it was decided to be a misdemeanor to carry away a dead body from a churchyard, although for the purpose of dissection, as an offence against common decency. In *Rex* v. *Young*, the master of a workhouse, a surgeon, and another person, were indicted for and convicted of a conspiracy to prevent the burial of a person who died in the workhouse. In *Rex* v. *Cundick*,* the defendant was found guilty of misdemeanor for not having buried the body of an executed felon, intrusted to him by the gaoler for that purpose. Lastly, in *King* v. *Davies and Others*,†

* Surrey Spring Assizes, 1822.

† Lancaster Assizes, March 14, 1828.

the defendants were convicted, and received sentence, for having taken into their possession, *with intent to dissect,* a dead body, at the time knowing the same to have been unlawfully disinterred.

Thus the law interdicts exhumation, yet it requires a proficiency in the medical practitioner that cannot without it be obtained. A surgeon performing an operation unskilfully is liable to punishment. He cannot even lawfully exercise his profession without having passed through an examination, which he is incompetent to pass, unless he has performed a certain number of anatomical exercises. Without dissection a knowledge of the organization of the human frame cannot be acquired, the causes of disease investigated, and the most certain and least painful remedies discovered. It tends to diminish the frequency of operations, and lessens the pain of those which are unavoidable. Surgeons, like others, can only acquire skill from practice, and they must learn their art either upon the living or the dead. But it is the poor who chiefly suffer from their ignorance,—as the Chinese proverb says, " the barber learns to shave on the orphan's face,"—and it is on the indigent the inexperienced operator commences practice, and to them the bunglers of the art are confined. It is the remains of the poor, too, that are mostly disturbed by the brutal resurrectionist; the rich can bury themselves deep, enclose their bodies in impenetrable cerements, or even appoint a watch to guard them from violation. Living or dead, therefore, the poor are the principal sufferers under the existing system: all suffer in some degree, because no specific class being set apart for the purposes of anatomy, every one, in the vicissitudes of life, is liable to fall into the hands of the unskilful, or be disturbed by the exhumator.

With a view of meeting these evils—of providing for

the wants of science—of extirpating a diabolical calling—and of maintaining the sanctity of the grave—it has been proposed to make lawful the practice of dissection, and to appropriate, for the benefit of the community, the bodies of persons dying under peculiar circumstances to anatomical purposes.

It appears there are about ten thousand general practitioners in England and Wales, and in the metropolis about eight hundred students of anatomy.* The number of students in 1823 was one thousand, but the difficulty of acquiring subjects has compelled many to resort to foreign schools, and it is thought there are not more than five hundred who actually dissect. Each student requires three subjects—two to learn the structure of the parts, and one to operate on. In order to obtain the necessary supply, it is proposed to take for dissection those who by will bequeath their bodies for that purpose—those who die in prisons while under sentence for a criminal offence—those who die in hospitals and workhouses, having no friends willing to undertake the expenses of their burial, and who have not expressed any wish to the contrary. The last source alone would probably yield an adequate number. By returns obtained by the Parliamentary Committee from 127 parishes of the metropolis, it appears that out of 3744 persons who died in the workhouses of these parishes in the year 1827, 3103 were buried at the parish expense; and that of these about 1108 were not attended to their graves by any relations. It is likely therefore that in the metropolis a regular supply of bodies might be obtained of those who have either no relations, whose feelings would be outraged, or such only who by not claiming the body evince an indifference to its future disposal.

* Report on Anatomy, Parl. Pap. No. 568, Sess. 1828, page 6, and Appendix, 155.

By a remedy so simple the cultivation of an useful science would be facilitated—the churchyard preserved from violation—an unnatural calling superseded—and the living not endangered by the temptation offered to the perpetration of the highest crimes from the scarcity of subjects.

We have thus brought together the chief facts connected with the horrid vocation of the resurrectionist, and shall offer a few concluding remarks on the principles involved in any future legislation on the subject. It is a question of very great importance, requiring to be seriously investigated, lest by too precipitate a proceeding, the most holy and venerable of human feelings be compromised, and their importance undervalued, merely because the immediate consequences are not apparent and their utility obscured in the antiquity of their origin.

One of the first considerations which ought to determine the character of a new anatomical law, is that it should contain no provision that can lessen in the public mind the sacred respect now felt towards the remains of the dead. We do not concur in the philosophy that would imply there is no ignominy, no punishment in the dissection of a body after death. It may be a *prejudice;* but if our moralities are to be submitted to this test, we do not know where we may be carried. If the dissection of a human body may be treated with indifference, so may the consumption of them for food. Incest, or a still more abominable offence; and patriotism, the love of fame, of offspring, and a regard to personal decency, may be all prejudices in the estimation of some, but they are prejudices which experience has proved more conducive to social happiness than their opposite truths. The dead we know cannot suffer; but in the inviolability of their remains is consecrated the safety of the living.

What would be the consequences of considering the

body of a man after death no better than that of a dog, or a regular subject of traffic? What a farce it would make of all the solemnities of a funeral and of the most imposing service in the Liturgy! What an opening for crime to the profligate mind! The murderer is often appalled at his deed by the sight of his victim. Death, it is known, may be effected by suffocation, by poison, and other means which leave no trace even to medical eyes. In numberless instances the removal of the living—of rivals, the aged, the incurably diseased, and the wealthy would make the fortune of survivors, or at least be of the utmost convenience. What often checks these private executions is, doubtless, the disposal of the body; or perhaps the dread of looking upon the lifeless corpse. By the institution of searchers and coroners' inquisitions, society has endeavoured to guard against these clandestine atrocities, but all precautions would be still more inadaquate than they now are, without the aid of what some may deem superstition; and we are convinced, were the horrible indecency of the sale of subjects tolerated, and the common mind thereby inducted to a familiar treatment of the body after death, one of the greatest safeguards of human life would be removed. It ought never to be forgotten that the Edinburgh murders commenced with the sale of a body arising from a natural death: the horrible wretches were at first appalled with the spectacle of their dreadful trade; but practice soon familiarized their minds, till at length they thought no more of the immolation of a fellow-creature than the strangling of a cat. The ferocious character of resurrectionists, and even the habits of some anatomists, show the hardening tendency of the principle we deprecate, and on which we could enlarge, had we not, perhaps, urged enough to establish the importance of the consideration for which we contend. One of the most favourable traits in the national character, in the paucity of personal crimes, may be ascribed to the uniform respect, which, before and after death, the person is treated in this country, and we trust no legislation will tend to impair this salutary feeling.

While, therefore, every facility ought to be afforded to science, it is important not to compromise the more important interests. Dissections ought, in our opinion, to be deemed an ignominy, and no one, without specific cause, denied those sepulchral rites and mode of decay which custom has sanctioned. To the philosopher it may be matter of indifference whether he be dissected by worms or the surgeon's knife, but laws are not intended exclusively for the learned. In the common mind dissection is considered an indignity—a depreciation of the earthly tabernacle; and were it openly tolerated, would lessen the respect for the dead and thereby remove one of the safeguards of the living.

In accordance with these views, the sale of bodies ought to be interdicted under severe penalties; they are too sacred to be made an object of traffic, and the toleration of it not only holds out a temptation to dreadful crimes, but is one step towards anthropophagy.

Secondly, women ought generally to be exempt from dissection, as inconsistent with the delicacy due to the female sex; but as a certain number is requisite to exemplify the partial differences of conformation, it might be obtained by appropriating those found dead and unknown, those dying in hospitals, or of peculiar diseases, the nature of which the surviving friends might wish to have investigated.

Having made these exceptions, we would offer up, as a sacrifice to science, all who die in prison, while under sentence for crime; all found dead and unknown; all who die in any hospital, charitable institution, or poorhouse, and not claimed and removed by friends or next of kin, in a state fit for interment, within forty-eight hours after death, and who have not by will or testament expressed any wish to be interred. To the devotion of these to public use no objection could be reasonably made; they are all either the victims of justice, or their lives have been so doomed or mispent that they have not a friend to close their eyes. In addition to them, any one should be freely allowed to bequeath, *as a gift*, his body to dissection; and the executors and next of kin should be allowed to offer, as a gift, a body for dissection, the deceased having expressed no wish to the contrary: but, in the two last cases, as well as in the case of women offered for dissection, under the circumstances mentioned in the preceding paragraph, no body should be removed to any school of anatomy, without a certificate first obtained from the coroner of the district, testifying that he had seen the body, and that there was nothing either in the last will of the deceased, or in the mode of dying, which prohibited its intended appropriation.

All bodies devoted to anatomical examination to be buried, with funeral rites, within a certain period,* and a certificate of such interment to be returned to the place from whence the bodies had been received.

Lastly, bodies to be removed to the dissecting-rooms either in the night, or in such private manner as not to be exposed to the knowledge of the public.

Under such regulations the practice of dissection might be rendered *lawful;* the safety of the living would not be endangered, no prejudice nor affection would be outraged, and the demands of science would be accommodated. But as a preventive to subjects being obtained in any other manner than that sanctioned by law, it

* Westminster Review, No. 19, p. 148.

would be necessary, *first*,—to make it a capital offence to steal the whole or part of any body from a churchyard or other place ; and, *secondly*,—to make it a misdemeanor in any medical person to buy or obtain the whole or part of a body in any other manner than the law prescribed.

There is in the cultivators of anatomy, as well as other pursuits, an enthusiasm, a mania, or morbid curiosity, which sometimes requires to be controled, as well as the ferocious practices of the resurrectionist. It is not long since a devotee of science actually unearthed the remains of his parent, in order to subject her head to phrenological scrutiny. A parallel outrage against general feeling was related by Mr. Brooke to the Parliamentary Committee.—A young lady suffering from a carious tooth, the lower jaw became so enlarged that she seemed to have a double head, formed by an immense secretion of osseous and cartilaginous substance. After her death, the grave being pointed out (no doubt by a disciple of John Hunter) to one of the resurrection-men, a party went in the course of a few nights and disinterred the body, which they decapitated, bringing away the head only, but leaving the corpse exposed upon the ground: the coffin-lid and shroud being also left in different places,—forming, with the empty coffin, a horrible exhibition to public gaze!

CHAPTER IX.

CAUSES OF THE INCREASE OF CRIME.

Amount of Crime in London and Middlesex, and its comparative Increase since 1811.—*Crimes against the Person as well as Property increased faster than Population.—Inadequate Causes of Crime assigned by Parliamentary Committees.—Additional Causes,*—1. *The Augmentation in National Wealth, especially Chattel Property;* 2. *The long continuance of Public Peace;* 3. *Ameliorations in Criminal Punishments;* 4. *Commercial Avidity and Speculation, involving a decline in Mercantile Principle and Character;* 5. *More extended Operation of the Debtor-Laws, from increased Mercantile Transactions;* 6. *Poverty occasioned by diminished Wages and Profits;* 7. *Pressure of Business at the Public Police-Offices.*—*Habit of Drinking among the Lower Classes of the Metroplis.—Influence of Popular Education on Crime.*

HAVING, in the three last chapters, given a general exposition of the predominant crimes in the Metropolis we shall conclude this branch of our subject with a few observations on the causes of the increase in the number of offences; premising that our remarks will apply to the metropolis only, and refer exclusively to causes tending to swell the criminal calendar within the last ten years,—the interval during which the augmentation has been most remarkable. Before we commence, it will be proper to trouble the reader with a few facts establishing the increase in delinquency, and the nature and character of the offences which have multiplied. The inquiries of Parliamentary Committees are mostly so complete and indefatigable, that it is impossible, aided by the lights they afford, any question connected with the public interests can be long obscured or misunderstood.

The total committals for offences in London and Middlesex, from 1811 to 1817, amounted to 13,415; in an equal period, from 1821 to 1827, to 19,883: being an average annual increase of 924, or 48 per cent. The increase of convictions was 642 per annum, or 55 per cent. But the population is computed to have increased 19 per cent; leaving, of the committals, 29 per cent., and of the convictions, 36 per cent., to be accounted for by other causes than the increase in population. The description of offences in the two periods, and their proportional increase, will appear from the following exhibition of crime in six classes; distinguishing those offences aimed at the person, those aimed at property under the protection of the person, those aimed at property most exposed to depredation, those of mere lust or appetite, those of rare occurrence, and those against the currency.

Offences in London and Middlesex, from the year 1811 *to* 1817, *compared with offences from the year* 1821 *to* 1827, *abstracted from the Report on the Police of the Metropolis,* 1828, *Appendix, B. page* 302.

	COMMITTED.		CONVICTED.		EXECUTED.	
	1811-17.	1821-27.	1811-17.	1821-27.	1811-17.	1821-27.
1st. CRIMES affecting the Person:						
Manslaughter	41	110	28	62	—	—
Murder	97	81	25	5	25	5
Stabbing, poisoning, &c.	48	66	14	17	4	6
	186	257	67	84	29	11
2d. CRIMES affecting Property:						
Burglary	442	428	221	245	19	34
Embezzlement (by servants)	141	295	71	196	—	—
Frauds	279	482	167	278	—	—
Housebreaking	106	144	52	103	—	1
Larceny, of all descriptions	10,223	15,892	6,378	10,495	7	19
Stealing from letters	12	6	8	4	1	2
Highway robbery	485	400	180	159	17	27
Receiving stolen goods	257	431	87	144	—	—
	11,945	18,078	7,164	11,624	44	83
3d. CRIMES against exposed Property:						
Cattle-stealing	14	14	10	6	—	—
Horse-stealing	51	108	32	65	—	8
Sheep-stealing	24	34	20	19	—	4
	89	156	62	90	—	12
4th. CRIMES of Lust or Appetite:						
Rape	38	33	4	5	2	2
—— Assault with intent	23	70	14	37	—	—
Sodomy	11	15	4	3	4	3
—— Assault with intent	68	96	38	52	—	—
	140	214	60	97	6	5
5th. CRIMES of rare Occurrence:						
Arson	8	10	2	3	2	1
Bigamy	46	54	30	39	—	—
Cattle-maiming	1	—	1	—	—	—
Child-stealing	9	6	7	3	—	—
—— concealing the birth of	1	—	1	—	—	—
Game-laws, offences against	—	2	—	2	—	—
Perjury	37	35	9	15	—	—
Piracy	6	27	4	2	4	—
Sacrilege	2	1	2	—	—	—
Sending threatening letters	3	1	3	1	—	—
Treason	7	—	2	—	1	—
Trafficking in slaves	—	1	—	—	—	—
Transports being at large	23	26	22	23	—	—
Felonies, not otherwise described	199	423	103	180	—	—
	342	586	186	268	7	1
6th. OFFENCES against the Currency:						
Coining	34	14	27	9	—	2
Uttering base coin	418	403	369	325	—	—
Forgery	118	87	64	46	44	19
Forged bank-notes, having in possession	143	88	140	86	—	—
	713	592	600	466	44	21

The increase or decrease per cent. in the preceding six classes of offences is as follow :—

	Committals.		Convictions.		Executions.
1st Class	inc. 40	..	inc. 28	..	dec. 65
2d Class	inc. 34	..	inc. 62	..	inc. 75
3d Class	inc. 80	..	inc. 50	..	———
4th Class	inc. 47	..	inc. 62	..	dec. 83
5th Class	inc. 73	..	inc. 46	..	dec. 14
6th Class	dec. 17	..	dec. 22	..	dec. 50*

It thus appears that the convictions for every class of offences, except the last, have increased, and in a much higher proportion than the increase in population. Offences against the currency have decreased almost entirely, from the withdrawal of the small notes of the Bank of England. Executions have decreased for every class of offences except the second ; but as convictions have increased, it has obviously resulted from a reluctance to inflict capital punishment, not a decrease in criminality. We regret to make this observation, because many benevolent persons entertained the hope, and even have so represented the fact, that the more *atrocious crimes*, especially those against the *person*, had diminished. But the returns to Parliament, from which the above statements are faithfully copied, warrant no such conclusion; the only consolation they afford is, that though personal crimes have increased, they have not increased so rapidly as depredations against property: and hence we must reluctantly conclude, that the great object of moral improvement and criminal legislation, during the last ten years, has failed, though not so pre-eminently, in checking the former as the latter description of delinquency.

A different result may be obtained by referring to the decrease in the number on whom *sentence of death* has

* Report on the Police of the Metropolis, 1828, pp. 4–5.

been passed; but this can be no exponent whatever of delinquency, and can only tend to mislead; for, as the number of convictions has increased, it only attests a more lenient administration of criminal law, not a diminution in any class of human depravity. A cursory inspection of the classes of crime might also induce more satisfactory conclusions. For instance, among the homicides, murder has actually decreased; but the kindred offence of manslaughter, for which, probably from disposition to lenity, the offender had, in many cases, been committed, has nearly trebled. In the committals for the capital crime of burglary there is a diminution: but this is more than counterbalanced by the augmentation in the secondary and neighbouring crime of housebreaking. Cattle-stealing has diminished, but horse and sheep stealing have doubled. Rapes have not increased, but assaults, *with intent*, which are almost as bad, have increased twofold. In frauds, embezzlements, and larcenies of every description, the increase is certainly the greatest: but this does not impugn our former melancholy deduction that every class of offence has increased more rapidly than even population.

Though crime has increased in the Metropolis, it has not increased so rapidly as in the country.* The population in England and Wales (London and Middlesex excepted) is computed to have increased only 16¾ per cent. in the two periods of 1811—17 and 1821—7; while, in London and Middlesex, the increase has been 19 per cent.; yet the comparative increase of crime is as follows:—

	England and Wales.		London and Middlesex.	
Commitments	86 per cent.		48 per cent.	
Convictions	105 ,,		55 ,,	
Executions	28 ,,	*decrease*	5 ,,	*increase.*

* Report on the Police of the Metropolis, 1828, Appendix C. p. 304.

It is a very extraordinary fact, that the comparative increase of crime in the Metropolis should have been *less* and the increase in executions *greater* than in the country—and this, too, in spite of the great diminution in London executions, from the cessation in Bank of England prosecutions. An argument might be deduced from hence in favour of the superior efficacy of *capital punishments:* but the circumstances influencing the relative state of crime in London and the provinces are foreign to our investigation; and having fairly inducted the reader to a knowledge of the facts establishing an increase in metropolitan delinquency, we shall direct his attention to the *causes.*

The late Police Committee did not enter very largely into an investigation of the causes of crime; nor did the evidence of the witnesses examined afford them materials for arriving at any very general conclusions on this subject. The causes principally relied upon were the increase in population—the cheapness of spirituous liquors—the neglect of children by their parents—the want of employment—absence of suitable provision for juvenile delinquents—imperfect prison discipline—and defects in the police. To these may be added certain other causes, applicable to the Metropolis, assigned by another Parliamentary Committee,* as accounting partly for the increase of crime, and partly for its "greater exhibition to public view," without evidencing any virtual increase of depravity—namely, the paying of prosecutors their expenses in cases of misdemeanour—the Malicious Trespass Act—decline in domestic superintendence—readiness with which magistrates commit for offences—defective and unsuitable punishments—and

* Report on Criminal Commitments and Convictions in England and Wales, Parl. Pap. No. 545, Sess. 1828, pages 4, 8, and 16.

the bringing before the tribunals petty offences, which were formerly either settled by summary chastisement, inflicted by the sufferer on the delinquent, or passed over without magisterial cognizance.

Some of these causes of delinquency are indisputable; others may be objected to as not peculiar to the period under review; and one at least has been too recently in operation to have contributed materially to that enormous increase which the criminal calendar has lately exhibited. In addition, therefore, to the causes assigned by the Parliamentary Committees, we beg to suggest the following:—

1. The enormous augmentation of national wealth, especially chattel property.
2. The long continuance of public peace.
3. Ameliorations in criminal punishment.
4. Commercial avidity and speculation, involving a decline in mercantile principle and character.
5. More extended operation of the Debtor Laws, from increased mercantile transactions.
6. Poverty, occasioned by diminished Wages and Profits.
7. Pressure of business at the public police offices.

With the exception of the last, all these causes of crime apply in almost an equal degree to the country; but we shall chiefly trace their operation in the Metropolis. Of the tendency of augmented wealth and commerce to multiply offences, we spoke at the commencement of the sixth chapter, and shall not repeat our observations. Indeed, the effects of accumulating property—the increase of houses, shops, warehouses, docks, wharfs, shipping, navigation, and conveyances of all kinds; the increase of commodities, their unceasing transfer from one to another, and the creation of additional objects of trust, confidence, and agency, consequent upon them; the multiplication of luxuries, enjoyments, and temptations: these and many others, having the same origin, tend so obviously to multiply frauds, embezzlements, larcenies, and that class of offences by which the criminal calendar has been chiefly augmented, that they need only to be adverted to in order to be readily admitted as one of the most prolific sources of crime. Waiving, therefore, a more particular consideration of effects which must be apparent to every one, we shall advert to the consequences of what may be now termed a long peace.

A moderate share of adversity is usually deemed favourable to the formation of virtuous habits; and, on the same principle, a long course of public prosperity may tend to national demoralization. It is certainly observable that every general peace is mostly followed by increased licentiousness in manners, selfishness, avarice, debauchery, and crime. The twelve years of uninterrupted peace during the reign of George I. were distinguished by the profligacy of individuals, impiety, and the indulgence of every criminal passion.* In like manner, the pacific era of George II. poured into the country a flood of national wealth and enjoyments, which were accompanied with their usual train of calamities. SMOLLETT, speaking of the general prosperity of the community, says, "Commerce and manufacture flourished again to such a degree of increase as had never been known in this island; but this advantage was attended with an irresistible tide of luxury and excess, which flowed through all degrees of the people, breaking down all the mounds of civil policy, and opening a way for licentiousness and im-

* Tindal's Continuation of Rapin, vol. xix.

morality. The highways were infested with rapine and assassination; the cities teemed with the brutal votaries of lewdness, intemperance, and profligacy. The whole land was overspread with a succession of riot, tumult, and insurrection, excited, in different parts of the kingdom, by the erection of new turnpikes, which the legislature judged necessary for the convenience of inland carriage."* The rage, too, for drinking GIN at this time exceeded all bounds. The populace of London were sunk into the most brutal degeneracy by drinking to excess this pernicious spirit, which was sold so cheap that the lowest classes could afford to indulge themselves in one continued state of intoxication, to the destruction of all morals, health, and industry. Such a shameful degree of profligacy prevailed, that the retailers of this poisonous compound set up painted boards in public, inviting people to be drunk for the small expense of *one penny*, assuring them they might be dead drunk for TWO PENCE, and have straw for nothing!

Descending to more recent periods, we find similar connexion between cause and effect. The country was intoxicated with prosperity at the commencement of the reign of George III.; and we have before had occasion to remark (page 148) the profligacy, both in private individuals and public men, which distinguished that era, and which far transcended any examples of the present day. The state of society immediately preceding the French revolutionary war, when the country had reached an unexampled pitch of prosperity, affords another proof of our general position. Many living individuals can bear testimony to the habits of drinking, licentiousness, and debauchery which then pervaded even the middle orders of the community; and we know,

* Continuation of Hume, vol. iii. page 275.

from the *Annual Register* and other cotemporary records, that the Metropolis was in a dreadful state of corruption and disorder. The environs and outskirts of the town were overrun with footpads and highwaymen; burglary and housebreaking were crimes of the most ordinary occurrence; and gangs of villains, fifteen or twenty in number, used to parade the streets, in open defiance of the police, and plunder and ill treat every passenger they met, with impunity. It was to remedy these enormous evils, and reform an inefficient and corrupt magistracy, that Messrs. Dundas, Wilberforce, and Burton introduced their plan of a permanent stipendiary police, which soon proved one of the greatest improvements ever introduced into the civil government of the Metropolis.

The last example we shall cite is still vivid in general recollection. The disastrous convulsions of 1824–5 were the natural consequences of causes which had been slowly operating from the general peace of 1815, and which, till then, had not reached their full developement. Over the character of this period we should wish to draw a veil; it grew out of vast accumulating capital; and men, intoxicated with wealth and prosperity, seemed absolved from moral and social ties. Every class was infected, from the peer to the commoner; those deemed respectable, as well as the reputedly infamous, appeared all promiscuously loosened to run a race of fraud, rapacity, and swindling. Can it be a matter of surprise that offences multiplied, when not a single class in the community remained whose entire purity and example could be said to offer a reproach to turpitude and crime?

But the effects of continued peace are not limited to the vices and extravagance produced by redundant wealth; a species of *immoral energy* is generated, for which there exists no legitimate outlet. Every one must have remarked in the circle in which he moves, whether living in a large town, or country village, at college or at school, in a counting-house or manufactory, that a number of depraved and uncontrolable spirits, in every grade of life, are constantly reaching maturity; possessed of strong passions, of ardent and irregular minds, they have no aptitude for habits of regular industry, nor the civil pursuits which are their natural inheritance. In time of war the Army and Navy open to them a field congenial to their character; the recruiting-sergeant, aided by "the soul-stirring drum," collects them through the country, and after being a source of domestic disorder and social annoyance, those of better families obtain commissions, while the less fortunate file in the ranks or man the fleet. But in peace these channels are closed, they hang loose and unamalgamated in society, and, having no external *debouchée*, they raise a sort of intestine commotion against the laws and usages of civil life. The unsettled, courageous, and enterprising among the working classes resort to poaching and smuggling—those of the middle orders, who have no alternative but commerce or trade, for which they are unfit, soon become bankrupt, from which they graduate as sporting men, gamblers, and fraudulent debtors. The remainder of the rout need not be described; from poaching, smuggling, habitual gambling, and unprincipled trading, the road to darker delinquencies is short, broad, and obvious.

It is scarcely necessary to explain that the preceding observations, on the derivation of the *personnel* of the army and navy, do not apply to the entire of these professions: many enter both branches of service of virtuous dispositions, of highly cultivated minds, and actuated only by a thirst for romantic adventure and chivalrous distinction. Our own first *penchant* was an enthusiasm for military glory, and, though we have long felt that war is the great reproach of civilized man, we still prefer in private life the freedom, sincerity, and frankness of the soldier's character, to the precision, real selfishness, and hypocrisy of more ostentatious moralists. Among a great proportion of wayward spirits in the navy and army, there are some of the best, as well as the bravest: the former has always been invincible, and the latter has conquered the conquerors; and there is nothing connected with the British name that stands on a prouder pinnacle of renown. There is no school of reform like His Majesty's service;—it transcends all our penitentiaries: while at Woolwich, we have often witnessed the improving effects of regular drill, compulsory cleanliness, order, and sobriety; and, no doubt, many whose boiling temperature was incompatible with the regimen of the civil state, have been saved in the service of their country from a disgraceful life and ignominious death.

Neither ought it to be inferred that peace is a national calamity; like every human good, it is not without alloy; but a small addition to the criminal calendar is a very inadequate set-off against the countless miseries of warfare. It must form an unimportant consideration to the legislator, that there are a few whose element is storm and strife, or whose prosperity renders them frantic and vicious, against the far greater number to whom peace yields plenteousness and quiet enjoyment, and against those national improvements in laws and institutions, in the general diffusion of science, in works of utility and magnificence, which her halcyon sway tends to promote. Our purpose has been to show the connexion between peace and the growth of immorality and crime, it would have been easy to point out overwhelming countervailing advantages to society, but that did not form the object of inquiry, and we shall now proceed to notice the tendency of recent *ameliorations in criminal punishment*.

Since the peace, there has been a constant effort on the part of humane individuals to obtain some mitigation in the severity of the criminal code; and this appears to have had an effect, both on the legislature and the administrators of penal law. The punishment of the pillory, except for purjury;* the public or private whipping of females;† the branding of culprits,‡ and the disembowelling of traitors§ have been abolished: in addition, the number of capital felonies has been reduced, by several statutes; and one statute, the 4 Geo. IV. c. 48, empowers the judge, in various felonies to which sentence of death is annexed, merely to order the sentence to be entered on the record. We have shortly before remarked that the number of executions, in proportion to the number convicted, and sentenced to death, has greatly decreased within the last seven years; but that in the Metropolis, where the proportional increase of crime has been *less* than in the country, the same proportional dimunition in the number of executions is not observable. We would not infer, from hence, that these ameliorations in the course of the law constitute one cause of the increase in crime; we have no authority for such a conclusion, and should be sorry to advance a conjecture so repugnant to humanity. It would be mournful indeed if an enlightened age had to retrace its steps, and again resort to torture, the thumb-screw, and the deleterious gaol to counteract augmenting depravity. Incidents in life are so often contemporary, which are wholly unconnected, as cause and effect, that one cannot be too cautious in drawing general inferences

* 56 Geo. III. c. 138.
† 1 Geo. IV. c. 57.
‡ 6 Geo. IV. c. 25.
§ 54 Geo. III. c. 146.

from their juxta position. We have felt it our duty, however, to submit these considerations to the reader, to whatever results they may lead, in order that he may be able to form a more correct judgment on the important question of the present chapter.

A less equivocal cause of crime may be found in the avarice of trade, and avidity of mercantile speculation. In no country are there so many worshippers of the *golden calf* as in England, where virtue and worth of every kind is measured by the standard of wealth. Every pursuit is chiefly valued as it conduces to the *accumulation of capital:* ethics, science, and popular knowledge, which, it might have been thought, would have been turned to more liberal purposes, are seldom directed to any other issue; no effort is made to inculcate a spirit of contentment even among those possessed of competence; all are excited into emulation, into pursuits of pride and ambition, and a rivalry of property, display, and ostentation. The fruits of this impulse were displayed in full maturity in 1824-5; the causes had been operating some years preceding, and a contempt for pecuniary mediocrity, mere industry, and probity gaining ground in public estimation; but it was not till that memorable era the tide of iniquity had reached the flood. On a superficial view it may appear too abstract to connect any deterioration in national morals with such recent vicissitudes, and that the causes were too ephemeral to have exerted a decided influence in the increase of crime. But it does not require long retrospection to be convinced how suddenly important changes are induced in the morals and character of nations by the influence of example, of high authority, or the catching fire of enthusiasm. A community of *Puritans* were metamorphosed, by the example of Charles II. and his courtiers, into a nation of profligate gallants. In France, the people passed at once from the idolatry of monarchy into the phrenzy of republicanism. Ireland has just presented the spectacle of her population being precipitated into almost rebellious clamourers for civil immunities, merely by the efforts of at most a trio of eloquent and relentless "agitators." The delirium of the South Sea scheme lasted only a few months: but the effect was general, and the entire country infected with a sudden fit of licentiousness, profligacy, and crime. Can any doubt, then, be entertained of the consequences ascribed to recent avarice, and the avidity of mercantile adventure. The schemes of rapacity and fraud, and the host of swindlers and unprincipled speculators generated in society from this cause, have produced an extensive deterioration in public morals; and, we are confident, any attentive observer of passing events will concur that, in the Metropolis, the pride of character, integrity, and honour has fallen at least fifty per cent. (to put our ideas in price current phraseology) within the last fourteen years.

An increase in bankruptcies and insolvencies is a constant accompaniment to augmented commercial activity. The avidity of trade induces improvident credit, and this, in its results brings into operation the machinery of the DEBTOR LAWS, with all their ruinous and demoralizing consequences. During the ten years, from 1817 to 1826, 13,416 persons have been *gazetted*, and 40,821 passed through the Insolvent Court: both of which may be esteemed so many contributions to the mass of incipient delinquency. In the five principal prisons of the metropolis, 6000 persons have been annually imprisoned for debt, where they had nothing before them but examples of idleness, drinking, low gaming, knavery, and every thing that is vile and base, and the very opposite of what it had been the object of all previous education, sermonizing, and legislation, to induce them to avoid and detest. The increased activity of the debtor laws is so obvious a cause of the increase of crime, that we do not think it necessary further to enlarge upon it, especially after what has been advanced on a former occasion; and we shall next advert to *poverty*, or more properly *indigence*, as tending to swell the criminal calendar.

That the wealth of the country is augmenting in the aggregate, no one at all acquainted with its situation can dispute; but this is a fact perfectly compatible with the existence of partial poverty that may be productive of crime. In order to satisfy ourselves on this point, we have examined, for the last ten years, such returns as are likely to indicate the general condition of the people; but, we confess, we have met with no results tending to establish the affirmative of the question. The consumption of the necessaries, and even some of the luxuries, of life, seems to have kept increasing, nearly in a ratio corresponding with the increase of population. The sale of cattle and sheep, at Smithfield market, has been yearly augmenting, with the increase in metropolitan baptisms, as well as the sale of corn and flour at Mark-lane. The sums received from the directors of Saving Banks and Friendly Societies, which, in 1817, amounted only to £328,281, had increased, in 1828, to £13,746,546. The consumption of coal in the metropolis has augmented from 980,372 chaldrons in 1810, to 1,558,810 in 1827. There has been a decrease in the consumption of porter, but this has been compensated by the increased sale of spirits, by the demand for intermediate beer, and the encouragement given to the retail breweries. Notwithstanding these statistical results it is impossible to shut ones eyes to the universal complaint of the diminution in the profits of trade, and the lowness of the rate of wages; the former no doubt resulting from the productive power and competition of capital; the latter from the unchecked progress of population. In the great woollen and cotton districts of the country, as well as in the Metropolis, there has long been advancing a process of *consolidation of capital*, or its accumulation into large masses, which have either swallowed up or reduced to the level of a very bare subsistence all the subordinate manufacturers, traders, dealers, and chapmen. But the depression in the price of labour below the means of comfortable subsistence, from the competition of workmen, is an evil of far greater magnitude. The statesman must be blind indeed who cannot forsee the dreadful catastrophe which must ultimately ensue from the indefinite increase in the number of the people, unaccompanied with a corresponding increase of employment and subsistence; still it is impossible to imagine how the legislature can successfully interfere, till some national distress, more palpable and convincing than the reasoning of philosophers, shall have demonstrated, even to popular conviction, its usefulness and necessity. Meanwhile the stream continues to flow; and when events shall occur which may cause a serious interruption to the ordinary means of employment and production we anticipate a revulsion of misery and discontent, like the retrocession of a torrent suddenly obstructed in its course.

In addition to the allowance of prosecutors their expenses in misdemeanour and the other causes, assigned for the greater exhibition of crime without a corresponding increase in depravity, there is another adverted to by Mr. Sergeant PELL,* and which partly appears to originate in the multiplicity of business, and inadequate provision for its discharge at the public police offices. A crowd of persons are sent to prison who either ought

* Report on the Police of the Metropolis, 1828, pp. 234–237.

never to have been committed at all, or whose offences ought to have been summarily adjudicated by the magistrate. To the two great gaols of the county of Middlesex 3306 persons were committed in one year, (1827) of which 2105 were committed from inability to find sureties until the sessions, comprising cases of assault, breaches of the peace, and disorderly behaviour: 571 persons were confined in the New Gaol, because unable to find sureties for *good behaviour;* on examining the commitments of these it was found their offences were such as came directly within the reach of the Vagrant Act, and as such ought to have been sent, not to the New Gaol, but to the House of Correction for a month, under a conviction by the committing magistrate, as vagrants. The prisons are filled with sailors, foreigners, and others; they get into difficulty, perhaps for an assault in an alehouse, or being found in a brothel at Wapping; they refuse or are unable to give an account of themselves, and, being strangers, they have no one to apply to for bail, and the magistrates forthwith commit them for want of sureties. Instances have occurred of persons being specifically committed for six months, or till they found sureties for their good behaviour, and of the committing magistrate, who relented probably of his severity, having ordered their discharge upon his *own authority* before either sureties were found or the six months had expired! There is no law empowering a single magistrate to demand sureties for general good behaviour, unless it be in a statute as old as Edward III. and which may be found in Burn's Justice of the Peace, entitled " Sureties of the Peace for Good Behaviour."

Another evil results, apparently, in the same necessity of using despatch in business at the police offices, from the practice of magistrates in committing under the Vagrant Act neglecting to return their convictions to the quarter sessions, as directed by the 5th Geo. IV. c. 83, and which is necessary to the ends of justice; because, in case of a second offence, a greater punishment is awarded, but of which second offence, no evidence exists, unless the first conviction has been returned. Of 3035 convictions in Middlesex, only seventy-three had been returned to the sessions; leaving nearly 3000 persons convicted of an offence without a single judgment having been passed upon them in the shape of a conviction. Many of these persons would probably not have been sent to gaol at all, had the trouble of drawing up the conviction been taken; but it is done with the stroke of a pen; no conviction is drawn up; they go to the gaol; and if an action were instituted against the magistrate for his conduct, (for it is illegal to commit, without following up the commitment by a conviction,) he is without defence; all he could produce would be some proof the plaintiff had been sent to gaol under a warrant; but the conviction being demanded, none could be produced, and the cause would be undefended.

Some of these abuses in justiciary proceedings have been partially remedied by Lord Lansdowne's Act, 9 Geo. IV. c. 32, s. 27, empowering magistrates to adjudicate summarily in common assaults; and the remainder are not likely long to escape the vigilance of the present Secretary of State for the Home Department.

We have thus briefly adverted to those peculiarities in the state of the country, and in the administration of the laws which may have tended to augment the criminal calendar; we shall next advert to a most pernicious vice, which both the Police Committee and the Committee on Criminal Commitments justly concur in ranking among the promotives of crime. The vice to which we allude is the vulgar one of *drinking spirits*, the tendency of which is to brutalize the character, to inflame the passions, and destroy all prudent and economical habits. From papers laid before parliament it appears that the quantity of foreign and British spirits entered for home consumption has, within the last few years, prodigiously increased. The average of three years 1820–1–2, is, in round numbers, 11,994,000 gallons, while the average of 1825–6–7, is 23,540,000; the last year gives 24,346,460, allowing (an extravagant allowance) that 6,000,000 of this quantity may be derived from the suppression of illicit distillation in Ireland and the decrease of smuggling in Great Britain; still the excess is equal to *one half of the whole quantity consumed in* 1821.*

It is an important fact connected with this subject that, during the period when distillers were stopped, in 1796–7, although bread was 15*d.* the quartern loaf, and other necessaries of life in proportion, the poor, in that part of the Metropolis where most of them reside, were apparently more comfortable, paid their rents more regularly, had fewer quarrels and assaults, resorted less to the pawnbroker, and were better fed than at any period for some years preceding. This could only be accounted for by their being denied the indulgence of GIN, which had become in a great measure inaccessible, from its very high price, and the money formerly wasted in this baneful compound being either saved or expended in wholesome provisions.

In the country, even in large manufacturing towns, this disgraceful vice is not so prevalent; but in London it may be said to be universal, and *decent* females, as well as those of dissolute character, are addicted to spirit drinking. It has been observed of a noted gin-shop, in Westminster, that the proportion of women who enter it to the men is as nineteen to one. It is to the predominance of this baneful habit

* Report on Criminal Commitments and Convictions, Parl Pap. No. 545, p. 14, Sess. 1828.

that the general inferiority of London females to those educated in the country may be attributed: in the furniture of their houses, economy, cleanliness, industry, and the whole circle of household virtues, there is no comparison between them. It is impossible to imagine a more dreadful vice in domestic life, and one is filled with horror at the bare idea of the neglect and suffering to which children must be exposed, while parents are under mental stupidity and moral degradation, from beastly intoxication. Women addicted to gin have been mostly found ready to commit any other offence, and we do not believe any single cause has contributed more than the cheapness of spirits to fill the workhouses and jails. We trust, therefore, the Legislature will interfere to check this pregnant source of moral and physical deterioration among the poor:—some there are, no doubt, who think the people ought to be left uncontrolled in what they choose to eat or drink; but these are little more than theorists, unacquainted with the character of the labouring classes, whom they look upon as creatures of pure reason, like themselves, and swayed in every movement by a careful balance of profit and loss; instead of viewing them as a great portion of them are, and, unavoidably, from their vocations, must be the victims of physical impulse, with little discretion, scarcely any forsight, and who seldom forego present indulgence for future benefits, and who, in short, can only be preserved from self-destruction by being removed out of the reach of temptation. Others, more profound, may contemplate, in the vice we deprecate, a means of counteracting the sanative effects of vaccination and a purer atmosphere, and who think that population had better be checked by *excess of drink* than starvation; but we believe these results have been deduced from too limited an inquiry, and that the more probable

Q

consequences are such as would multiply the number of puny and destitute objects in our streets, without lessening the claimants for employment and food.

There only remains one more object to which we wish to advert, namely,—the *Influence of Popular Education on Crime;* and that we shall do merely to explain what seems a certain degree of misapprehension on both sides the question.

To us it appears too much importance has been attached to education, both as an incentive and preventive of crime: knowledge, so far as it refers to human action, teaches to discern good from evil, and obviously directs and induces us, from mere self-love, to seek the one and avoid the other. But from the knowledge now sedulously diffused as popular instruction, we ánticipate no injury whatever, and certainly no great benefit;—much of it will never reach those for whom it is benevolently intended; and if it did, their lot forbids, without a previous change in their condition, that they can ever be able to appreciate and enjoy its objects, pleasures, and advantages.

Of teachers of science we have abundance, of morality very few: yet the former is little more than the art of gain, the latter of happiness. Reading and writing, an acquaintance with natural philosophy, law, and jurisprudence,—these of themselves are chiefly valuable as professional attainments, qualifying for the counting-house, the bar, the senate, and the laboratory;—they give intellectual power, but have no tendency to render the possessor either more virtuous or more vicious. Let us submit an example in illustration. The legal classes, medical practitioners, and mercantile men are mostly tolerably endowed with the information we have enumerated; but can it be said we find among them purer and more disinterested conduct, the natural affections stronger, more humanity, patriotism, and self-denial than among those whose knowledge scarcely extends beyond the Liturgy, or the inheritance of a few traditionary maxims of life? Unless, therefore, popular education includes morality as well as science, it cannot be said to operate either as an instrument or preventive of depravity; it is simply an engine of power, and, whether perverted to evil or good, depends on impulses derived from other sources. By morality, it is almost unnecessary to explain, we do not mean that which precludes enjoyment, but that which augments it; being, in fact, little more than prudence, teaching us to shun whatever is hurtful to ourselves and fellow-creatures.

Precepts derived from experience, often repeated, and strengthened by example, form the basis of popular instruction. A deeper philosophy may be necessary to some; but, to the bulk of the community, it is incompatible with their social state; nor would its attainment compensate them for the sacrifices necessary to its acquisition. The progress of science may be compared to the advancement of agriculture; the farther it is carried, and proportionably less becomes the produce, till, at last, it barely defrays the cost of production. The most useful truths are seldom those most difficult to be comprehended; and knowledge is like the earth, whose most valuable treasures lie near the surface, and those who dig lower are often repaid with much toil and little profit.

CHAPTER X.

COURTS OF JUSTICE.

Five Jurisdictions for the Administration of Criminal Justice in the Metropolis.—Number of Gaol-Deliveries in the County of Surrey.—Inequalities in Period of Confinement before Trial.—Courts for Adjudication of Civil Suits.—Sittings of Nisi Prius.—Synoptic View of Metropolitan Courts for Administration of Civil and Criminal Justice.—Number and Income of the Legal Classes.—Improvement in Administration of Justice at the Old Bailey.—Utility of more frequent Sessions of the Peace in the Metropolis, and the Advantages of a Perpetual Tribunal for the Trial of Offences.—Suggestion for augmenting the Judicial Powers of the Stipendiary Magistracy.

Our exposition of the protective institutions of the Metropolis would be incomplete without some account of the courts established for the administration of civil and criminal justice, and of the prisons for the detention and punishment of offenders.

In the several districts of the capital are no fewer than five jurisdictions, each possessing exclusive or concurrent authority within its respective limits. 1. The city of London, where the lord mayor and aldermen have exclusive jurisdiction within the ancient boundaries. 2. The city and liberty of Westminster, where about 100 justices have jurisdiction in that particular district; but where the magistrates of the county of Middlesex have equal jurisdiction. 3. That part of the Metropolis which is situate in the county of Middlesex, without the limits of the city; and in which the magistrates for the county have jurisdiction. 4. The district included in the ancient liberty of the Tower, containing about 700 inhabitants, has its distinct magistracy, who hold separate sessions of the peace. 5. The borough of Southwark, and that part of the Metropolis adjoining, where city magistrates have jurisdiction, besides the whole of the magistrates of the county of Surrey.

Under these five jurisdictions are as many courts of general sessions of the peace, for the trial of the lesser offences, as larcenies, frauds, and assaults, which are punishable by transportation, fine, imprisonment, or whipping. 1. The general sessions of the peace for the city of London are held eight times a-year, by the lord mayor and aldermen. 2. The general sessions of the peace for the city and liberty of Westminster were only held quarterly, prior to the 9 Geo. IV. c. 9, but may now be held eight times a-year. 3. The general sessions for the county of Middlesex are held eight times a-year, at the New Sessions House, Clerkenwell-green, by the magistrates of that county. 4. The general quarter sessions of the peace are held in the Sessions House, Wellclose-square, by the justices for the Tower Liberty, for the trial of minor offences committed within the Royalty. In the borough of Southwark, and that part of the Metropolis situate within the county of Surrey, are fifteen gaol-deliveries in the course of the year; the four borough sessions, held by the aldermen of the city, at the Town-hall; the four quarter sessions, with as many adjournments, held at intervals of about six weeks from the original sessions, by the magistrates of the county of Surrey, at the New Sessions House, Newington, at Ryegate, Guildford, and Kingston; besides the three assizes, at which forgeries and other capital felonies are tried. The more atrocious crimes in

London and Middlesex are tried at the Old Bailey sessions, held under a special commission of *oyer* and *terminer* to a certain number of the judges, the lord mayor, recorder, and common sergeant of the city.

Thus it appears that five inferior and two superior courts are established for the trial of all offences committed in the Metropolis not determinable, on summary process, before the magistrates. From this mode of emptying the gaols, prisoners are liable to a longer term of confinement before trial for offences committed in the borough of Southwark, whether such offences be of a lighter or more atrocious character: in the former case, they must remain till the quarter sessions (there being no intermediate general sessions of the peace); and, in the latter, till the assizes. Thus, in London and Middlesex, a person can never be confined longer than six or eight weeks before trial; but, if he cross over the bridges, and commit an offence, his confinement, previous to trial, may extend to two, three, or even four months.

The courts for the adjudication of CIVIL SUITS, in the Metropolis, are extremely numerous, and of jurisdictions more or less extensive; several are confined to the city of London, others to the Borough, some to the city of Westminster or county of Middlesex; and the jurisdiction of others is limited to manors, liberties, precincts, or a determinate circuit round the royal palaces. The courts of *Nisi Prius*, in London and Middlesex, called the *Sittings*, are held by the judges of the superior courts for the trial of all issues joined in the courts of Chancery, King's Bench, Common Pleas, and Exchequer; and those for Middlesex were established by the legislature in the reign of Queen Elizabeth. The time for holding these courts was first limited to four days after term, but this period has been successively extended, and now, by 1 Geo. IV. c. 59, continues unlimited during the vacation next after term.

Prior to the 1 Geo. IV. the *Nisi Prius* sittings, in Middlesex, were confined to Westminster-hall, but, by that act, they may be held at any other fit place within the city of Westminster. It would be impossible to notice, in detail, all the courts for the administration of civil and criminal justice in the Metropolis; we shall, therefore, subjoin a brief enumeration of them from Dr. COLQUHOUN, introducing a few remarks and such alterations as have been made since the time of that writer.

COURTS OF JUSTICE IN THE METROPOLIS.

Supreme Courts.

The High Court of Parliament.

The House of Lords; being the appeal in the last resort in all causes criminal and civil.

The Court of Exchequer-chamber, before which writs of error are brought on judgments in the Court of King's Bench and other Courts; it is composed, in certain cases, of all the Twelve Judges, and the Lord Chancellor; but sometimes of a smaller number.

The High Court of Chancery—at Westminster-hall—and Lincoln's-inn-hall. Auxiliary and subordinate to this Court are the Courts of the Master of the Rolls and the Vice-Chancellor.

The Court of King's Bench, held in Westminster-hall.

The Court of Common Pleas, held in Westminster-hall.

The Court of Exchequer—a court of law, equity, and revenue; held at Westminster-hall and Sergeant's Inn.

The Court of Appeal in Colonial and Prize Causes; before the Lords of his Majesty's Privy Council, at the Cock-pit, Whitehall.

The High Court of Admiralty, for prizes, &c. at Doctors' Commons; and, in criminal cases, twice a-year, at the Old Bailey.

Four Ecclesiastical Courts. (Doctors' Commons.)

- Prerogative Court, for wills and administrations.
- Court of Arches, for appeals from inferior Ecclesiastical Courts in the Province of Canterbury; the Court of Peculiars is a branch of this court.
- Faculty Court, to grant dispensations to marry, &c.
- Court of Delegates for ecclesiastical affairs.

Sixteen Courts in the City of London.	The Court of Oyer and Terminer and Gaol-Delivery, for trying Criminals at the Old Bailey.	Held by His Majesty's Commission to the Lord Mayor, Judges, Recorder, Common Sergeant, &c.
	Court of Hustings.	The Supreme Court of the City for pleas of land and common pleas.
	The Lord Mayor's Court.	For actions of debt, apprenticeships, and for appeals from inferior courts and for foreign attachments: giving decisions in all cases whatever, in fourteen days, at an expense of about 50*s*. Held in the King's Bench, Guildhall, by the Recorder. Appeal allowed to a superior court if the debt exceed £5.
	Sheriffs' Court.	Held every Wednesday, Thursday, Friday, and Saturday, at Guildhall; where actions of debt and trespass, &c. are tried by the Sheriff and his Deputy, who are Judges of the Court.*
	Court of Requests.	Held in Guildhall-buildings, by two Aldermen, under 39 and 40 Geo. III. and not less than twenty inhabitant householders, appointed for a month, in rotation from the several wards. If only three meet on the day appointed for a sitting, their jurisdiction is limited to debts of 40*s*.; if seven, it extends to £5. Monday, Tuesday, Thursday, and Friday are days for issuing summonses and executions; Wednesday and Saturday for hearings. No counsel or attorneys are expected to attend.
	Chamberlain's Court.	Held every day, to terminate differences between masters and apprentices; and to admit those qualified to the freedom of the city.

---

* Both the Lord Mayor's Court and the Courts of the two Sheriffs are held by prescription: process may be issued to any amount, and they may hold to bail for debt. The following is a statement, from Parl. Pap. No. 117, Sess. 1828, of the number of writs issued from these courts during the last five years:—

Lord Mayor's.	Under £20.	£20 to £30.	£30 to £50.	£50 to £100.	£100 & upwards.
1823	228	110	130	144	253
1824	217	92	114	99	245
1825	261	109	132	155	240
1826	364	169	168	208	384
1827	321	130	137	33	233
Sheriffs'.					
1823	141	84	65	34	34
1824	164	89	67	50	41
1825	302	123	116	74	63
1826	383	148	113	73	51
1827	199	151	88	58	29

Sixteen Courts in the City of London.	Court of Orphans.	Held before the Lord Mayor and Aldermen, as guardians of the children of deceased freemen, under twenty-one years of age, &c.
	Pie Poudre Court.	Held by the Lord Mayor and Stewards, for the administering of instantaneous justice between buyers and sellers at Bartholomew-fair, and to redress all such disorders as may arise therein.
	Court of Conservancy.	Held by the Lord Mayor and Aldermen four times a-year, in Middlesex, Essex, Kent, and Surrey; who inquire, by a Jury, the abuses relative to the fishing on the River Thames, and redress the same; from Staines *west*, to Yenfleet *east*.
	Court of Lord Mayor and Aldermen.—Court of Common Council.—Court of Common Hall.—Court of Wardmote.	These relate principally to matters of civil government in the City—the regulation of municipal officers—the election of Lord Mayor, Sheriffs, &c.—the appointment of the several committees for letting city lands, the Gresham trust, the Thames navigation, the Bridge-house estates, and the Corn and Coal meters—and the removal of nuisances, and the regulation of the police and nightly watch. The Wardmotes are held chiefly for the election of Aldermen and Common Councilmen.
	General and Quarter Sessions of the Peace, held by the Lord Mayor and Aldermen, eight times a-year.	
	Coroners'Court.—To inquire into the causes of sudden deaths.	
	Court of the Tower of London.	Held within the verge of the City by a Steward, appointed by the Constable of the Tower, before whom are tried actions of debt, trespasses, and covenants.
Courts of Justice within the City and Liberty of Westminster.	Court of the Duchy of Lancaster.	A supreme Court of Record, held in Somerset-place, for deciding by the Chancellor of said Duchy, all matters of law or equity belonging to the County Palatine of Lancaster.
	Quarter Sessions of the Peace.	A Court of Record, held by the Justices of the City and Liberty of Westminster, eight times a-year, at the Guildhall, Westminster, for all trespasses, larcenies, and other small offences, committed within the City and Liberty.
	Westminster Court.	Or Court Leet, held by the Dean of Westminster, or his Steward, for choosing parochial officers, preventing and removing nuisances, &c.
	Court of Requests, Castle-street, Leicester-square.	Held by Commissioners, being respectable housekeepers, for deciding, without appeal, all debts under 40*s*. for the parishes of St. Margaret, St. John, St. Martin, St. Paul, Covent-garden, St. Clement Danes, St. Mary-le-Strand, and that part of the Duchy of Lancaster which joins Westminster. Monday, Tuesday, Wednesday, and Saturday are days for taking out summonses; Thursday for hearings.

Court of Requests, Vine-street, Piccadilly, within the City and Liberty of Westminster.	Held in the same manner, and for the same purposes; for the parishes of St. Anne, St. George, Hanover-square, and for St. James, Westminster.

Courts of Justice in that part of the Metropolis which is within the County of Middlesex.

St. Martin's-le-Grand.	A Court of Record, subject to the Dean and Chapter of Westminster, held every Wednesday, for the trial of all personal actions. The process by *capias* against the body, or an attachment against the goods, in this particular Liberty.
Marshalsea, or Palace Court.	A Court of Record, having jurisdiction twelve miles round Whitehall, (exclusive of the City of London,) for actions of debt, damages, &c. and subject to be removed to a higher court of law when above £20. Sits every Friday.
East Smithfield Court.	A Court Leet and Court Baron, held for this Liberty, to inquire into nuisances, &c. In the Court Baron, pleas are held to the amount of 40*s*.
Finsbury-Court	A Court Leet, held once a-year, by a Steward of the Lord Mayor, as Lord of the Manor of Finsbury, for inquiring into nuisances, competent for leet-juries, and swearing in constables for the manor.
St. Katharine's Court.	Two Courts to be held within this small precinct, for actions of debt and trespass; but we apprehend the suitors have been swallowed up by the erection of the new docks of St. Katharine's.
Hackney and Stepney Court.	A Court, instituted under a charter of Charles II. and regulated by 21 Geo. III. c. 73; held by the Steward of the Manor of Stepney, by whom, and a jury, are tried actions of debt, on assumpsits only, above 40*s*. and under £5. Imprisonment is at the rate of a week for 20*s*. of debt; and the jurisdiction includes Bow, Clapton, Homerton, and Kingsland, round to Whitechapel. From fifty to sixty causes are usually decided at a sitting.
County-Court, Kingsgate-street.	For debts under 40*s*. in which the County Clerk presides, with a Jury, and proceeds by summary process, under 23 Geo. III. in lieu of the old County-Court process. Court sits 104 days in London, 12 days in Enfield, and 12 days for the Western Hundreds of Brentford and Uxbridge. Upon an average, 150 causes are decided each day.
Quarter and General Sessions of the Peace and of Oyer and Terminer.	Held by the Justices of the County of Middlesex, at the Sessions House, Clerkenwell-green, for felonies, misdemeanors, &c. and for roads, bridges, prisons, and other county affairs.

Ditto.	Two Coroners' Courts.	For inquiring into the causes of sudden deaths.
	Court of Requests.	For debts under 40*s*. without appeal, held in Osborn-street, Whitechapel, by commissioners under the act of parliament, chosen annually by the parishes in the Tower Hamlets.
	General and Quarter Sessions of the Peace for the Liberty of the Tower.	Held by the Justices of that Liberty, eight times a-year, for larcenies, trespasses, felonies, misdemeanors, &c. within that district.
Southwark.	Court of Record.	Held at St. Margaret's Hill, Southwark, by the Lord Mayor's Steward, for actions of small debt, trespass, &c.
	Court of Record.	For the Clink Liberty, held near Bankside, by the Bishop of Winchester's Steward, for actions of debt, trespass, &c. within that Liberty.
	Court of Requests.	Held in Swan-street, for debts under £5, within the Town and Borough of Southwark and the eastern half of the Hundred of Brixton, including the parishes of St. Saviour, Newington, Bermondsey, Lambeth, and Rotherhithe, and their several liberties and precincts. Summonses may be had any day; and hearings Tuesday and Friday. By 4 Geo. IV. c. 123, plaintiffs to make deposit proportioned to the debt. Commissioners not to determine titles to land, nor decide any debt being the balance of an account originally exceeding £5.
	Coroner's Court.	To inquire into cause of sudden deaths.
	Quarter Sessions of the Peace.	Held by the Lord Mayor and Aldermen, at St. Margaret's Hill, for the Borough of Southwark.
	Quarter Sessions of the Peace for the County of Surrey.	Held by the Magistrates of the County of Surrey, at the Sessions House, Newington, and at Ryegate, Guildford, and Kingston; and the four adjourned sessions, at intervening periods, at the same places.
	Court for Relief of Insolvent Debtors.	Held twice a-week, in Portugal-street, Lincoln's-inn-fields, for receiving the surrender of property and effects, for the benefit of creditors, of persons in actual confinement for debt, damages, or costs.
	Eleven Police Courts or Petty Sessions.	Two of these are held in the City; one at the Mansion-house, the other at the Justice-room, Guildhall, and the remainder in different parts of the Metropolis. As before explained, they are open daily for the purposes of police, and such matters of a summary nature as are within the cognizance of justices of peace.

Attached to these different courts are about 800 officers; to which may be aded 450 barristers-at-law, 2000 attorneys, 130 conveyancers and equity draftsmen, 67 special pleaders, 84 proctors, 40 public notaries, 4000 clerks, assistants, and others; besides doctors-at-law, masters in chancery, sergeants-at-law, and king's counsel, making a legal phalanx, in the Metropolis, of nearly 8000. Dr. COLQUHOUN estimated the total income of the legal classes, when the amount of property and professional practice was much less than at present, at £7,600,000,* and two-thirds, probably, of this sum is absorbed by *legalists* resident in London. The adage says—*Many hands make light work*,—but the maxim is reversed in law, and the multitude of practitioners is one cause of litigation and the pressure of business on the tribunals.†

In the administration of criminal justice, in the City of London, a beneficial change has been introduced within the last five or six years, which, it is hoped, will be followed by more important improvements throughout the Metropolis. The sessions at the Old Bailey used to last from sixteen to nineteen days; they are now over in five or six, and very often in four days, to the great

* Treatise on the Wealth and Resources of the British Empire, p. 124.

† The increase of litigation, and, consequently, of profit to the profession, has been prodigious of late years; as is shown by the following statement of the number of causes entered for trial in the superior courts:—

Years.	King's Bench.	Common Pleas.	Exchequer.
1823	1474	445	162
1824	1695	472	222
1825	2164	500	157
1826	3112	1021	245

The multiplication of law-suits in the two last years may be ascribed to the winding up of the vast number of bill and credit transactions, which chiefly contributed to the overtrading and speculation prior to 1825, and to the bankruptcies, insolvencies, and arrests resulting from that great mercantile catastrophe.

convenience of prosecutors and witnesses, and a vast diminution of expense. This increased despatch is effected by two courts sitting at the same time; both courts commence each day at nine o'clock in the morning, and do not cease to sit every day, during the trials, till nine in the evening. During the first days of the sitting, the capital cases, which take more time than the other, are tried by the judges; meanwhile the city magistrates are proceeding with the minor offences, which formerly did not begin till the fourth or fifth day of the sessions.

A still more important improvement in the criminal administration of the Metropolis would consist in having more *frequent gaol deliveries.* Between 3 and 4000 persons are yearly committed for offences in London and Middlesex; some of these are for crimes of the most atrocious character, others are of a nature so venial that one day's deprival of liberty would be too severe a punishment. Of 6862 commitments to the New Gaol, Clerkenwell, only 170 were for offences of the highest class; 3306 were for larcenies, misdemeanors, conspiracies, frauds, and uttering base coin; and 2530 of the remainder were for assaults, riots, military desertion, and bastardy.* Offenders of this different description, and even those totally innocent, are all liable to different terms of imprisonment *before trial,* varying from one day to thirteen or fourteen weeks, if incarceration happen to have taken place at the commencement of the long vacation. Injustice to the accused is not the worst evil of the existing system; in the long intervals between the sessions, the gaols become crowded to excess, classification and other rules of prison discipline can only be imperfectly enforced, and the innocent, the juvenile offender, and the hardened criminal, become

* Report on the Police of the Metropolis, 1828, p. 71.

mingled together in one promiscuous mass of delinquency.

To remedy such serious evils, two suggestions have been submitted to the late Police Committee; one, to have a weekly or perpetual sessions of the peace for the trial by jury of all offences less than capital; the other suggestion, we believe, was advanced by W. H. Bodkin, Esq. and recommended the institution of a moveable tribunal, consisting of two or more magistrates, to try, in succession, in the different divisions of the metropolis, offences of the last-mentioned description. Either of these plans would be great improvements, and we are not aware of any serious objections having been urged against them, beyond certain provisions contained in three or four acts of parliament of no great utility, the increased duty it would impose on clerks of the peace and grand juries. The last, perhaps, might be got rid of by dispensing with the attendance of a grand jury; some consider this branch of judicial administration superfluous in every case; but, without going this length, there is obviously less need of such preliminary inquest in the class of offences proposed to place under the jurisdiction of the new tribunals.

The institution of an ambulatory tribunal possesses considerable advantages: it might be moved in the vicinity of the prisons; sit at Clerkenwell one week, at Westminster another, and at Newington the third; and, if thought advisable, Greenwich, Woolwich, and other places without the limits of the metropolis, might be included within its jurisdiction. The expenses of erecting prisons for the detention of offenders before trial, and conveying prosecutors and witnesses to Maidstone, Guildford, and other distant places, falls very heavily on the county rate, and any plan which would lessen it is entitled to attention.

Besides these plans, we would beg to suggest another

of a very simple nature, requiring nothing more than an act of parliament, creating no additional functionary nor expense. Of those persons committed for trial, upwards of one-half are for offences which are not visited with severer punishment than fine, whipping, or not exceeding a year's imprisonment :* now, there does not appear any cogent reason why all offences of this description should not be finally adjudicated by the *stipendiary* magistracy. Each public office of police forms a petty sessions of the peace, and we think two or three magistrates might be safely trusted with the final punishment of the class of offences to which we refer, without risk of committing any egregious error or act of oppression. It would certainly not be advisable such large increase of judicial power should be entrusted to the country magistracy, for two reasons; first, there is not the same publicity in their proceedings; and, secondly, they do not generally possess the same experience and legal knowledge as the London justices.

The notoriety of every justiciary act in the metropolis, by the admission of the public into the police offices, aided by the agency of the press, and combined with the late act, requiring all appointments to the stipendiary magistracy to be made from barristers of at least three years' standing, afford sufficient guarantee against enormous abuse either from individual character or professional incompetence.

We shall not enlarge further on the suggestion we have ventured to propound, satisfied with submitting it to the notice of those more competent to form an opinion of its practical utility. It would have the effect of obviating the great evil of the metropolitan gaols being crowded with untried prisoners.

* Report on the Police of the Metropolis, Sess. 1828, page 288.

CHAPTER XI.

PRISONS OF THE METROPOLIS.

Observations on Prison Discipline.—NEWGATE, *General Arrangements of.*—*Number of Prisoners, their Diet, Treatment, and Character.*—*The Condemned Cells.*—*Improper Indulgence to Prisoners.*—GILTSPUR-STREET—*Objects for which established.*—*Food, Employment, and Education of Prisoners.*—CITY BRIDEWELL—*Origin and Management of the Hospital.*—BOROUGH COMPTER.—*Improvements made therein.*—NEW PRISON, *Clerkenwell*—*Description of, and Number of Prisoners*—*Defects in Management and Structure of this Prison.*—COLD-BATH-FIELDS—*Number and Trades of Prisoners.*—*Hours for Admission of Visitors.*—*Salaries of the Officers.*—TOT-HILL-FIELDS—*Proposed New Gaol.*—WHITECROSS-STREET—*City and County Gaol for Debtors.*—*Charities for Poor Prisoners.*—*State of this Prison.*—*Exemplifies Evils of Imprisonment for Small Debts.*—*Tally-Shops.*—THE FLEET—*Objects of this Prison.*—*The Rules, the Master's and Common Side.*—*Officers of the Prison, and their Emoluments.*—MARSHALSEA—*Origin and Jurisdiction.*—*Regulations of.*—KING'S BENCH—*A National, not a County Prison.*—*Chummage.*—*Provisions for Poor Debtors.*—*The Rules, Day-Rules, and a Run on the Key.*—*The Marshal, his Appointment, Emoluments, and Powers.*—*The Strong Rooms.*—*Observations.*

PRISON is a general term, applied either to a place of confinement, intended for the safe custody of the person to answer a civil action; or a *common gaol,* for the detention of those apprehended under a criminal charge; or a *bridewell,* for the amendment of the idle and disorderly; or a *house of correction,* for the punishment of those convicted of more serious crimes. Merely as places of security, the objects of a prison may be easily attained; but, as places of punishment, they involve principles more difficult to be comprehended. Imprisonment, when applied as a penal infliction, ought to operate as a warning to others, and to the privation and reform of the delinquent; but it is obvious these ends may be counteracted by inadequate discipline in houses of correction; either from too much indulgence to the offender, by which the just severity of the law is evaded, or by his being exposed to society as corrupt, and intercourse as impure as that to which he had been previously accustomed, and which had probably contributed to his incarceration.

During the last twelve years, the best system of prison-discipline has formed a subject of much discussion and inquiry; and this has contributed to introduce many improvements, both in our metropolitan and provincial gaols. It is to be regretted, however, that all the advantages anticipated have not been fully borne out by actual experience. "As places of reform only," observes a late Parliamentary Committee, "gaols have not succeeded; as places of reform only, they ought not to be considered." That they have failed in effecting permanent improvement in the criminal mind is only a result they share in common with whipping, the treadwheel, the hulks, and terminal transportation; and it is from a conviction of the inutility of these punishments, that we have been led to recommend a system of *perpetual exile to a penal settlement,* embracing different kinds of treatment, according to the various shades and classes of delinquency. This, however, would not dispense with the use of prisons, either as places of detention or punishment; and, consequently, the best mode of conducting them would still form a subject of inquiry.

Two of the most material ends in the discipline of gaols are, first, to render them, not as some still are, a source of moral contagion and depravity; secondly, to render them places of real suffering, discomfort, and humiliation, and such as removes all pretext of competition between the accommodations of a prison and the situation of the most wretched in a state of guiltlessness and liberty.

With a view of establishing uniformity and better discipline in gaols and houses of correction, the *Prison Act** introduces many excellent regulations, providing for the classification of prisoners; for the maintenance of order, sobriety, and decorum; for the exclusion of luxuries; and guarding against the improper admission of visitors and the misconduct of gaolers. Under the 5 Geo. IV. c. 85, s. 10, classification is to be made by the visiting magistrates, regard being had to "the character and conduct of prisoners and the nature of their offences." Character is a much more important consideration than offences, as it is obvious a returned transport, or other hardened offender, may be sometimes imprisoned for an assault, or trifling misdemeanor; and it would be highly improper he should be classed among minor delinquents of this description. Perhaps it would be better to leave the determination of the class in which an offender should be placed to the committing magistrate, or judge presiding at the trial, as these, from developments during the examination or trial of

* 4 Geo. IV. c. 64, amended by 5 Geo. IV. c. 12, and 5 Geo. IV. c. 85.

the accused, have the best opportunity for becoming acquainted with his real character and previous history. The regulations of the Prison-Act extend to London as well as the country; but we shall find, in the following exposition of metropolitan gaols, that, either from the unfitness of the buildings now erected, and reluctance to incur expensive alterations, or from neglect in the magistracy, that the provisions of Mr. Peel's statute are only imperfectly carried into execution.

NEWGATE.

This is a common gaol for the city of London and county of Middlesex, and is under the jurisdiction of the lord mayor, court of aldermen, and sheriffs. According to the present arrangement it is divided into stations, yards, day-rooms, and wards. Of the three stations, the first is wholly occupied by transports; in the second are three yards occupied by persons for fines, misdemeanours and untried prisoners, and the further end of the passage leading to the cells is for capital convicts; the third station is wholly occupied by females, divided into yards for the tried and untried. A turnkey and under-turnkey are appointed to each station. From the construction of the prison the occupants of several wards have access to the same yard, and though no prisoner is allowed to visit a ward to which he does not belong, yet they meet and associate in a common yard. Upwards of 120 prisoners sometimes belong to one yard. Of the nine yards two are appropriated to the females, one to the sick, one to the convicts under sentence of death, one to the boys and prisoners of a respectable situation in life; so that there are only four yards more for the classification of the remaining males; the consequence of which has been the admixture of prisoners for trial with convicts. There are fifteen condemned cells; their

R 2

dimensions are $6\frac{1}{2}$ by 10 feet each, which are much too small for the number of persons often confined in them. It is thought advisable never to have a condemned felon alone, as suicides have often occurred; and when only two have been together crimes have been committed of a nature not to be more particularly described.*

Newgate is intended not only for the reception of those directly committed for trial, but for a still greater number who are removed there from other prisons just before the sessions commence, and it is frequently crowded with convicts waiting to be sent out of the country. Mr. Wontner considers 350 as many as ought, under any circumstances, to be at one time in the gaol; but it generally occurs this number is greatly exceeded. In September, 1826, there were 643; and about thirteen years ago there were upwards of 900. The consequences are very imperfect classification, and neglect of the salutary provisions of the Gaol-Act.

No prison-dress is adopted in Newgate. Destitute prisoners are clothed at the expense of the City; each suit costs 12*s*. The prison allowance of bedding consists of a hempen mat, worked with a portion of tar, to prevent the lodging of vermin, and to exclude damp,

* Lately upwards of sixty felons were confined in the condemned cells, chiefly from an interpretation given in the metropolitan district to a late act, the 4th Geo. IV. c. 48; which provides that in various felonies to which the punishment of death is annexed, the court, if it think proper, may abstain from pronouncing sentence of death and merely direct it to be recorded. The grounds on which this salutary act were passed are stated to be general; but the statute has been held not to apply to London and Middlesex, and the ancient form of proceeding consequently continues unchanged. The results are the accumulation of numbers in the press-yard or condemned cells, the diminished effect and solemnity of the judgment of death, and the severe suffering which cannot but result to these criminals in whose cases the law is likely to take its course, in being precluded from the seclusion most appropriate to their melancholy situation.

and two rugs. The allowance of food is a pint of gruel for breakfast; for dinner, alternately, half a pound of beef, and a quart of soup, in which the meat was boiled the previous day, with barley and a variety of vegetables. Religious service is performed on Sunday, Wednesday, and Friday. A school is provided for youthful offenders under sixteen years of age, untried and convicted.*

When Newgate was visited, last year, by some members of the late Police Committee, it contained 348 prisoners: 281 males and 67 females. Of the whole number, 221 could either *read or write*, and 129 could do neither: 47 had been there before, but how many times could not be ascertained. Excluding the women, 142 were mechanics, 128 labourers, and 11 mariners.

The Police Committee animadvert, in strong terms, on the general state and mismanagement of this prison, especially on the permission given to the prisoners, both tried and untried, to receive any quantity of cooked food their friends may bring, and a quart of porter a day. It, besides, frequently occurs that the prisoners who have money employ others to draw their full allowance of beer, so that some obtain a very considerable quantity of liquor. On the female side, a chandler's shop is kept, from which the men, also, obtain tea, sugar, tobacco, and similar luxuries. Indeed, their situation, as justly remarked, is in "*many respects superior to that of the labouring poor;*" enjoying an ample allowance of fuel and food, exemption from labour, and, if necessary, clothed at the public expense; besides permission to see visitors to an almost unlimited extent.

It is unnecessary to exhibit, in more detail, the existing defects in this great metropolitan *depôt* of delinquency, as we believe the City of London, at the instigation of

* Report on Prisons, p. 8, vol. viii. of Parl. Paps. Sess. 1818.

Mr. Peel, is about adopting measures to remedy the more glaring abuses.

GILTSPUR-STREET PRISON.

The Giltspur-Street Prison, until the end of the year 1815, was denominated *The Giltspur-Street Compter*, for debtors and delinquents apprehended in the City of London, and connected with the Ludgate Prison solely for debtors who are freemen of the City, and both were exclusively, as the prison now is, for commitments within the jurisdiction of the City. On the removal of the debtors to Whitecross-street, that part of the prison formerly occupied by such persons was converted into a house of correction for felonies and misdemeanors.

The objects of police for which this prison is set apart are three :—1. For the reception of what are called *night-charges;* that is, all disorderly persons apprehended and lodged there for the night in a lock-up room; and such persons are regularly reported to the magistrates every morning.—2. For the detention of accused persons until examination; or who are remanded for further examination; or for vagrants—natives and foreigners.—3. What is called the House of Correction, where those sentenced to hard labour are confined, and those committed for assaults and misdemeanors.

The prison-allowance of food is the same as that allowed in Newgate, excepting that an additional half-pound of bread has been given to those working at the mill. In the House of Correction, each prisoner has a separate bed, though all the beds nearly join each other, and numbers sleep in the same room. The bed consists of a tick paillasse, stuffed with straw, placed on canvas; and, for covering, two rugs, or three, according to the season of the year. Male House of Correction prisoners are employed in grinding corn with a hand-mill, for the supply of this prison and the gaol of Newgate with bread; in breaking flax with machines; in picking oakum; in whitewashing and painting the prison; as carpenters, shoemakers, &c. Females, in spinning flax; picking oakum; in washing, making, and mending for the prison; and occasionally in needlework for the Ladies' Association.

From October, 1826, to October, 1827, the number of persons committed to this prison was 5287. When visited, last year, by Lord Blandford and Messrs. Calvert and Hobhouse, it contained 64 males and 18 females; of whom 21 were artizans, the remainder labouring people: 47 males and 7 females could read and write. No fault was found with the general state of this prison as to cleanliness and the disposition of the yards; but the vagrant-ward and that part of the prison appropriated to committed females require ventilation. The governor, chaplain, and surgeon are appointed by the court of aldermen. The keeper's salary is £800 per annum.

THE CITY BRIDEWELL

Is one of the three hospitals named in the charter of Edward VI., by which he granted to the corporation of London the manor and messuage of Bridewell, with appurtenances and privileges, for the purpose of maintaining these hospitals instituted for the education and relief of the poor; for the cure of the sick and diseased; for the employment of the idle and correction of the disorderly. Bridewell is that hospital devoted to the latter objects, namely, employment and correction of the idle and disorderly; vagrants are, also, frequently confined here a few days previously to being passed to their respective parishes.

Serious complaints were made against the state and

general management of this place, by a Parliamentary Committee, in 1818; but some reforms have since been introduced. The principal work at present performed by the male and female prisoners is turning the tread-wheels, by which corn is ground and dressed for the supply of the prisoners and the patients at Bethlem Hospital with bread, the same being baked at Bridewell. The difficulty of finding ordinary work for male prisoners (where the terms of confinement are short, as at Bridewell) has always been found great, except when they have already attained the knowledge of a trade; but the females are employed, in addition to the tread-mill, in needlework. The governors have determined, under a report of their own body, made some time since, to extend the occupation branch of this establishment on part of the site of their ground at Bethlem Hospital, where space will be afforded for external work, and the drying of linen can be provided for better than in the City.

Seven hundred and thirty-two persons were committed to Bridewell in 1827. When visited, in 1828, it contained 49 males and 14 females, of whom 33 could read and write; 28 of the male prisoners were labourers, the remainder seamen or artizans. The revenue of the hospital, amounting to about £7000 per annum, is ample enough to support a much better establishment. No airing-yards are attached to the prison, and the intercourse between the different classes of prisoners is not prevented.

BOROUGH COMPTER.

Although the jurisdiction of the City over a part of Southwark was established by ancient charters, yet the court of aldermen did not, for a long period, exercise their authority, and, in consequence, the Borough

Compter, a very mean and confined place, was, according to the ideas of prisons formerly entertained, sufficient for the purposes to which it was applied, as few prisoners were there confined; but, after the appointment of a resident magistrate to act and hold courts in the Borough, various descriptions of persons were committed to the Compter which had formerly been committed elsewhere; and, when a Committee of the House of Commons visited the prison, in 1817, it was found totally inadequate to the purpose. In consequence of their representations, the common council resolved to appropriate a house adjoining for additional accommodation, and enclose a considerable space with a wall, so as to afford airing-ground for the prisoners; and also to erect additional buildings to admit of classification; the whole at an estimated expense of £5500, and the sacrifice of a rental of £70 per annum. In going over the prison, in the month of March, of the present year, we found these projected improvements had been fully executed, and it is now a compact and well-arranged place: the sleeping-rooms are well contrived; there are yards for airing and exercise; work is provided for convicts; and the different classes of offenders are kept separate. The only defect we could discover was in the accommodation of one of the turnkeys; owing to the smallness of the lodge in which he is cribbed up in the night, he is compelled to sleep in a sort of canine posture, forming almost a circle with his head and heels.

NEW PRISON, CLERKENWELL.

This is a common gaol for the county of Middlesex, and persons are committed to it for every description of offence, from the lowest to the highest, known in the criminal code. It is one of the most important and extensive gaols of committal in the kingdom; the average number of persons who annually pass through it is upwards of 5000. There are six yards on each side of the prison; each yard has its dormitory; these have each a soldier's barrack-bed; no straw is allowed, but each prisoner has a rug and a blanket; in addition to which there are beds provided with flock and feather bedding, and clean linen once a fortnight. These beds any one can have on paying 6*d.* a-night; but the poverty of the inmates is generally such that few are able to avail themselves of the indulgence. Each prisoner is allowed 1lb. of wheaten bread a-day; and meat or soup on alternate days. Those prisoners for trial at the Old Bailey are removed to Newgate a week previous to each session; and those for trial at the Middlesex sessions are taken direct and there disposed of.

The defects in this prison have long been a subject of animadversion, without leading to any substantial reform. The keepers and turnkeys have no means of overlooking the conduct of the prisoners, so that riots and assaults are of daily occurrence, without the possibility of detecting the aggressors. On the side of the gaol appropriated to the male prisoners there are but three ward-rooms and airing-yards, independent of the reception-ward and the small ward set apart for the boys. The male prisoners, therefore, of every description, are necessarily distributed into these divisions; hence it is frequently impracticable, from the fluctuation of numbers and the crowded state of the prison, to make a proper distinction between the various classes. The well-known offender, who has been repeatedly in confinement, and is fully committed for an aggravated crime, is confined with individuals whose guilt is comparatively trifling, and associated with others who have been committed for re-examination only, many of whom are discharged without prosecution. But, if this indiscriminate association, during the day, be pregnant with mischief, how greatly are its evils aggravated by the want of separation at night! Such is the number of prisoners that *not more than sixteen inches* are sometimes allowed for sleeping room. In order to remedy this, it has been found necessary occasionally to appropriate to the men two of the wards and yards on the female side of the prison; an arrangement that is never resorted to without great inconvenience to the general discipline of the gaol. To shut up such an assemblage of characters without the slightest control over their language or their actions, and this, too, as is the case during the winter season, for not less a period, at one time, than fifteen hours, is an evil of very serious magnitude. The night-rooms in question are rendered most disgusting scenes of riot, and no doubt of obscenity—scenes which cannot fail to render the guilty more depraved, while they operate upon many who are but young in crime, or committed merely for re-examination only, with peculiar cruelty and injustice.*

When visited, last year, the New Gaol contained 121 males and 55 females; of whom 73 could read and write, 30 could read only; 60 of the males had trades, and the remainder labourers.

COLD-BATH-FIELDS PRISON.

This is the house of correction for the county of Middlesex, established under 26 Geo. III. c. 25, and is under the jurisdiction of the county magistrates. In the year ending March, 1828, the number of males committed was 3848, of females 1657. Their employment is the tread-wheel, picking oakum, menial offices in the prison, and needlework. When visited by the Police Committee, there were 555 males and 143 females; of whom

* Report of Visiting Magistrates of Prisons in Middlesex.

332 could read and write, 118 could read only. Among the males were 11 bakers, 13 smiths, 26 shoemakers, 8 tailors, 4 butchers, 8 painters, 4 plasterers, 6 brass-founders, 4 barbers, 5 plumbers, 1 printer, 3 coopers, 3 dyers, and 6 seamen; among the females, 3 shoe-binders, 4 dress-makers, 2 silk-weavers, &c.

The regular hours of visiting the prisoners are from twelve to two each day. No convict-prisoner can see his friends without an order from a magistrate; but the practice is to admit all to the grating, between the hours above-named, and, if they come from a distance, some additional time is allowed; no one, however, is suffered to enter within the walls or into the yard, but strangers are admitted on one side of the grating within the principal gate of the prison, and the prisoners are on the opposite, a turnkey walking in the space between.

The salary of the governor is £400, with perquisites; the surgeon £200 a-year for his attendance here and at the New Gaol; and the chaplain £120 per annum.

TOTHILL-FIELDS PRISON

Is a place of confinement within the City and Liberty of Westminster; and prisoners are committed there from the neighbouring police offices. These prisoners are of various descriptions, comprehending felons, mis-demeanants, disorderly persons, vagrants, and debtors. In the year 1827, there passed through this prison 350 persons. The gaoler is appointed by the magistrates of Westminster, at a salary of £400; he has a house to live in, free of taxes, but no other perquisites. He has under him five turnkeys and a watchman. Great defects prevail in this gaol; but, as an act of parliament has been obtained to erect a new one, we shall not do further than express a hope that this will be done with as little delay as possible.

WHITECROSS-STREET PRISON.

This prison is set apart for debtors, and has three distinct divisions: Ludgate side, for those who are freemen of the City of London, and who, on commitment, produce a certificate, called a *doucee*, of their being freemen; London side, for all other debtors arrested within the jurisdiction of the City, including such freemen as, at the time of arrest, neglect to procure a doucee; and Middlesex side, the third and largest division, for those arrested in the County. Persons, by warrants from the court of requests of the City and the court of requests of the County, are also committed to this prison. A separate division is provided for all females, whether of the City or County.

In this prison there is a provision made, at the expense of the City, for the absolute wants of those confined, by an allowance of food and fuel beyond what is distributed in any prison of the kingdom. This allowance is given to all who produce a certificate that they are poor. The consequence is, that almost all have obtained such certificates. Certain divisions of the prison have peculiar benefits, arising from charitable donations and bequests. In the case of those imprisoned for small debts, the keeper is authorized to receive the amount of debt and costs from the county prisoners; and, provided no detainer is lodged, forthwith to liberate him: but a debtor committed from the court of requests of the City cannot obtain his liberation till he procures what is termed a *scrutatus*, which is a certificate signed by the clerk in the Secondaries' Office, by the clerk of the Giltspur-street prison, and by the clerk of the Poultry Compter, vouching that no detainers have been lodged against him in any of these offices. This is stated by a Parliamentary Committee, in 1818, to have formed a grievance where the debt was trivial, and an impression having existed that no prisoner, not a Court of Conscience debtor, could obtain a scrutatus out of office-hours, or on a holiday, without paying a fee of 12*s.* 6*d.* many individuals remained in prison several days after compromising with their creditors, or after the term of their sentence had expired.

Alterations of the most important kind have been projected in this prison, and some of them have been carried into effect, as far as the structure of the place admits. The chief defect is the unequal apportionment of the prisoners in the several yards, which renders classification almost impracticable. In the Giltspur-street, Ludgate, and women's yard there are seldom more than thirty persons each; while in the Middlesex yard, which is not more than one-third larger than either Ludgate or Giltspur-street, there are sometimes from 400 to 500. All the acts of violence and insubordination are, as may be supposed, committed in the Middlesex-yard. By a division of this yard into three compartments, it is submitted that classification, agreeably to the directions of the act of parliament, may be partially effected. The power to do mischief would be greatly diminished by a judicious separation of the lower order of debtors from those who are called gentlemen; and of those who are known to be swindlers and cheats from the tradesmen who owe their imprisonment to misfortune. To prevent such acts as *catting* (stripping new prisoners for what are called " ward-fees"), a separation of the tempters and the tempted ought to be accomplished. So ill regulated was the place lately that when any individuals became offensive to the other prisoners, there was no place to which to remove them, except the infirmary.

The evils of imprisonment for small debts are strikingly

exemplified in this prison. During the last eight years, 1500 persons have been annually incarcerated for sums below £5 each. Persons may go and swear a debt of a shilling or sixpence before the City court of requests, and have the debtor locked up for twenty days; the expenses are treble or quadruple the debt; the maintenance of the debtor costs the Corporation 2*s.* 6*d.*; and this not being sufficient to support the debtor's family, they are probably cast upon the parish. Numbers of labourers and artizans are imprisoned in this way by tally-shop-keepers; at these shops, goods are sold to the working-people at so much per week, at a profit of 100 per cent.

THE FLEET.

This is a prison for the confinement of persons under process of debt issuing out of the courts of Common Pleas and Exchequer; and for persons committed for contempt by these courts; and, also, by the Court of Chancery and by the Duchy Court of Lancaster.

The building is modern, strong, solid, and protected from fire by stone staircases and stone floors in the galleries and rooms, except in the upper story, where the floors are boarded; it is in general clean, healthy, and free from offensive smells; the rooms sufficiently lighted: though the cleanliness of the rooms must, in a great degree, depend upon the habits of the respective occupants, and their attention in preserving it, quickened by the means which the deputy-warden may exercise to enforce it. The infirmary is large and airy; the strong room, or place of confinement for refractory prisoners, is sufficiently secure, well lighted, and provided with a fire-place; the chapel is commodious. Within the interior walls of the prison there is an area, affording sufficient space for exercise; these walls are of considerable height, and guarded by a *chevaux de frize;* but their contiguity to houses on the outside, and their proximity, in some parts, to the interior buildings of the prison, must lessen the difficulty of escape, though very few instances have occurred in which it has been attempted with success.

The space without the prison called "The Rules" is about three miles in circumference, including the London Coffee-house and several public-houses; within which space the prisoners are permitted to reside, upon giving security against an escape: this is done by a warrant of attorney to confess judgement; and, on payment, to the warden, of a certain per centage upon the debt according to the circumstances of the debtor and the magnitude of the debt, but which never exceeds five per cent. upon the first £100, and two and a half per cent. on the second.

Day-rules may be obtained every day during term on which the Courts of Common Pleas and Exchequer respectively sit, by applying to the warden, and giving the same sort of security as in the last case; such day-rules enable the prisoner to go at large during the day for which they are granted, from the time of opening the gates in the morning till eleven o'clock at night. The expenses of the day-rule, exclusive of the expense of the security, consist of 1*s.* to the warden; 1*s.* 10*d.* to the clerk of the papers; and 1*s.* 8*d.* to the officers of the court who grant the rules. A fresh warrant of attorney is required every term to obtain a day-rule, unless the party is within the rules; in which case, no fresh security is taken.

The prison is divided into the Master's side and Common side. The Master's side consists of 109 rooms; of which, 106 have fire-places, and all of them admit what are called *chums,* except fifteen, which are on the ground-floor, called "Bartholomew-fair," and which are small and low; the other three, which have no fire-places, are called slip-rooms: for each of the above rooms a rent of 1*s.* 3*d.* is payable, weekly, to the warden. The Common side consists of four large rooms, with fire-places; the beds are placed in small recesses, called cabins, separated from each other, leaving a sufficient space in the rooms for the prisoner to work in: three of these rooms contain seven cabins, the other only six, and the number of prisoners in each room never exceeds the number of cabins in it; for these rooms no rent is paid, the bedding and furniture for the rooms on both sides are found by the prisoners; and, in cases where the prisoner is unable to procure any for himself, which very rarely happens, he is supplied by the profit arising from the begging-grate, or by the charity of his fellow-prisoners.

The warden or deputy-warden has the disposal of all the rooms, and allots those on the Master's side to such prisoners as previously pay the admission of £1:8:8; and he allots the cabins on the Common side, without any admission-fee: those who are lodged on the Common side, and not sworn on the begging-grate, are liable to an admission-fee of 15*s.* 4*d.*, which, in fact, is usually paid on their discharge; but those who are so sworn are not liable to any such fees. The rooms on the Master's side are allotted to the prisoners, in rotation, from the time of the payment of their admission-fee; the first who takes possession of a room is called the owner; and when every room is occupied, and fresh prisoners brought in, every prisoner who pays the admission-fee is lodged, together with the owner, upon the same principle of regular rotation, and is called a *chum;* and if the number of prisoners should make it necessary that more than two should be lodged in the same room, the same system of chummage and rotation continues to take place.

The officers of the prison are a warden, deputy, clerk of the papers, three, or more, turnkeys, a crier, watchman, and scavenger. The warden is appointed by the Crown, and the other officers of the prison by the warden. To the offices of warden, deputy, and clerk of the papers no salary is attached, but the first and last are remunerated by fees and perquisites; those of the warden, after all deductions and subaltern payments are made, average about £2000 per annum; those of the clerk of the papers to about £800.

There are various charities applicable to poor prisoners, amounting to about £48 a-year, which are divided among those who swear they are not worth £5, and cannot subsist without the charities of the Fleet. There is, also, the begging-box, in which a sum is collected averaging about £130 per annum, of which no account is kept; the donations of the day being appropriated to the prisoner who stands at the grate to receive them, which all the prisoners who take the oath mentioned are permitted to do, in turns. There is, also, the sum of £500 a-year raised on the several counties of England and Wales, under the 53 Geo. III. c. 113, which is appropriated to prisoners who swear they are not worth £10. When a prisoner has no means of subsistence, he is either supported out of these charities or by waiting on the prisoners who are in better circumstances.

The average number of persons in this prison, at the time of the Inquiry of a Parliamentary Committee in 1816, was 250 within the walls, and about 60 in the rules. This is about the number in custody last year, which may be seen, as well as the sums for which they were imprisoned, by referring to page 124 of this publication. As part of the projected improvements in the

City, for which an act of parliament has been obtained, it is intended to remove the Fleet; and a new prison is about being erected in a very eligible situation in St. George's Fields.

MARSHALSEA PRISON.

This prison has no Rules like the Fleet. It was formerly attached to the jurisdiction of the King's Palace-Court of Westminster, the Court of the Marshalsea of the Royal Household, and the High Court of Admiralty; but the jurisdiction of the second of these has long since fallen into disuse, and the High Court of Admiralty has not been in the practice of committing its prisoners here; so that the only prisoners now confined in it are, first, officers and privates of the royal navy, under sentence of naval courts-martial for mutiny, desertion, or other offences; and, secondly, persons committed for debt, or contempt, by the Palace-Court, the jurisdiction of which extends to the distance of twelve miles round the palace at Westminster. The entrance to the prison is through the house of the deputy marshal; it is separated into two divisions, one, called the Admiralty Division, is appropriated to criminal prisoners; the other division is for the reception of debtors.

The prison is kept in repair by the Board of Works, under the direction of the Treasury; and the power of making regulations for its government is vested, by 32 Geo. II. c. 28, in the two chief justices, the chief baron, or any two of them, with three or more justices of the peace for the county of Surrey. The knight-marshal, as he is commonly called, is constituted by letters patent; his emoluments arise from a salary of £271, payable out of the Civil List, and certain fees, a schedule of which is annexed to his patent, amounting to about £20 a-year. A surgeon and chaplain are attached to the hospital. The prisoners find their own bedding, furniture, and fuel. The practice of chummage prevails here, as described under the head of "Fleet Prison." For a statement of the number of prisoners and the sums for which they were in custody, last year, see page 124.

THE KING'S BENCH PRISON.

This is a national and not a county prison, and the Marshalsea is under the jurisdiction of the Court of King's Bench.* It is situate in the Borough of Southwark, standing upon an area of about four acres, and enclosed by a wall 35 feet high, surmounted by iron spikes. The principal building is upward of 300 feet long, and has very much the appearance of an extensive barrack. It contains, within the walls, 225 rooms, 8 of which are called "state-rooms," and are reserved by the marshal for the better class of prisoners; the remainder, with the exception of a few back rooms, which poor debtors have rent free, are occupied by the prisoners, who pay 1*s*. weekly, for a single room, unfurnished: if two persons live in the same room, 6*d*. each; if three, 4*d*. Besides these rooms, there is a coffee-house and public kitchen, which are separate erections, and two public-houses, one on either wing of the principal building, or terrace. Between the terrace and the boundary wall are spacious racket-grounds and fives' courts, celebrated as the best in the kingdom. At the end of the prison is a sort of market, consisting of a few sheds, occupied, at a rental of 1*s*. weekly, by butchers, poulterers, green-grocers, &c.

Persons arrested for debt, or confined under the sentence or for contempt of the Court of King's Bench,

* Parliamentary Report on the King's Bench, vol. iv. p. 1, of Parl. Paps. Sess. 1815.

are imprisoned in this place. It was not originally intended for the general reception of debtors, as now appropriated. The vast number incarcerated arises from the facility of removal, by *habeas*, from the less-comfortable accommodation afforded in other gaols, and from the circumstance of debtors, sued in the supreme court, having put in special bail in different parts of the kingdom, being obliged to surrender, in the Metropolis, in discharge of bail.

A Committee of the House of Commons, which sat several days, engaged in an inquiry into the state and management of this prison, in 1815, reported that it was not capable of containing properly more than 400 prisoners; WILLIAM JONES, Esq. the marshal, thought it would hold 500; it, however, frequently happens that 800 or 900 are confined here.

Every prisoner, on his entrance, pays 6*s*. 2*d*. and, on his discharge, 14*s*. 2*d*. as gate-fees. But, whether the entrance-fees are paid or not, the debtor receives, on demand, a *chum-ticket*, which is a ticket of admission to some room in the prison. The rule of chummage is, that the person who has been longest in prison keeps his room free from having another prisoner chummed or billetted on it, till all the rooms held by those of a junior date to himself have each a prisoner chummed on them. The system purports to be one of rotation; and, if the prisoner be poor, and wishes to be bought out, he is chummed upon one who can afford to pay him; if he wish to remain, he is placed in the room of a person who will keep him, and he has accordingly a chum-ticket upon the youngest prisoner in one or other of these classes. The person chummed out seeks lodgings in another part of the prison among those of his own class; the price for the share of a room is 5*s*. a-week; and it is not unusual to find eight or more persons of the poorer classes sleeping two in a bed, or on the floor, in rooms of the dimensions of 16 feet by 13.

The prison was formerly divided into the Master's Side and Poor Side: that distinction has long ceased, though there are a few of the lower rooms, at the back of the prison, exclusively occupied by the poorer classes. Those may be considered, however, on the poor side who receive the county allowance under the 53 Geo. III. c. 113.

Besides those confined within the walls of the prison there are several hundreds who enjoy the benefit of the "*Rules,*" extending, in circumference, about two miles and a half, and containing about six miles of open road and street. By a rule of the Court of King's Bench, of the 35th Geo. III. all taverns, alehouses, and places licensed for public entertainment should be deemed to form no part of the Rules. The marshal, on application for the Rules, takes security from the applicant by way of indemnity for the debt with which they stand charged:—If the prisoner takes the Rules for a debt of £100, or more, £8 is demanded for the bond, stamp, and other fees, and £4 for every succeeding £100; if the sum be large, and the security good, a fee is sometimes taken in a smaller proportion; if the debt be under £100, six or five pounds are demanded. But, in many instances, the Rules are given without expense, as a mode of clearing the prison. The chief profit of the marshal arises from granting the Rules, and, in 1815, averaged £2600 per annum.*

There are, also, "*Day-Rules,*" which any prisoner can obtain, during term-time, by permission of the marshal, on sending a petition to the clerk of the day-rules, which is presented to the Court of King's Bench;

* Parl. Report on the King's Bench, Parl. Pap. vol. iv. p. 7, Sess. 1815.

the fee paid on this is 4*s*. 2*d*. daily. The safe return of the prisoners, within the Rules, is considered as sufficiently secured by their recognizances; and those within the walls give a bond to the tipstaff, renewable every term, the expense of which is three guineas. Besides these, there is a device by which a prisoner has been permitted to go out of the prison, which is known by the name of a "*run on the key*." It is a liberty granted by some of the officers of the prison to any of the prisoners to go into the Rules for the day. This last is not a recognized mode of obtaining a furlough, and ostensibly is done without the knowledge of the marshal.

As a strict observance of the limits of the Rules is not generally enforced, many have availed themselves of the privilege to visit the watering-places, and enjoy as much personal liberty as if entirely at large; it follows that a committal to the Bench of those possessed of money, either of their own or creditors', becomes only nominal punishment; while those without this needful auxiliary, though unfortunate, are subjected to as great privations as actual delinquents.

On the 25th of March the gates are opened at eight in the morning and closed at nine; but no person can come into the prison before eight nor after half-past eight, except in term time, when strangers may get in until half-past nine, and prisoners till ten. On the 29th of September and until the 25th of March the gates are not open, for the admission of visitors, until half-past eight in the morning. A prisoner may walk over any part of the interior at any hour of the day or night, as there is no fear he will escape the vigilance of the turnkeys, who, on his first admission, by minute examination, make themselves well acquainted with his person and countenance.

Poor prisoners are entitled to the allowance, under

the Lords' Act, of 3*s*. 6*d*. a-week; in addition to which they receive a share of all the charities and benefactions paid for the use of the common-side prisoners, on taking *an oath* (which, it is said, some are not very scrupulous in doing) that they cannot command the sum of £5, and cannot subsist without the charities. Those who claim these charities are, besides, compelled to hold alternately the begging-box at the grate.

The marshal is nominated by the Chief-Justice of the King's Bench, and appointed by the King, either by sign manual or letters patent. The present marshal, WILLIAM JONES, Esq. was appointed in 1791. No salary is attached to the office of marshal; his income is derived from granting the Rules, fees on commitments and discharges, and from other sources, such as the rent of rooms, profits on the sale of porter, ale, and wine, the rent of the coffee-house, market-sheds, &c. The average gross amount of revenue derived from these sources averaged, in the three years preceding 1815, £5000; the outgoings, including salaries of clerks, turnkeys, &c. £1730. To these emoluments of the marshal may be added £320 per annum for fees on bails and judgments. The profits on beer, sold in the prison, amounted, at the same time, to £872 per annum. The admission of spirituous liquors, into this as well as every other prison, is prohibited by the Gaol-Act; considerable quantities, however, are smuggled in and vended in the tape-rooms, and a prisoner recently placed himself in great personal jeopardy by publishing the fact. The marshal is a magistrate, but acts only as such within the district of his own prison. He has the power of committing riotous and disorderly prisoners to Horsemonger-lane, which, however, is seldom exercised. The places of confinement, within the walls of the prison, are called the "*Strong Rooms*," consisting of two cells and an apartment of a better description; as these form the "lower hell" of the place, their *agrémens* are inferior to those afforded in the larger *depôt*.

The prison is managed and governed by rules laid down from time to time by the Judges of the Court of King's Bench, and these are printed, and ought to be hung up in different parts of the gaol. The earliest rules bear date the 30th Geo. II. and others have been continued down, at intervals, to the 3d Geo. IV. They are much too voluminous to be inserted here, nor would they be of much utility; for, as the penalties, when any are annexed, are seldom enforced, they form a small portion of the practical code of the place. One of the greatest defects in this establishment, we apprehend, results from its legislative government being vested in the same authority as that which appoints the head officer. Had the Secretary of State for the Home Department the framing and enforcing of the rules for the regulation of the prison, it is not improbable a more impartial system of judicial administration between the governor and the governed would be established. No particular blame is imputable to the present marshal; considering the difficulties of his situation, and the peculiar class of subjects under his sway, the bulk of whom owe their incarceration to misfortune, folly, or dishonesty, and who, in consequence, are either melancholy or vicious, and a prey to perpetual *ennui*, discontent, and irritation, from the absence of accustomed occupations, society, and enjoyments, and being the victims of the petty extortions peculiar to such places, and of which persons, in their circumstances, are singularly susceptible: with such lieges we repeat—always prone to dissatisfaction and complaint, under a system more in fault than the instruments who carry it into execution—we do not think the government of the marshal is justly chargeable with any particular degree of harshness or indiscretion, and that he is not likely to be guilty of any deliberate act of inhumanity or oppression.

In going over the prison, in the middle of the present month (March), we were glad to find some of the abuses, reported by the Parliamentary Committee had been remedied. It was painful enough to see so many persons in a state of idleness and misery, without profit either to themselves or others. They evidently require *more space*, and, if the odious system of imprisonment for debt is to be continued, a suggestion has been offered not unworthy attention, namely, to remove the Fleet prisoners to the Bench, for whom it would be sufficiently large, and, in lieu of erecting a new Fleet, to erect a new King's Bench prison in St. George's Fields.

CHAPTER XII.

PUBLIC SEWERS.—WATER COMPANIES.—GAS-LIGHT ESTABLISHMENTS.—FIRE-POLICE.

General Observations on the Sub-Works of the Metropolis.—PUBLIC SEWERS.—*Origin and Laws relative to Commissions of Sewers.—Number of Commissions, and their Districts.—Mode of Applying, by Individuals, to the Commissioners.—Expenditure for Sewers in the Metropolis.—Rules established for the Construction of Sewers by the Holborn and Finsbury Divisions.—Table of Levels in different Parts of the Metropolis.*—WATER COMPANIES.—*Effects of Competition among Water Companies.—Account of the several Companies, and the Mode of Supplying the Metropolis with Water.—Observations on the Conduct of the Companies and the late Complaints on the Supply of Water.—Increase of Rates, and Inconsistencies in the Mode of fixing them.—Proposal to vest a Control over the Companies in the Home Office.—On the Salubrity of Thames Water.—Statement of the Profits and Income of the Water Companies.*—GAS-LIGHT ESTABLISHMENTS.—*Importance of well-lighted Streets to Protective Justice.—Establishment of Chartered Gas-Light and Coke Company.—The City of London.—The South London.—The Imperial.—Rapid Progress of Gas-Lighting.—Inconveniences from the Intermixture of Mains and Services.*—FIRE-POLICE.—*Parochial Fire-Police.—Provisions of the Building Act.—Hints to Individuals in case of Fires.—Insurance Offices the most efficient Protection.—The Fire-Patrol.—Fires in the Metropolis, and Losses consequent upon them.—Fire-Police more Perfect, as regards the Protection of Property than Person.—Laws for guarding against Fire.—Great Fire at the Custom-House.*

PEOPLE commonly undervalue the benefits of which they have been long in possession; and it is an admirable expedient for bringing ourselves to a due sense of the advantages we enjoy to revert to the inconveniences and annoyances we sustained before these advantages were obtained. The utility of this retrospection is strikingly illustrated in contrasting the past and present state of the Metropolis. We are so familiar with well-lighted streets, free from nuisance or obstruction, that we are apt to deem them almost "native" to the place, instead of being the slow product of many salutary laws, and of the skill, capital and enterprise of individuals. Among the contrivances more particularly ministering to the public health and convenience, three are entitled to particular notice; namely, the construction of sewers, the conduits for the conveyance of water, for domestic uses; and the various methods adopted, by gas and otherwise, for lighting the public thoroughfares. The benefits derived from these sources will be readily appreciated by adverting, for a moment, to the state to which our streets would be reduced if deprived of their aid; without sewers for carrying off the waste water, the houses would be constantly exposed to damp and inundation, and every hollow and vacant spot filled with pestilential pools, equally offensive to the eye and injurious to health; the pipes for the conveyance of pure water are still more useful than the aqueducts for carrying off that which is foul and superfluous; the precarious supplies derived from springs and brooks would be totally inadequate, and nothing less than a river, distributed through thousands of channels, is commensurate to the wants of so dense a population: the advantages resulting from a well-regulated system of lighting are too apparent to be pointed out; it supplies the absence of the solar luminary, and forms no inconsiderable branch of the police by guarding both persons and property from violence and depredation. One great excellence in these contrivances consists in the manner in which they are arranged; by the works being all laid under ground, they present neither obstruction nor annoyance to the passenger; they form an invisible agency, the benefits of whose operations are hourly experienced, though the means by which they are produced be concealed.

Leaving these introductory remarks, we shall come to the institutions and laws which regulate what may be termed the sub-machinery of the Metropolis. It forms an important branch of our civic establishments, and the expense is defrayed either by a compulsory or voluntary assessment on the inhabitants.

PUBLIC SEWERS.

The sewers of the Metropolis are subterranean channels for conveying into the river Thames the foul and redundant water. The main, or principal sewer is for the drainage of a whole level, and runs down the lowest part of the district; in some cases, it is an original water-course, covered with streets and buildings, and extending the distance of four or five miles: such is King's Scholar's Pond sewer, running from Hampstead southward, and draining the principal parts of the parishes of St. Mary-le-bone, St. George, Hanover-square, St. James, St. Margaret, and St. John the Evangelist, and emptying itself into the Thames westward of Vauxhall-bridge. From the several mains, collateral branches extend through the different streets, and communicate, by means of drains, with the houses and premises of individuals. All who receive a benefit, or avoid a damage, are liable to contribute to the maintenance of the sewers; but the private drains, carried from the premises of individuals, must be made, and maintained, at the cost of the owners. The jurisdiction of the commissioners extends only to the common, or public sewer: in laying out new streets, the sewers are made by the proprietors, and afterwards taken under the management of the commissioners.

From the lectures of the learned CHALLIS, at Gray's Inn, in 1662, public sewers appear to have been first vested in commissioners in the reign of Henry III.;* and, after several acts to extend their powers, became consolidated in the 23d of Henry VIII. c. 25, when authority was granted to certain individuals, in various districts of the kingdom, to construct sewers for drainage, and levy rates for the purpose. The authority of the commissioners is almost absolute, and still continues, with little abatement. They can summon, examine, and even imprison; and it is doubtful whether even the courts of law can interfere. As regards the appointment and qualifications of the commissioners, the statute of Henry VIII. directs that substantial persons, having a freehold qualification of £20 per annum, shall be nominated by the lord chancellor, lord treasurer, and two chief justices, for "making and repairing ditches, banks, gutters, gotes, sewers, calcies, bridges, streams, trenches, mills, ponds, and locks." Each commission is to continue ten years; and six are to form a quorum.

* The chief statutes relating to sewers are 6 Hen. VI. c. 5, regulated by 6 Hen. VIII. c. 10; 23 Hen. VIII. c. 5; and 25 Hen. VIII. c. 10, amended by 3 and 4 Edw. VI. c. 8; 1 Mary, stat. 3, c. 11; 13 Eliz. c. 9; 3 Jac. I. c. 14; and 7 Ann, c. 10.

Commissioners acting without being duly qualified to forfeit £40 each sitting; they may proceed either by inquisition or survey; each commissioner to be allowed 4*s*. a day while engaged in the duties of the commission; and the rates are to be assessed in proportion to land, rents, profits, and fisheries.

Besides this and other general acts, local acts have been obtained by several commissions, the provisions of which extend only to the particular jurisdiction for which they have been granted. In that part of the Metropolis north of the Thames there are four principal commissions:—1. For the City of London. 2. For the division of Holborn and Finsbury; extending to the parish of St. Leonard, Shoreditch, and the Liberty of Norton Falgate. 3. For the City and Liberty of Westminster and part of the County of Middlesex; including Hampton, Isleworth, Acton, Hanwell, Hammersmith, Fulham, Kensington, and Chelsea; and to and within the City of Westminster to Temple Bar; and to parts of St. Pancras, Mary-le-bone, Paddington, and Hampstead. 4. For the Tower Hamlets; including Spitalfields, Hackney, Mile End, and part of Limehouse, &c. Commissioners of sewers and pavements in the City are appointed by the corporation, whereof the recorder and common sergeant are required to be two; the members of the other commissions are appointed by the lord chancellor, and consist of the principal inhabitants resident in the respective districts. The mode of procedure is much the same under each commission; and consists of a view, a survey, and assessment. The Westminster jurisdiction is divided into districts; and a survey and presentment is made by the intervention of a jury of each district. A similar course is adopted in the jurisdiction of the Tower Hamlets. But the city commissioners, and those for the Holborn and Finsbury divisions, act without a jury.

The officers attached to each commission consist of a clerk, surveyor, inspector, clerk of the works, messengers, &c. The general courts are mostly held four times a-year; and committees assemble monthly, or oftener. The only direct remuneration, either to commissioners or juries, (where the latter are employed,) is a dinner on days of business. The assessment is made by a poundage on the rental, same as the poor rate, and is mostly paid by the landlord, unless upon agreement to the contrary with the tenant. The last commission granted to the Tower Hamlets is dated in February, 1821, and contains 150 names; in the Holborn and Finsbury district are 196 commissioners; in the Westminster district 196, many of whom are peers and members of the House of Commons.

An individual having any complaint to make, or improvement to solicit, should apply at the office of the commissioners; the office of the city commissioners is at Guildhall; of the Holborn and Finsbury divisions at 7, Hatton-garden; the office of Westminster in Greek-street, Soho-square; and of the Tower Hamlets 15, Great Alie-street. A complaint-book is kept, in which the representations of individuals are entered, and a surveyer goes to inspect; if it is a private drain, the business belongs to the individual; if a public sewer, the repairs are made, and expense defrayed by the commissioners.*

The average expenditure, under the Westminster commission, is about £24,000 per annum; the Holborn

* Report of the Select Committee of the House of Commons on the Powers vested in Commissioners of Sewers in the Metropolis, Parl. Papers, vol. v. No. 542, page 41, Sess. 1823.

and Finsbury £10,000; the Tower Hamlets under £2000; the City of London £8000: making an annual average expenditure for the maintenance of the old, and the erection of new sewers, of £44,000.

We shall conclude this article with the insertion of the following statements, for the convenience of builders and others, abstracted from Parliamentary Paper, No. 542, Session 1823, pages 26 and 46.

Regulations for the Construction of New Sewers within the Limits of the Holborn and Finsbury Divisions.

That all main or leading sewers receiving water from more than one street or place exceeding forty houses, shall not be less than five feet high, and three feet wide, formed on an oval plan, of one brick and a half in substance, from the bottom to the springing of the arch, and one brick for the arch.

That all branch sewers for streets or places containing less than forty houses shall be four feet six inches high, and two feet six inches wide, and one brick in substance, of an oval form; also, that the current of such sewers be not less than a quarter of an inch to every ten feet in length, but as much more as the situation will admit; and that the bottom of every public sewer leading into any other public sewer, be six inches above the bottom of such original sewer.

That apertures for cleansing the sewers be formed at the corner of each street or place, or at a distance not exceeding seventy feet from each other, covered with moorstone kirb; and that the top of the same shall be eighteen inches below the surface of the street.

That the bottom of all private drains be twenty inches above the bottom of the public sewers, with which they communicate, and that such drains shall not be less than nine inches in diameter in the clear.

That all the bricks to be used in these works be sound hard-burnt stocks, and the mortar compounded of good lime, and clean sharp drift sand, well mixed together; and that the whole be executed in the most workmanlike manner, under the directions of the Commissioners.

By the Court,

STABLE and LUSH.

Sewers must be made in the form directed by the Commissioners, and builders and others, on application in writing at the office, will receive the necessary instructions.

To prevent the inconvenience arising from ground being excavated too deep, the Commissioners have directed that, on application being made at the office previous to the excavation of such ground, information will be given as to the lowest depth at which the same can be drained.

The Commissioners also give notice that whenever the lower floors or basements of buildings have been laid so low as not to admit of drainage with a proper current, they will not allow any sewers or drains into sewers to be made for the service of such buildings; and further, that no building or erection of any kind will be permitted to be made upon or over any sewer.

The Levels or Altitudes of certain Streets above the highest High Water of the River Thames, measured from the Surface of the Carriage-Road.

	Above the highest High-water Level. Ft.	In.
The STRAND:		
At the north end of Northumberland-street	19	7
end of Wellington-street	35	6
north end of Essex-street	27	0
HAYMARKET:		
At the west end of Coventry-street	52	0
PALL-MALL:		
Opposite the south end of St. James's Street	13	3
PICCADILLY:		
At the south end of Air-street	49	8
north end of St. James's Street	46	7
south end of White-Horse-street	24	6
PRINCES-STREET:		
At the west end of Gerrard-street	61	4
BROAD-STREET, BLOOMSBURY:		
At the west end of Drury-lane	65	0

Oxford-Street:		
At the south end of Berners-street	74	3
Near to Stratford-place	59	4
Crossing the Regent-street	76	0
At the south end of Orchard-street	70	4
New-Road, St. Mary-le-Bone:		
Opposite the north end of Cleveland-street	80	10
Centre of the Regent-circus	77	2
At the north end of Gloucester-place	72	3
Regents' Park:		
At the road on the north side of the aqueducts crossing the Regent's Canal	102	6
Great George-Street:		
Opposite the south end of King-street	5	6

Westminster:

The whole surface of Westminster, excepting a small space surrounding the Abbey, and a very small part of the Horseferry-road, is below the level of the highest tide.

SUPPLY OF WATER.

The supply of water to the metropolis has recently formed a subject of anxious inquiry and discussion. Next to the atmospheric fluid it is the most essential of natural substances, and to the inhabitants of a large city more especially it is the first requisite, both for cleanliness and health. Some of the most splendid remains of antiquity are those acqueducts by which this article was conveyed to the ancient cities; but though these were mighty works, the supply which they afforded was not ramified over the whole population, and given to every house, and almost every room, as in London. Upwards of a million of human beings, a countless number of other animals, and many works and manufactories of great magnitude, are regularly furnished with this indispensable ingredient, by the agency of subterraneous machinery of immense extent and intricacy. What is most extraordinary is, that this vast convenience has not been achieved by the power of the state, but is the gradual result of individual skill, capital, and enterprize.

The companies which supply the metropolis with water are the following:—

New River,	Grand Junction,
Chelsea,	The Lambeth,
East London,	Vauxhall, or South London, and
West Middlesex,	Southwark Water-works.

The five first supply London and Westminster, the three last that part of the metropolis on the south of the Thames. The New River and Chelsea are the oldest establishments, and, with three smaller companies, now no longer existing, provided the whole supply north of the River, previously to the year 1810. In that year the East London, West Middlesex, and Grand Junction Companies were formed, under the authority of several acts of Parliament, in order to encourage competition;* but it is obvious, from the peculiar nature of these undertakings, that the principle of competition, without regulation, might operate to the destruction of the parties, and thereby be ultimately injurious to the public. Competition, in ordinary cases, adjusts the supply to the demand, through the liberty which the sellers have to go out of the market, as well as to come into it; but, in trades carried on by means of large capitals, vested in fixed machinery, and furnishing a commodity of no value but for consumption on the spot, the sellers are confined to the market by the nature of their trade; and

* Report on the Supply of the Metropolis with Water, Parliamentary Paper, Session 1821, No. 537, page 3.

if the new comer has to seek immediate employment for large works by taking custom from the established dealer, as there can be no great difference in the quality of what they sell, they must vie *in lowness of price*, and will probably be driven to underbid each other down to the point of ruin, because it is better to take anything than nothing for that which cannot be carried away, and this must continue till both or one is worn out, or till, by some arrangement between themselves, they can put a stop to their mutual destruction.

These consequences followed from a competition between the water-companies on the north of the river; it was carried on, during several years, at a very ruinous loss, and must, in all probability, have led to the extinction of all, except one or two of the wealthiest, as it actually did to that of the smaller companies, but for an arrangement which took place, by which the supply of the town was partitioned between them, and the several companies bound themselves, by penalties, to abstain from serving with water beyond the line agreed upon. Though this was a measure of self-preservation, on their part, it clearly gave them a power over the public never intended by Parliament, and which might be abused to any extent. The water-rates were soon after increased to the amount of *twenty-five per cent.* and which have been since still further augmented: strong complaints have also been made both on the purity and quantity of the water supplied; circumstances which sufficiently indicate that the united companies have assumed the absolute dictation of monopolists over their customers, and that they are no longer compelled to the observance of those easy terms to which they had been reduced during the late contest. Before, however, making any observations on the points at issue, it may be proper to give an account of each company, as developed in recent Parliamentary Reports :—

1. *The New-River Company* get their supply chiefly from the spring at Chadwell, between Hertford and Ware. It comes in an open channel, of about forty miles in length, to reservoirs at Clerkenwell, which, the town having now stretched completely round it, must receive a considerable quantity of charcoal, coal-tar, and ammonia from the smoke. There are two reservoirs, having between them a surface of about five acres, and an average depth of ten feet. These reservoirs are eighty-four feet and a half above low-water-mark in the Thames, and, by means of steam-engines and a stand-pipe, an additional height of sixty feet can be given to the water, so that all the mains belonging to this company are kept full by a considerable pressure of water. The highest service given by the New River is the cistern on the top of Covent-Garden Theatre. The aqueduct, by which the water is brought has only a fall of two inches per mile; thus it wastes, by evaporation, during the drought of summer, and is impeded by frost in the winter. At these times the company pump an additional supply from the Thames, at Broken Wharf, between Blackfriars and Southwark bridges. To this, however, they seldom have recourse; and their engine, which they have erected only since the works at London-bridge were broken down, has worked only 176 hours in the year. The New-River Company supply 66,600 houses with water, at an average of about 1100 hogsheads each in the year, or, in all, about 75,000,000 of hogsheads annually.

2. *The East-London Water-works* are situated at Old Ford, on the river Lea, about three miles from the Thames, and a little below the point to which the tide flows up the Lea. By the Act of Parliament, this company must take its water when the tide runs up and the mills below have ceased working. The water is pumped into reservoirs and allowed to settle; and a supply of 6,000,000 gallons is daily distributed to about 42,000 houses. This company supply no water at a greater elevation than thirty feet, and the usual height at which the delivery is made to the tenants is six feet above the pavement; they have 200 miles of iron pipes, which, in some places, cost them seven guineas a yard. This and the New River are the only companies which do not draw their supply of water entirely from the Thames.

3. *The West Middlesex* derive their supply of water from the Thames, at the upper end of Hammersmith, about nine miles and a half above London-bridge, and where the bed of the Thames is gravel. The water is forced, by engines, to a reservoir at Kensington, 309 feet

long, 123 wide, and 20 deep, paved and lined with bricks, and elevated about 120 feet above low water in the Thames. They have another reservoir on Little Primrose-hill, about 70 feet higher, and containing 88,000 hogsheads of water, under the pressure of which the drains are kept charged, in case of fires. They serve about 15,000 tenants, and the average daily supply is about 2,250,000 gallons.

4. *The Chelsea Water-works* derive their supply from the Thames, about a quarter of a mile east of Chelsea-hospital, and they have two reservoirs, one in the Green-park and another in Hyde-park, the former having an elevation of 44 feet, and the latter of 70. These reservoirs, till within these few months, had never been cleaned, nor had there been any preparation made for that purpose in their construction. About one-third of the water served out by this company is allowed to settle in these reservoirs, and the remaining two-thirds are sent directly from the Thames. Latterly, the company have been making preparations for filtering the water, and also for allowing it to settle in reservoirs, at Chelsea, before it is delivered in the mains. The Chelsea Company serve about 12,400 houses, and the average daily supply is 1,760,000 gallons.

5. *The Grand Junction Company* derive the whole of their supply from the Thames, immediately adjoining Chelsea-hospital; thence it is pumped, without any filtration or settling, into three reservoirs at Paddington. These reservoirs are about 71, 86, and 92 feet above the high-water-mark in the Thames; their united contents are 19,355,840 gallons; and, by means of a stand-pipe, the water is forced to the height of 147 feet, or about 61 feet above the average reservoir. The number of houses supplied by the Grand Junction Company is 7,700, and the average daily supply is about 2,800,000 gallons.

6. *The Lambeth Company* take their supply from the Thames, between Westminster and Waterloo bridges. It is drawn from the bed of the river by a suction-pipe, and delivered to the tenants without being allowed to subside, there being only a cistern of 400 barrels at the works, as a temporary supply, until the engines can be started. The greatest height to which the company force water is about 40 feet, the number of houses that they supply is 16,000, and the average service is 1,244,000 gallons daily.

7. *The South-London*, or *Vauxhall Company*, take their supply from the river Thames by a tunnel, which is laid six feet below low-water-mark, and as far into the river as the third arch of Vauxhall-bridge. At that particular place, the bed of the Thames is described as being always clean, and without any of those depositions of mud

and more offensive substances that are found in many other places. Besides the greater purity of the bed of the Thames here than where any other compauy on the south side take their supply, the company allow the water to settle in reservoirs. The Vauxhall Company supply about 10,000 houses with about 1,000,000 gallons of water daily.

8. *The Southwark Water-works* (the property of an individual) are supplied from the middle of the Thames, below Southwark and London bridges; and the water thus taken is sent out to the tenants without standing to settle, or any filtration further than it receives from passing through wire grates and small holes in metallic plates. The number of houses supplied by these works is about 7000, and the average daily supply about 720,000 gallons.

The elements of this supply will be better understood by collecting the results into a table, as follows:—

Companies.	Services.	Average per Day. Gallons.	Gallons Annually.	Average per House.
1. New River....	67,000	13,000,000	4,056,000,000	182
2. East London ..	42,000	6,000,000	1,872,000,000	143
3. West Middlesex	15,000	2,250,000	702,000,000	150
4. Chelsea	12,400	1,760,000	549,120,000	142
5. Grand Junction	7,700	2,800,000	873,600,000	363
6. Lambeth	16,000	1,244,000	388,128,000	77
7. South London	10,000	1,000,000	312,000,000	100
8. Southwark....	7,000	720,000	224,540,000	102
Total..	183,100	28,774,000	8,977,388,000	157

Average per house, north of the river............ 196 gallons.
Average ditto south ditto .... 93 ditto.

Observations.—From this table it appears that the average supply, per house, is more than twice as much on the Middlesex side of the Thames as on the Surrey side, and that the district supplied by the Lambeth Works does not receive one-fifth of the quantity which is supplied by the Grand Junction. It is true that, in many places of the Lambeth district, the houses are much smaller than in the other, and it is also true that not so much is consumed in watering the streets, the supply for that purpose being in some places taken directly from the Thames, and the watering very imperfectly done in others; but still, as the population is very dense, it is possible that these small houses contain, upon the average, as many inhabitants as the largest houses in other districts. Hence it should seem that either the one district has an over supply, or that the other has not enough. In cases of fire, too, on the Surrey side, frequent and serious complaints have been made of the damage that has ensued from the delay and difficulty of obtaining water. The services, too, are less frequent (some houses being only supplied once a-week) on the south side of the river.

With respect to the *quality* of the water, some distinction must be observed in speaking of the several companies, since they derive their supply from different sources and under different circumstances, and convey it in different states of preparation to the consumer. The chief objections have been made to the Thames water; but the two largest companies, the New River and East London, which furnish eleven-eighteenths of the whole, do not derive any, or a very small portion of their supply from this source. All the others draw their supplies from the Thames, though under different circumstances, some taking it up more, some less pure; some of them purifying it in cisterns ere they send it out to the public, others not. By the Chelsea and Southwark works, the water is conveyed direct from the river to the mouths of the consumers. By the other companies the process of filtration and settlement is very inadequately performed, and the water received in a state of great impurity. The quality of the water varies, also, according as it is taken from the top or bottom of the river, or in the vicinity of sewers. The water formerly raised at the old London-bridge, near the surface, being purer than that taken from the bottom in the vicinity; and the water of the South London, at Vauxhall, is purer than that taken higher up by the Chelsea and Grand Junction; and that taken by the last is the least pure, though taken farthest up the river, probably from the proximity of that company's *dolphin* to the great Ranelagh sewer.

The increased rates imposed by the companies have been justly complained of. The increase of 25 per cent., on the rental of 1810, was thought sufficient by the Parliamentary Committee of 1821, but, since then, a gradual increase has taken place, amounting to £44,000 annually, to the companies, on the north of the river. It is, also, objected* that no scale of rates exists by which to form a judgment upon the reasonableness of the rate imposed: no two companies agree in their mode of rating; on the contrary, as the amount is unlimited, so is the proportion altogether uncertain; it is not regulated either by the quantity of water consumed, or the distance to which it is conveyed, but appears to be left to the agents of the different companies to charge as they shall think fit. The increase in the rates and profits of the companies, since 1820, will appear in the following statement, abstracted from Parliamentary Paper, No. 567, Sess. 1828:—

* Report on Supply of Water, No. 567, p. 5, vol. viii. of Parl. Pap. Sess. 1828.

WATER-WORKS.

Statement of the Comparative Income, Expenditure, and Profits of the Five Water-Companies North of the Thames, in the Years 1820 *and* 1827 :—

Years.	Houses.	Rate per House.	Gross Annual Income.	Gross Expenditure.	Net Profit.
		WEST MIDDLESEX.			
1820	10,350	47*s.*	£24,252	£ 9,000	£15,252
1827	14,500	51	37,000	13,000	24,000
		GRAND JUNCTION.			
1820	7,180	57	20,153	8,916	11,237
1827	7,809	61	24,702	10,674	14,027
		CHELSEA.			
1820	8,631	35	15,150	12,255	2,894
1827	12,409	30	18,589	12,532	6,027
		EAST LONDON.			
1820	32,071	22	35,358	16,836	19,022
1827	42,000	21	45,442	14,050	31,392
		NEW RIVER.*			
1820	52,082	25	67,275	48,109	19,165
1827	66,600	28	95,657	59,204	36,453

Without competition, or the apprehension that it will arise, the companies may continue augmenting their rates almost without limit. But experience has shown that competition among water-companies is like civil strife in a nation, which, after inflicting mutual loss on the contending parties, terminates in the absolute despotism of the most powerful. In order, therefore, to protect the companies from the ruinous consequences of rivalship, and the consumers from the exactions of a monopoly, it would be expedient a *scale of rates* should be established under the sanction of public authority.

* The Dividend on the New-River Company, for 1827, was £516 : 11 : 11; in 1770, £255 : 13 : 11.

This would not be introducing any new principle into municipal regulation; it has been adopted in the regulation of hackney-coachmen, watermen, and the rates of postage. After a scale of water-rates had been fixed, any further augmentation might be prohibited without the previous sanction of the Secretary of State for the Home Department, or the Lords of the Treasury.

It would also tend greatly to the satisfaction and security of the public if a power of control and inspection of the works of the water companies was given to the Home Office, as a protection against water being sent out to the consumer of an impure and unwholesome quality. In the acts of parliament granted to the gas companies of the Metropolis, such protective power is reserved to guard the public from injury and annoyance; and a similar superintendence is demanded in respect of the supply of water, especially if the existing establishments are to enjoy (what appears almost unavoidable) a monopoly of the market.

Much of the alarm felt on account of the impurity and unwholesomeness of the Thames water has subsided since the commissioners appointed to investigate the subject have published the results of their inquiries. A great part of the extraneous matter impregnated in the Thames is not held in a state of solution, but only mechanically combined, and may be separated by filtration through sand; and still more effectually by a mixture of sand and charcoal. The argument founded on the disappearance of fish from the river, that the water had undergone a serious deterioration within the last ten years, never appeared to us quite satisfactory. The fish may have been driven from their usual resort by the disappearance of their food, the greater disturbance of the channel, or, perhaps, they have been exterminated in the endeavour to supply the wants of a vastly-increasing population. However this may be, we believe the companies on the north of the Thames have been some time adopting measures, and introducing such improvements in their works as are likely to remove all just complaint, as regards the insalubrity of their beverage.

Upon the whole, we cannot conclude this section without observing that there is room for important improvements both in controlling the powers exercised by the water companies, and in improving the supply of the water of the Metropolis; and the individuals who first called attention to the subject are entitled to the gratitude of the community. It does not, however, appear an evil of the magnitude that was at first surmised; and, so far as the salubrity of the fluid is concerned, the recent alarm may be likened to that felt some years since respecting supposed adulterations in our daily food. Certain it is that it has not been usual for physicians to refer metropolitan diseases to the deleterious quality of the water; and the vast improvement in the health of the capital shows that it cannot have exerted a very fatal influence. Still it is an inquiry of the very highest importance: the water for the domestic uses of a great city ought not only to be free from defect, but, like Cæsar's wife, above suspicion. It is an element with which we are in such constant communion, in one shape or another, that we say it not only ought to be exempt from all taint, but from all disagreeable associations; and, considering the immense population and wealth of London, the expenditure of a million (were that requisite) would be amply compensated in obtaining a plentiful, wholesome, and unsuspected supply of this indispensable element of life and cleanliness.

GAS-LIGHT ESTABLISHMENTS.

Robberies are mostly effected in the winter months, the darkness of the nights affording shelter to the operations of the depredator; and, in consequence, every improved mode of lighting the public streets is an auxiliary to protective justice. Among the regulations introduced by Lord Burleigh for improving the police of Westminster, in the time of Elizabeth, one of them directed every householder to suspend a lantern over his door. In this way the City of London was lighted by those who chose to do so; afterwards, it became imperative, in consequence of the streets being infested with robbers and housebreakers, owing to the insufficiency of the lights in the night. Application was made to Parliament, by the Corporation, to enable them to light the streets in a more effectual manner; in compliance with which, an act was passed, empowering them to erect a sufficient number of glass lamps in such places as they should judge proper, to be kept burning from the setting to the rising of the sun, throughout the year; and giving them power to make a rate to defray the expense thereof. London was accordingly lit by the Corporation in, and the respective parishes out of the City, together with several private lamps in various parts of the Metropolis. In this state street-lighting continued, without any material alteration, till the discovery of gas lighting almost entirely superseded the oil-lamps. This beautiful application of science, after struggling through much opposition, and experiencing considerable vicissitudes in its progress, has at length attained great perfection; and, in the present section, we intend giving a short account of the principal gas-companies in the Metropolis. Though private establishments, they form a part of our protective institutions; and, by tending to the security of persons and property, are as much a branch of our general police as the sewers and water-companies, which contribute to public health and cleanliness.

In the Metropolis there are four great gas-light companies—the Chartered, or London Gas-Light and Coke Company; the City of London; the South London; and the Imperial. Our notice of them will be very brief, and chiefly founded on the Report of Sir William Congreve to the Home Office in 1823, which is the latest official account published of the London gas establishments. We shall begin with the Chartered Company; it is the oldest established, and it is partly to the perseverance of the original projectors, under many discouragements, that we are indebted for the brilliant illumination which nightly adorns the first capital in Europe.

The London Gas-Light and Coke Company obtained their charter on the 30th of April, 1812. They have three establishments; namely, in Horseferry-road, Brick-lane, St. Luke's, and Curtain-road. The extent of mains belonging to the Horseferry station is about fifty-seven miles; there being two separate mains in some of the broadest streets. The mains run east to Temple-bar; west to Brompton; north to Tottenham-court-road; south to the Asylum, branching in collateral directions.

The Brick-lane establishment supplies Cornhill and Wormwood-street; the east side of Tottenham-court-road, Holborn, and Islington. At this station, the mode of getting rid of the nuisance of the lime-water (in which the gas is purified), by evaporation, in cast-iron troughs, in lieu of passing it through the sewers into the Thames, was first introduced. The mains of this station extend forty miles.

The Curtain-road establishment supplies Whitechapel,

Crown-street, Finsbury-square, Kingsland-road, and Wellclose-square; extending through about twenty-five miles of main.

The whole annual consumption of coal by the three different stations of this company may be stated at 20,678 chaldrons, producing about 248 millions of cubic feet of gas annually. The whole number of lamps lighted by the company is 30,735, through an extent of 122 miles of main. The capital of the company is stated at £600,000, and their rental £125,977. The dividend paid, in 1822, was eight per cent.; the price of shares £70, being a premium of £20 upon the original shares of £50.

The City of London Gas-Light and Coke Company, Dorset-street. The mains of this company are fifty miles in length; and extend eastward to Somerset-street and Whitechapel; westward to Temple-bar; northward to St. John's Street; southward to Blackfriars' Bridge, subdivided into collateral branches. They light about 5,423 private lamps, and 2,413 public lamps. The annual consumption of coal is about 8,840 chaldrons. The rental is £30,839, and the capital, limited by act of parliament, to £200,000. The shares of £100 each are at a premium of £38.

The South London Company have two establishments, namely, Bankside and Wellington-street, in Great Surrey-street, Southwark. From the former station the mains extend about forty miles: eastward from Marsh-gate to Dockhead; southward to toll-gate, beyond Walworth; south-east nearly to the Green-man turnpike, Kent-road, and toward Mansion-house-street beyond Newington; northward over Southwark-bridge into Thames-street. The gasometer at the Wellington-street station communicates with same main as the gasometer at the Bankside station. The capital of this company is £120,000.

Their rental £14,962. These shares are at the same premium as the City of London company.

The Imperial Gas-Light and Coke Company, at their station in Great Cambridge-street, Hackney-road, had their buildings and erections in a state of great forwardness when Sir W. Congreve made his Report; three gasometers were nearly completed, and twenty miles and upwards of mains laid down. At their station at Pancras two cisterns for gasometers were in active preparation. The company chiefly lights the north-west part of the Metropolis. By a return made to Parliament last year (Parl. Pap. No. 116), it appears they had expended in the purchase of land, works, pipes, machinery, and other matters connected with their establishments, £539,723. Their rental amounted to £70,000; and the net profits had increased from £8,162, in 1824; to £27,452, in 1827.

Observations.—The first observation that arises on taking a general view of the gas-works in the Metropolis is the immense extent to which they have been carried since the year 1814, when there was only one gasometer in existence; whereas, at present, there are four great public companies established, having altogether forty-seven gasometers at work, capable of containing, in the whole, 917,940 cubic feet of gas, supplied by 1,315 retorts, consuming upwards of 33,000 chaldrons of coal in the year, and producing upwards of 41,000 chaldrons of coke. The whole quantity of gas generated annually being upwards of 397 millions of cubic feet, by which 61,203 private, and 7,268 public or street lamps, are now lighted in the Metropolis. In addition to the great companies, who are placed by legislative enactment under the control of the Secretary of State, there are several private companies, whose operations being of a more confined nature they are omitted in this statement.

It might have been imagined that the enormous quantity of coal consumed in the generation of gas would have greatly enhanced the price and increased the quantity of coals brought into the port of London. This, however, has not been the case; on the contrary, the increase in either of these is inconsiderable, owing to the compensation arising from the quantity of the surplus of coke produced, being in the proportion of 120 or 130, for every100 chaldron of coals carbonized. The fall in the price of oil is also another source of saving to the public.

The intermixture of the mains and services of different companies is a source of nuisance and inconvenience; for it frequently happens, in case of leakage, it is not known from whose pipes the damage proceeds. Hence, a hesitation is manifested as to which company should open the ground, and delay and inconvenience arise not only from the nuisance being thus prolonged, but from the more frequent breaking up of the pavement, arising from a double set of mains and services. Some of the companies are anxious for a limitation of districts. The latter charters, indeed, have proceeded on this principle: the Imperial Company, for instance, is limited to a particular district. The chief argument that could be adduced against it is the effect it might have on prices, by limited competition, and thereby giving a monopoly to the companies in their respective districts; but this might be obviated by regulating the price.

The Coal Gas Companies were subjected to a severe trial in opposing the attempt to intruduce oil gas, as a substitute and improvement on coal gas; the expenses of the different companies, in opposing the bill for the establishment of the London and Westminstor Oil Gas

Company amounted to £30,000.* The rapid progress of gas-lighting, from the time Murdoch exhibited at Birmingham coal gas, as a substitute for lamps and candles, affords a striking proof of the spirit of inquiry and intelligence which animates the community, and of the power of that spirit, aided by capital, successfully to advance a novel and useful invention. It is only twenty-four years since, Winsor, a Prussian, gave lectures, and exhibited gas-lights as a philosophical toy, at the Lyceum, and now there are upwards of 200 gas establishments in the country; and there is hardly a town, or manufactory, or place of public resort unembellished with this splendid illumination.†

FIRE-POLICE.

The fire-police of London consists of two parts; the one the parochial police, appointed by statute; the other, if they may be so considered, the establishment of the fire-offices. The first originated in the great fire of 1666, which was followed by many legislative enactments, in the reigns of Charles II. and Queen Anne, for the greater security of buildings, and which were improved and consolidated in the *Building-Act*, the 14 Geo. III. c. 78, extending to all buildings erected, or to be erected hereafter, in any parish within the Bills of Mortality, or the parishes of St. Mary-le-bone, St. Pancras, Chelsea, and Paddington.

These acts, besides regulating the mode of building houses in future, so as to render them safe, ornamental,

* Matthews's Origin, Progress, and Present State of Gas-Lighting, page 227.

† Mr. Williams, in his late work on "Subways," relates an anecdote strikingly illustrative of the untoward commencement of gas-lighting in the Metropolis. After the practicability and importance of lighting the streets with gas from coal had been ascertained, leave was obtained

and commodious, renders it obligatory on every parish to keep one large engine and one hand-engine, and also ladders to favour escapes. These are to be kept in known places; and, that every facility may be afforded with regard to water, it is incumbent on churchwardens to fix stop-blocks and fire-plugs, at convenient distances, upon all the mains of water-works within the parish; and to place a mark in the street where they are to be found, and to have a key or instrument ready to open such fire-plugs, so that the water may be accessible on the shortest possible notice: the penalty on the parish-officers, for neglect of these provisions, is £10. In case of fire, the turncock whose water comes first is entitled to 10*s.*; the person bringing the first parish-engine to 30*s.*, the second to 20*s.*, and the third to 10*s.*, to be paid by the parish; excepting in cases where chimneys are on fire, and then the expense falls ultimately on the person inhabiting the house or place where it originated. No reward is to be paid without the approval of an alderman or two common-councilmen in the City, and, elsewhere, a justice of the peace. On the breaking out of a fire, constables and beadles are required to repair to the spot with their staves, and to protect the sufferers from the depredation of thieves, and to assist in removing effects and in extinguishing the flames.

At a convenient distance all over the Metropolis are placed watch-houses, where a parochial constable attends, in rotation, every night, to receive disorderly and criminal persons, and to carry them before a magistrate next

from the Commissioners of Pavements of St. James's, to lay down pipes and light up Pall Mall. For a considerable time an immense concourse of people came from all parts to see these lights, which pleased the public exceedingly; but, after the street had been lit a few months, an order came from these sage Commissioners to take the posts, pipes, and all away, as a public nuisance!

morning. In each watch-house, also, the names of the turncocks and the places where engines are kept are to be found. This circumstance is mentioned for the information of strangers, to whom it is recommended, in case of fire, or any accident or disturbance requiring the assistance of the civil power, to apply immediately to the officer of the night, at the nearest watch-house, or to the watchman on the beat.

Application, also, on the breaking out of fires, may be made at the station-houses belonging to the several insurance-companies, and which are found in all parts of London. At each of these a fireman resides, and an engine and horses are promptly prepared to proceed to any place on the alarm of conflagration. In fact, the most efficient protective police is in the almost universal practice of insuring, and in the interest of the insurers to adopt every precaution for the prevention and ready extinction of fires. The parish engines have almost fallen into disuse; the large one is seldom kept in repair, and the smaller engine is only useful to take into chambers, or small apartments. Some years since, the *Sun* and *Phœnix* established a fire-patrol, to be in constant motion in the streets of the Metropolis, and give notice in case of the breaking out of fires: this establishment cost them £3000 per annum, and, the other offices declining to contribute towards the expense, and not being productive of any equivalent advantage, it was discontinued.

Some of the fire-offices are of very old establishment, and have been founded by royal charter or act of parliament, others by deed enrolled, and others give security upon land for the payment of losses. The rules by which they are governed are framed by the managers, and a copy given to every person at the time he insures; so that, by his acquiescence, he submits to their proposals, and is fully apprised of the terms by a compliance with which he will be entitled to indemnity. The firemen are all watermen, and protected from impressment by statute. They are paid by the job, at so much per hour, and receive, besides, gratuities for chimney alarms. Under 55 Geo. III. c. 184, a duty of 3*s.* per cent. per annum, on all property insured from fire, is payable to Government. The vast amount of property insured will appear from the following return to Parliament of the amount of duty paid into the Stamp-office, by the London fire-offices, for the year 1827 :—

	£	*s.*	*d.*
Sun	111,521	10	2
Phœnix	62,482	1	0
County	43,522	16	11
Royal Exchange	38,034	2	1
Protector	37,063	12	7
Guardian	29,063	14	11
Imperial	28,334	2	7
Globe	26,169	14	9
Atlas	20,898	16	3
Alliance	14,746	16	4
Union	15,705	7	1
British	15,464	3	3
Westminster	14,359	9	7
Hand-in-Hand	11,704	1	7
London	7,177	4	11
Palladium	4,721	5	9
Beacon	726	13	1

The chief seat of metropolitan fires is in the waterside district, where manufactories are most numerous, and where there are numerous old houses and buildings for which there has been no opportunity of erecting party-walls and complying with the other provisions of the Building Act. Mr. Wilkinson, a gentleman who had bestowed much pains in the inquiry, calculated, some years since, that, in London, there are, upon an average, every year, 35 serious fires, that five lives are lost, and that property is destroyed to the amount of £100,000. The average loss, both in lives and property, for the last ten years, has far exceeded this estimate. Half the fires in the Metropolis are supposed to be the work of incendiaries.

As regards the security of property, the fire-police is nearly unobjectionable; but, as respects the security of persons, there cannot be said to be any provision whatever, unless the ladders which the parishes are obliged to keep can be considered as such. The fire-offices, having no interest in saving life, it would be an important improvement to allow a reward to the firemen, or others, for every person rescued from the flames, and to render it obligatory, either on the parishes, or the fire-offices, to be provided with fire-escapes and such means of personal relief as science and experience had proved best adapted to the purpose. The importance of some public provision of this kind is self-evident in so vast a metropolis, where, in spite of every precaution, fires are almost of daily occurrence: during the last twelve months, twenty-three persons have lost their lives from inability to escape from buildings on fire—namely, seven in Red-Lion-street, five in Field-lane, three at Camberwell, one in Cross-street, and seven in Crutched-friars.

We shall conclude this section with a short notice of the laws in force for guarding the public against fires. By 7 Ann, c. 17, not above 10 gallons of turpentine are allowed to be boiled or distilled, at one time, in any place contiguous to other buildings, (except in houses already built in Southwark,) under a penalty of £100 and treble costs. By 14 Geo. III. c. 78, servants, carelessly setting fire to any house, are subject to a penalty of £100, or to be imprisoned eighteen months. By 12 Geo. III. c. 61, no one is to keep above 200lbs. of gunpowder, nor any person, not a dealer, above 50lbs. in the cities of London or Westminster, or within three miles thereof. By 3 Geo. IV. c. 55, s. 32, any vessel, above Blackwall (except a king's ship), having on board more than 25lbs. of gunpowder, the same may be seized. Section 36, of the same act, prohibits, under penalties, the master of any vessed, between Westminster-bridge and Blackwall, having on board guns loaded with ball, or discharging any gun, so loaded, between sun-set and sun-rise; it also prohibits the melting of pitch, tar, rosin, tallow, or other combustible matter aboard any vessel, while in the same line of river.

A knowledge of these enactments is sometimes of the utmost importance to those who insure against the risk of fire. At the great fire at the Custom-house, the quantity of gunpowder lodged there was such as precluded all legal claim to compensation from the fire-offices; actions were brought against all of them, and failed.

CHAPTER XIII.

BREWERS—LICENSED VICTUALLERS—HOTEL, COFFEE-HOUSE, AND TAVERN KEEPERS.

Historical Summary of Laws Regulating Inns and Alehouses.—Consequences of Free Trade in the sale of Ale and Spirits.—Inconsistent Objects sought to be reconciled by the Legislature.—Deductions applicable to future Legislation.—Inutility of Certificates and Recognizances for regulating Alehouses.—Increase of Public Houses, and corrupt Influence exercised over the Magistracy.—Brewers become the Mortgagees and Purchasers of Alehouses.—Its Consequences in deteriorating Beer and promoting Consumption of Spirits.—Proportion of Free Houses and Houses belonging to the London Brewers.—Different Conduct of a Brewer's Tenant and Free Publican.—Better Beer supplied to Free Houses.—Petition of the Inhabitants of London against the High Price and inferior Quality of Porter.—A Parliamentary Committee exonerate the eleven great Brewers, from the charge of mixing Drugs in their Beer, but not the lesser Brewers and Publicans.—Monopoly of Brewers as great in the Country as in the Metropolis.—Differences between the Trade of a Butcher or Baker and that of a Victualler, and the Necessity of a Magistrate's License for the latter.—Abuses in the Licensing System, and Petition of the Licensed Victuallers of the Metropolis.—Publicans do not possess a vested Right in their Trade and not Inviolable as private Property.—Proof of the exorbitant Profit of Brewers.—Decrease in the Consumption of Beer: not caused by National Poverty, but greater Sobriety in the People.—Unequal Operation of the Beer Duties.—Intermediate Beer Act.—Encouragement afforded to Retail Breweries.—Injurious tendency of the Alehouse Licensing Act of last Year.—Measure for Relief of Hotel-Keepers.—Wine-Rooms, Shades, and Oyster-Rooms.—Proposal to vest a Power of Licensing Houses, in particular Cases, in the Home Office. — Suggestions for encouraging the Retail Breweries.—Benefits resulting from the late Regulation of closing Alehouses at early Hours.—Effects of Saturday-night-drinking on the Working Classes, and Proposal for not allowing Alehouses and Spirit-shops to be opened, on Sunday, till after Morning Service.—Statement of the Consumption of Malt, Beer, Wine, Spirits, Tea, and Butchers' Meat, for the last Forty Years.—Number of different Kind of Brewers in England and Wales, and Quantity of Strong, Intermediate, and Table Beer brewed.—Number of Licenses granted at different Periods.

PRIOR to the reign of Edward VI. ale or tippling houses, or houses of public refreshment, were set up at the free will and pleasure of any person who thought fit to vest his property in that manner. In the old law-books it is held, "that, before that period, it was lawful for any one to keep an alehouse without license, for it was a means of livelihood which any one was free to follow: but, if it was disorderly kept, it was indictable as a common nuisance." Parliament, however, taking into consideration the mischief attendant on the abuse of this liberty, as affecting the morals of the people, gave, by statute, in the reign of Henry VII. a power to justices of the peace to suppress useless houses. The evil not being diminished by this law, by the 5th and 6th Edward VI., justices were empowered to *put away* common alehouses as they thought expedient; and none were to keep such houses in future but such as should be allowed in open session, or else by two justices, who are directed to take bond and surety by recognizance of the alehouse-keepers, for preserving good rule and order therein.

In the 1st James I. c. 9, an act passed which sets forth in the preamble, " that whereas the ancient, true, and principal use of inns, alehouses, and victualling-houses, was for the resort, relief, and lodging, of wayfaring people, travelling from place to place, and for such supply of the wants of such people as are not able by greater quantities to make provision of victual, and not meant for entertainment and harbouring of lewd, idle people, to spend and consume their money and their time in lewd and drunken manner;" it then proceeds to subject to penalties the keepers of alehouses who suffer people to tipple therein. The 7th James I. c. 10, disables an alehouse-keeper, convicted in these penalties, from keeping an alehouse for three years.

From the period of Edward VI. to the reign of James II. the Legislature, in imposing the necessity of a license had solely in view the question of police: all their regulations were principally directed to the good and orderly management of public-houses as connected with the preservation of public morals. Early, however, in the reign of William III. an act passed which produced the most important effects: it was for the avowed purpose of encouraging the distillation of British spirits; and, by this act, *all persons*, whether licensed or not, were authorized to distil and sell British spirits by retail, provided only the duties were paid. This law gave such an encouragement to the manufacture and consumption of spirits that it was found necessary to check their sale. By 12 and 13 William III. c. 11, s. 18, all persons were prevented selling distilled liquors, to be drank in their houses, unless licensed in the same manner as common alehouse-keepers.

At this period spirits were retailed by tradesmen and sold like any other commodity to be consumed off the premises: this increased the trade to such an extent, that, by 2 Geo. II. c. 17, a duty or £20 was imposed on the retailing license to sell spirits, which, for the first time, was directed to be *renewed yearly;* and by the 11th section of the same act, no license is to be granted to keep a common inn or alehouse, or to retail spirits, except at a general meeting of the justices of the peace, to be held for that purpose, on the 1st of September yearly, or within twenty-one days after. This statute is the origin of the present system of licensing public houses at a general annual meeting; and the object of which is set forth in this act, namely, that the magistrates may be truly informed as to the want of such public inns or alehouses, and the characters of persons applying for licenses for the same. The £20 duty on the license for the sale of spirits having given rise to a clandestine sale of them, injurious to the revenue, it was repealed, and a penalty of £10 imposed on all who should sell spirits in stables, sheds, or wheelbarrows, or in any other place than a dwelling-house.

But that this did not remedy the existing evils is apparent; for, by the 9 Geo. II. c. 23, called the Gin Act, no person is permitted to vend spirits in any manner in a less quantity than two gallons, without first taking out an annual license, for which he should pay £50; by the same act 20*s*. a gallon is laid on British spirits; and a license for the sale of them is prohibited, except granted to those who keep victualling-houses, inns, coffee-houses, alehouses, or brandy-shops; and who exercise no other trade whatever.

In these different enactments, the Legislature had two

objects in view not easily reconcileable :—first, to promote the distillation and sale of spirits, as a profitable source of revenue, as well as an encouragement to the agriculture of the kingdom ;—secondly, to prevent abuses in the consumption of spirits, arising from their cheapness, and the manner in which they were vended. The plan then adopted was, to prevent all private sale, to make the retail of spirits public, and to take the trade out of the hands of hucksters, barrowwomen, and salesmen, and place it in those of reputable tradesmen and housekeepers. That these were the intentions of Parliament, and that they failed, is certain ; for the heavy expense of the license, and the duties on the spirits gave such a bounty on illicit distillation and illegal sale as produced consequences the very opposite to those which the legislature contemplated ; the revenue was injured, and the trade thrown into the hands of those who took out no license and paid no duty. The testimony of contemporary writers, and the authority of parliamentary debates, show the dreadful excesses which these ill-advised laws produced ; when, at last, after a trial of seven years, an act passed by which the duty of £50 was taken off, and one of £20, imposed in its place ; and the duty on spirits from malt and corn was lowered from 20*s*. a gallon to 3*d*. : a spirit license is restricted as before to those who keep taverns, victualling-houses, coffee-houses, or alehouses, with a proviso, that nothing in the act shall be construed to enable any one to sell spirits by retail unless first licensed to sell ale or other spirits.

In the next year an explanatory act, the 17 Geo. II. c. 17, passed, in order to check a practice which had grown up, namely, of persons who came under the operation of the law, authorizing them to hold licenses, yet who separated the spirit-house from the alehouse, and opened and kept a shop for spirits in other situations: this practice is declared illegal, and a penalty of £10 affixed to the offence. Upon the authority of these provisions the magistrates of the Metropolis have exercised a power of taking away licenses from old established victuallers, who either turned their houses into shops more for the sale of spirits than that of malt liquors, or who held houses constructed in the form of a "spirit-shop" rather than an alehouse.

By 24 Geo. II. c. 40, s. 8, no person within the limits of the Head Office of Excise shall be licensed to retail spirituous liquors, unless occupying, as tenant, a tenement of the yearly value of £10 or upwards; or in any other part of the kingdom, unless he pay to church and poor.

The multiplicity of robberies, thefts, disorders, and licentiousness of every description which prevailed in the country gave rise to the 25 Geo. II. c. 36; and was intended, among other things, to restrain a practice very prevalent among publicans of having concerts, balls, and other gaieties at their houses; the second section prohibits the keeping, within the cities of London and Westminster, and twenty miles thereof, without license from the quarter sessions, any house, garden, or place for public dancing, music, or other public entertainment of the like kind, under a penalty of £100 on the keepers, and the houses to be deemed disorderly. Constables, or other persons authorized by warrant, may enter such places, and seize any person found therein, in order to their being dealt with according to law. Places licensed are directed to have an inscription over them, setting forth that they are licensed pursuant to the statute: but places licensed by the Crown, or lord-chamberlain, are excepted from the act.*

* The Licensing Act of last session, the 9 Geo. IV. c. 61, repeals a great many restrictions on the victualling trade; but having left un-

The 26 Geo. II. c. 31, after declaring the insufficiency of the existing laws to prevent disorders and abuses in victualling-houses, inns, &c. proceeds to make enactments requiring, from the applicant for a license, a certificate of good character, signed by the minister of the parish and certain inhabitants, and securities, by recognizance, that he shall be of good fame and sober life: the forfeiture of the recognizance is to be determined by the verdict of a jury; and a power is given, under such verdict, to disqualify an offender from selling beer or spirituous liquors for three years.

Under this statute the licensing of publicans continued to be regulated, without any important alteration, till the year 1822: and we have been induced to present the foregoing epitome of legislation in order to exhibit the opposite effects resulting from a free trade in intoxicating liquors and one placed under different degrees of municipal regulation. In departing from the ordinary rules of commercial freedom, and in subjecting individuals to be restricted in the manner their property should be employed, for their own profit, the Le-

touched the 25 Geo. II. (and also 32 Geo. III. c. 59, affecting hotel-keepers), and it being common in the Metropolis for publicans, without a music-license, to have balls, concerts, and other entertainments at their houses, the informers set to work, during the winter, to reap an abundant harvest from the penalties. From one unfortunate victualler they modestly demanded £3,600 " of lawful money of Great Britain," he having, contrary to the statute, on sundry occasions, tolerated, in his house, room, garden, or other place, divers posture-makings, jigs, and violin-scrapings. Upwards of 400 actions were instituted, by low attorneys, in a short time, and more than two-thirds compromised. In some instances £20, and even £30, were given to escape from the nets of the fraternity. The privileges of the lord-chamberlain not being infringed by the statute, and as a license from the king's sergeant trumpeter may be obtained for a trifle, many licensed victuallers avail themselves of this protection.

gislature clearly had in view,—first, the advantage and security of the revenue against the unlicensed sale of exciseable liquors; secondly, the conservation of public peace and morals. From their endeavours to attain these ends, two conclusions of considerable importance, at the present period, may be deduced, and which will serve to shew the probable tendency of future legislation on the subject. The first is, that when the trade was free it was productive of so much immorality and disorder, that it became indispensable, as a matter of police, to place it under magisterial control. The second is, that where habits of drinking have become too prevalent, an increase of duty, either on the commodity itself, or on the retailer's license, may, instead of checking the evil, only be productive of smuggling and other illegal practices.

Before adverting to the alterations introduced by the licensing act of 1822, and subsequent statutes relating to the manufacture and sale of beer and spirits, it will be proper to give some account of the state of the victualling trade prior to the 3 Geo. IV. and which still, in a great measure, continues, both as affecting the mode of licensing by magistrates, the monopoly of the sale of the common beverage of the people by great brewers; the security of property vested in public-houses; and the protection afforded to the public against the imposition of a deteriorated and unwholesome article of general consumption.

The securities of certificate and recognizance, provided in the 26 Geo. II. against the admission of improper characters as publicans, proved of little practical utility. In the Metropolis it was a common practice for the beadles of the different parishes, for a small gratuity, to obtain the signatures of the number of inhabitants required by law; the certificate so signed was then delivered to the high constable, and by him to the clerk of the justices, who laid it before them for their approval: all the parties, between the applicant for a license and the magistracy, had mostly a private interest in forwarding or thwarting the application; the beadle being influenced by the amount of his gratuity; the high-constable (probably a coal-merchant) from the prospect of the publican's custom; and the justice's clerk, in some divisions, was actually the retained agent to one of the great breweries.* The recognizance degenerated into mere form; magistrates have been in the commission thirty years, and never knew an instance of a recognizance being estreated.

Under this system public houses fell into the hands of the most disreputable characters, and they were multiplied without regard either to public morals, justice to the old-established houses, or the wants of the neighbourhood for such accommodation. In some streets four or five public houses have been opened within a few doors of each other. The Police Committee, in 1817, found, in High-street, Shadwell, one public house to every twelve other houses; in New Gravel-lane, in the same district, they were established in the proportion of one to eight; in Lower Shadwell in the ratio of one to six; in Norton Falgate there were twenty-four to a population of 1752, being as one public-house to every seventy-three persons, including men, women, and children; and, in Whitecross-street, in the distance of

* One of the great brewing firms of the Metropolis informed the Police Committee, in 1817, that they employed Mr. Thompson, one of the clerks to the justices of the Tower Division, as their agent, to forward their interests with regard to licenses. The same firm retained, with similar views, Mr. Lush, a clerk in one of the police offices, and to apprise them and lend his aid when informations were laid against their tenants.

300 yards, there were twenty-three public-houses.* Many of these houses were of the lowest description: they were flash-houses, and the resort of the profligate and abandoned of both sexes. Owing to the corrupt influence acting on magistrates, licenses for houses, in neighbourhoods where actually wanted and petitioned for by the inhabitants, were often refused, while those petitioned against, as nuisances and unnecessary, were granted.

Of late years, a practice has grown up for brewers to become the owners, purchasers, or equitable mortgagees of the leases of public-houses; nearly one-half of the victualling-houses in the Metropolis are held in this manner; and it cannot be doubted that, under the confined and restricted power which the public at large possess of employing their capital in the trade of victualling-houses, this system is very prejudicial to the interests of the community. The consequence of this monopoly is, that the beer is of an inferior quality, and that the poor and middling classes of the community, living in those districts, justly complain of the badness of the commodity they are compelled to drink, no other being in the market, and are driven thereby to the use of spirits. In houses where good beer is sold, the consumption of spirits is trifling, but, when beer becomes bad, the consumption of spirits increases. In short, these results uniformly follow, namely, that where the beer is deteriorated, either by the effect of monopoly, or from the result of the demands which the Government make, in the nature of revenue, from the manufactured article, or from adulteration, the immediate and invariable effect has been an increased demand for spirituous liquors.

* Parl. Report on the Police of the Metropolis, Sess. 1817, p. 10.

Mr. Barclay informed a Parliamentary Committee that, in his trade, which is the greatest in London, one-eighth of the houses they served were their own property; that about three-eighths of the remainder were engaged to them by the advance of money, leaving four-eighths free. In the Messrs. Whitbread and Co.'s one-seventh are their own houses, or held on lease, and about three-sevenths free trade; and in that of Messrs. Truman and Hanbury about the same proportion. But, in order to show the zeal with which some brewers push the system of monopoly, Mr. Hanbury, speaking of his partner, Mr. Aveling, said that no plot of ground had been laid out for building without his obtaining immediate notice of it, and, in cases which he thought advisable, without his purchasing the most eligible spot for a public-house, or at least obtaining for himself the offer of it. Many houses, not under the control of the brewers, are the property of the malster or spirit-merchant, by whose agency the seignorial powers of the former are as effectually maintained as if they held the direct proprietary: the brewer binds his houses to the spirit-merchant, who, in his turn, performs the same service for the brewer; and the malster, from similar interests, has obvious motives for directing the custom of any house under his influence.

Great difference is observable in the conduct of a brewer's tenant and the occupier of a free house, the latter being more tenacious of his character, for upon that he can only depend; whereas, the tenant of the brewer is generally careless of reputation, trusting to the influence of his landlord to secure to him the continuance of his license; add to this, a landlord is frequently a magistrate, and, though the law prevents his sitting on the bench on the licensing-days, yet his weight and authority is still there, and it is through his influence with his brother magistrates that he supports the credit of his houses.

It is obvious that, in the Metropolis, there will of necessity be found many disorderly public-houses, and that a constant struggle may be considered as taking place between the magistrates in suppressing these houses and the many causes that exist to create them. It is then the union between the magistrates whose duty it is to put down those places of low resort, which, for their superior infamy, are called *flash-houses,* with those who have a direct interest to promote them, that is so injurious to the public. Without meaning anything invidious towards so respectable a body of men, it is yet evident that brewers and distillers and all who deal in wine and spirits make fortunes in proportion to the sale of their respective commodities; and it is known that some of the most profitable and worst-conducted houses either belong to brewers, or are held in mortgage by them. The disorderly and licentious conduct of these houses does not insure the loss of the license; but that if, at last, from the notorious infamy of the parties complained against, the magistrates are compelled to interfere, the least possible punishment is inflicted, the tenant is shifted, a real or fictitious transfer is made, and a new landlord takes possession, to follow the old practices in the same house with aggravated misconduct; the maxim is, "the house, being brick and mortar, cannot be guilty of any crime," and the old system is revived with the same profit as before.

The interest of the brewers in public-houses not only interferes with magisterial regulation, but also limits the benefit the public ought to derive from open competition in the sale of beer. In London, within the limits of the Head Office, there are 4397 victuallers, of whom only 31 brew their own beer, nearly the whole of the remainder being served by the eleven great breweries. As a majority of the victuallers are the dependents or mere servants of the brewers, they have no option in the purchase of the commodity they retail, they must receive such beer as their landlord thinks proper to send them, and the consumer is placed in similar bondage, as he cannot conveniently go out of his neighbourhood for an article of constant use. Among the brewers themselves there is not likely to be any rivalry beneficial to the public; the smallness of their number is favourable to a good understanding among them, and they have obvious motives for acting in concert. They accordingly meet to fix and lower prices at pleasure, and quality, not price, is the only object of competition. But quality can only be an object when a publican is opposed by the house of another brewer, or a free house. In those streets, hamlets, and parishes in which the public-houses are the property of the same brewer there is no competition of any kind, and the consumers are entirely at his mercy, and in such districts, of which there are many in the Metropolis and vicinity, the beer is universally found to be of a very inferior quality. The only obstacle to the entire monopoly of the brewers is the free houses; the owners of these can choose their market; and it is constantly observed that the brewers supply houses of this description with a superior liquor to that the proprietary houses are compelled to take.

On the 10th of March, 1818, the inhabitants of London and the vicinity presented a petition, containing 14,000 signatures, to the House of Commons, complaining of the high price and inferior quality of beer; and a Committee of the House was appointed to inquire into the truth of these allegations. The Committee, in their Report, do not admit there is any evidence of the principal brewers realizing more than a fair profit on the capital employed in their trade; but it is allowed that the property invested by loans and mortgages creates a necessity of selling beer at such a price as may secure a trade-interest on the money advanced. After calling for the officers of excise, and making every inquiry into the truth of the imputation, they entirely exonerate the eleven great brewers from the charge of mixing with their porter any deleterious ingredient; and they affirm "that their beer has been and now is composed of malt and hop, legal colouring, and finings only."* But the conduct of the lesser brewers and publicans is not so innoxious, as appears from the following extract:—

"But your Committee must, in justice to the petitioners, state, that they do find, both from the Excise-returns and from the seizing officers, that drugs, of a very *nauseous, and some of a very pernicious quality*, are still vended by persons, as a trade, and bought by the lesser brewers and publicans; by both of them infused into their vats, and mixed in their barrels respectively, and in that state retailed to the public. That this practice is not confined to the Metropolis, but extends to the country; and that travellers, from London houses, have been known to possess and offer cards, containing a list of articles, together with instructions adapted to the adulteration of beer. It is evident that the use of such articles by the lesser brewers and publicans, together with the practice of both, in many instances, (as proved by the Excise-returns,) of mixing table-beer with strong beer, must have a tendency to bring the general beverage of the eleven great breweries also into a degree of discredit; to excite distrust in the minds of the public; and strongly to induce them to lay their claims before the legislature, without being able distinctly to point out the real author of their grievances."—*Report on Public Breweries, p.* 3.

* Report of a Committee of the House of Commons on Public Breweries, vol. iii. p. 3, of Parl Paps. Sess. 1818.

The Committee reprobate, in strong terms, the practice of the great brewers, furnishing free publicans with better liquor than their own tenants; and Mr. Barclay and another principal brewer admitted, in their evidence, that brewers becoming the proprietors of public houses would inevitably tend to deteriorate the beer, and the ultimate injury of their own trade. These consequences are so apparent they scarcely require proof; that the brewer will manufacture a cheaper and inferior article to be retailed in houses where he is exposed to no competition, every one must be convinced, and every one who has had an opportunity of comparing either the beer, wines, or spirits, vended at a free house and a brewer's house so circumstanced, must have experienced such to be the case. There is, in fact, no more comparison between the beverage retailed under such different circumstances, than there is in the getting up of the *Morning Advertiser* (a product of the same monopoly), and the daily journals open to competition, and which depend for their success solely on the superior *materiel* and ability with which they are conducted.

Bad as the system is in the Metropolis, it is still worse in some parts of the country. In Portsmouth there were, a short time since, 231 public houses; of these 168 were in the hands of brewers, 34 in the hands of spirit-merchants, and 29 were free houses. In King's Lynn there were 68 public houses, all in the hands of the corporation or of brewers. In Brighton there were 66; of which 55 were in the hands of brewers. In Watford, St. Alban's, and Reading, all the public houses were in the hands of the brewers.

That the existing system has produced many evils is sufficiently evident, from the returns laid before parliament last session. It appears that in sixty collections of excise into which England and Wales (London included) are divided, there are 49,500, publicans, of whom 23,000, being one-half the country publicans, brew their own beer, the rest being served by brewers. These collections may be included in six districts, in three of which the population drink brewers' beer, and in the remainder victuallers' beer. In the London district, as before observed, there are 4,397 publicans, of whom only 31 brew their own beer. The second district comprehends Kent, Sussex, Surrey, Hants, Berks, Middlesex, Hertfordshire, Cambridgeshire, Norfolk, and Essex, in which there are 9,984 publicans, of whom only 820 brew their beer at home. The third district comprises Northumberland, Westmoreland, Cumberland, and Durham, and extends across the kingdom to Manchester and Liverpool: in this there are 5,871 publicans, of whom only 587 brew at home. Of the whole 20,252 publicans only 1438 brew at home. These vast districts, containing between four and five millions of people, are supplied by 1472 brewers out of London, and 99 in it; making but 1571 in all. In the three remaining districts, comprising part of Gloucestershire, Herefordshire, Worcestershire, Salop, all Wales, part of Somersetshire, Lancashire, Devonshire, &c. there are about 14,892 publicans, and 12,543 brew at home. The beer so supplied is decidedly the best, as the trade is not injured by monopoly.

Leaving, as indisputable, the injurious operation of the brewers' proprietary in public-houses, both in the Metropolis and the country, we shall next advert to the operation of the present mode of licensing publicans. The abuses that have crept into the system, and the difficulty of devising an adequate remedy, are such that it was in contemplation, by the framers of the licensing act of last year, to throw the trade open and abolish licensing altogether; but the magistrates made such strong representations on the disorders and mischiefs that would ensue, the intention was ultimately abandoned. Between the trade of a baker or butcher, for example, and that of a victualler, no one can deny there exist substantial distinctions; the former may be safely left to be regulated by their own interest, both as to their number, local situation, and mode of conducting business; but as regards the latter, the case is wholly different. The publican deals in commodities to be consumed on the premises; they are of a nature tending to produce intoxication; they are vended early and late, and collect men together in companies. The mere fact of houses being places of nocturnal resort, and of a promiscuous assemblage, is sufficient to bring them within the jurisdiction of a special police. In the theatres, and other places of public amusement, individuals cannot assemble in numbers without being liable to disorder; and the presence of an officer is requisite for the maintenance of the peace; but how much more necessary is some analogous precaution in public houses, where strangers not only assemble, but often also in a state of unusual excitement. Experience, too, has demonstrated the necessity of magisterial control. Formerly, as we have seen, the publican carried on his trade without a license; but the disorders which grew out of an unrestricted trade were such that the Legislature was obliged to interfere. It is not, however, the public peace only, but the public accommodation, that often requires a judicious system of licensing. In many situations the convenience of travellers, or the wants of a small neighbourhood call for the establishment of an inn; but, owing to the limited return no one would venture his capital in the undertaking, without a protection against competition. Throwing the trade open would multiply alehouses beyond the wants of the public, and thereby deteriorate beer more than the monopoly of the brewers; every house almost would be an ale-shop; their numbers would make them an impoverished and disreputable class; and the diminutive sale of each would render the liquor undrinkable —vapid in winter, and sour in summer.

However much, therefore, the abuses of the licensing system may be regretted, we apprehend, it had better be reformed (if possible) than abolished. The evils now complained of are,—1. The power of the brewers to procure licenses for their houses to the exclusion of other candidates, either by their influence as magistrates, or by their connexions with magistrates. 2. Arising from the same influence the difficulty of punishing the misconduct of publicans, and maintaining public order and morals. 3. The insecurity of property, and the vast amount of it placed at the arbitrary and almost irresponsible disposal of justices of the peace. 4. The deterioration in the common beverage of the people, the consequence of monopoly in the beer trade, and its injurious effect on public health and consumption. On the two former propositions we have already enlarged, and on the remainder we shall only submit a few brief observations.

The number of publicans in England and Wales is 49,359, and the amount of property invested in their trade has been estimated, by Mr. Buxton, at fifty millions.* Over this number of persons, and over this mass of property, the magistrates have almost absolute power, which may be exercised as their interests, caprice, or personal feelings dictate. By their fiat property, to which long possession has given at least a

* Hansard's Parliamentary Debates, Sess. 1822, vol. vii. p. 1694.

plausible right, and upon which the support of a family depends, may be suddenly rendered comparatively valueless; while, on the other hand, their sovereign permission to hang out a sign, may render a mere hovel as valuable as a gentleman's estate. They may give a license to one of the most unfit, or refuse it to the most fit, person possible. They may continue a license to some person who has had it but a twelvemonth, and who, during that time, has made his home a nuisance to the whole neighbourhood; or they may take away a license from a house to which it has been attached for a century, and the enjoyment of which has not only been attended by no evil, but has been productive of great public benefit;—and all this they can do without the shadow of control.* That such unlimited and almost irresponsible power should be exercised without abuse it would be contrary to all experience of human nature to suppose; and that it is abused there are abundant examples to prove. An individual has been deprived of the license to a house for the lease of which, only a year before, he had given £1000, merely because he had changed his brewer and coal-merchant. Houses for which £4000 have been paid have suddenly had their license taken away, even when the minister, parish-officers, and principal inhabitants have petitioned against it.† A license for a house, eligibly situated, both for travellers and the neighbourhood, has been refused, while one has been granted to another in the vicinity possessing none of these recommendations, but which happened to be the property of a person who had a better understanding with the clerk of the licensing justices.‡ A dentist has got a license for a house,

* Mr. Brougham, House of Commons, Feb. 7, 1828.

† Report on the Police of the Metropolis, 1817, p. 20.

‡ Mr. Beaumont's Petition to the House of Commons.

though another public-house was close by, apparently for no other reason than he was a particular friend of an influential magistrate. Lastly, a house has been sold for £1100, and immediately after, when a license had been obtained for it, by the intervention of a great brewer, it has been estimated to be worth £3000.*

In 1816, the licensed victuallers of the Metropolis, to the number of 2200, petitioned the House of Commons against the arbitrary power exercised by magistrates of granting or refusing licenses to old established victuallers, and prayed that better security might be afforded for the enjoyment of their property. In the able Parliamentary Report, on the Licensing System in 1817, to which we have often referred, this power of the justices is justly brought into question and treated as a recent assumption, unsanctioned by the existing law. The observations of the Committee are so important that we beg leave to transcribe them.

"The power assumed of late years by the magistrates to deprive an established house of its license, is in no statute given them by express words; on the contrary, when a license was to be suspended even for three years, it was to be done by the verdict of a jury, upon proofs of misconduct, and forfeiture of recognizance being brought before them. When, however, the legislature looked to revenue from the licensing of public-houses they were directed to be renewed annually, and in this manner the magistrate has assumed an authority of refusing to grant such license, with which it is by no means clear the law ever intended to invest him. The primary object in giving to justices a controlling power over all tippling-houses, was to prevent

* Petition of John Brown, presented by Mr. Huskisson to the House of Commons, May 6, 1822.

improper people from keeping them and to limit their number, as heretofore, by the common law. As long as they were not disorderly, no power centred in the magistracy to lessen their number or to regulate their trade. The legislature, in course of time, thought fit to collect, through this medium, a considerable revenue, by imposing stamp-duties on the various licenses to retail ale and beer, wine and spirituous liquors, which has gradually increased from 1*s.* in the reign of Queen Ann, to £15 or £20, and to make this tax annual, an annual license was directed to be taken. This then was the reason why the power of annually licensing was given to justices; but the legislature never contemplated that magistrates would assume the power of considering old licensed houses as new ones; or that without trial, without inquiry, without hearing the parties, without a conviction of any sort, with not even alleged misconduct, they should be able to deprive, by their sole will and pleasure, persons of their property, to which long enjoyment had given them a right, and upon which their existence and that of their families depended. The result of this system has been to lessen the security of all property vested in the trade, to drive people of capital out of it, and to have the tendency of replacing these persons of credit by adventurers, who will look to other sources of obtaining licenses, than the fair one of good character."—Parl. Report, p. 20.

Whether the power of magistrates to deprive old or new established houses of their licenses has been lawfully exercised does not form a question so important as might at first be supposed. The security of a victualler's property would not be greatly augmented, if the power annually to withhold his license were taken away; unless, at the same time, the power to grant new licenses was recinded. The value of a publican's trade consists as much in being protected from competition as in the perpetuity of his license. Magistrates by opening new houses in opposition to old ones may as effectually undermine their value, as by depriving them of their license. In fact, this is the way the justices in Wiltshire proceed when they wish to open a monopoly; and it would be well if the example were more frequently followed. If the brewers in that county have got a monopoly of licenses in any one district, the magistrates immediately grant a new license, by which the monopoly is destroyed. Hence the power of appeal in all cases afforded to publicans by the Licensing Act of last session, is not so great a boon as was contemplated; their bondage to the magistrates, resulting as much from the power to open new houses as to withhold the licenses of old-established ones.

That a special jurisdiction should be exercised over publicans, for the purposes of police, we have before explained the utility, and all that they have a right to expect is that the power granted for this end should not be partially, oppressively, or corruptly exercised. This is all they can justly demand. The Legislature is too wise to venture on any sudden changes in the property of victuallers, or property of any other description, no matter how acquired; but it is quite unlikely it will ever allow that publicans possess a *vested right* in their trade, or that capital embarked therein can be assimilated in its pretensions to private property. Such an assumption is wholly indefensible. Ever since the reign of Edw. VI. inns and alehouses, except as places of refreshment for travellers, have been considered only tolerated nuisances, always liable to be abated; and, with the ordeal of a yearly license to undergo, to remind them of their precarious tenure, it is inconceivable how it could enter into the minds of men, even in a dream, that their calling was a freehold inheritance which could not be lawfully disturbed. So long as the trade of victualler is conducted conformably to the conditions under which it has been placed, they are entitled to protection and exemption from acts of partial oppression and interference; but that their interests, as publicans, shall be placed in competition with the public health and morals, (to which it has always been the policy to make them subservient,) is a position that can never be countenanced.

The disadvantages sustained under the existing system deprive the community of all interest in supporting any extravagant pretensions either of brewers or their vassals, the licensed victuallers. Were the beer-trade free, the profit on capital embarked in it could never rise above the average profit of other trades; but, restricted as the trade is in the Metropolis and many parts of the country, the consumer has no security against exorbitant price, or, which is the same thing, being compelled to take an inferior article. Owing to the constant fluctuations in the price of malt and hop, it is impossible to say at what price beer ought to have been generally sold during the last twenty years; but there is one collateral incident connected with the trade which demonstrates that beer of a better quality might have been supplied at a fair profit. The fact to which we allude is the circumstance of the free houses being furnished with better liquor than proprietary houses. Now, it is quite obvious, the brewers would not supply the free houses at a loss, they obtain what they consider a remunerating profit: but, in dealing with their own tenants, they are not content with a remunerating profit, they seek an exorbitant one, by taking advantage of their monopoly in compelling them to vend an article of less costly manufacture and production.

The returns of the Excise-Office to Parliament show that the beverage of the people has been undergoing deterioration for the last forty years, and that more beer has been made out of a less quantity of malt. The average consumption of malt, in the five years, from 1819 to 1823, was less than in the five years from 1792 to 1796; though the average quantity of beer brewed in the former period exceeded the latter by one million of barrels.* In short, the brewers have found it advantageous gradually to reduce the quantity of malt and hop in their beer, until at length it is no longer that liquor of which Boniface once declared that he could eat, drink, and sleep upon it, and which was also clothing to him.

How far this deterioration may have affected the consumption, and driven the people to the use of other liquors, it is impossible to affirm. It is, however, most extraordinary, that no more beer is consumed now than 26 years since, though the population has increased 36 *per cent.* We are not inclined to ascribe this result altogether to the decline in the quality of beer, nor to the increase in the poverty of the consumers, because such conclusions would be unsupported by facts. Unquestionably, as a nation, we have become more *sober* than formerly, and the fashion of drinking to excess has abated. This change is indicated by the altered character of diseases, in the diminished mortality from fevers, consumptions, dropsies, and other disorders usually supposed to supervene from hard drinking. Except in the increased consumption of gin, during the last four years, caused by its cheapness, and the vast number of Irish immigrants, there has been a diminution in the consumption of intoxicating liquors, in wine and spirits, as well as beer: and that this has not resulted from national

* Statistical Illustrations of the British Empire, 3d edit. p. 73.

poverty, but a change of manners is evinced by the increased consumption of other articles in lieu of them—namely, of tea, bread, and butchers' meat.*

Beer has been always considered the national beverage of Englishmen; and it is truly an object of public policy to prevent the substitution in its place of any less wholesome liquor. The heavy tax, however, cannot fail to have this tendency, and promote the sale of spirits. It is a tax which bears with peculiar hardship on the poor, and very slightly on the rich; for a duty of 20*s*. a quarter is paid on malt, besides another duty of 10*s*. a barrel on strong beer, 5*s*. on intermediate, and 2*s*. on table-beer.† Supposing three barrels to the quarter, a duty of 50*s*. is paid by the consumer, who purchases it at the retail price. Three-fifths of the tax are avoided by those who brew their own beer. The rich, who brew their own beer for domestic use, pay only 20*s*. where 50*s*. is paid by the poor. Not only is the tax unequal as regards the rich and the poor, but also as regards different districts of the kingdom. In many parts of the country the cheapness of fuel and lowness of rent afford facilities for brewing which do not exist in the Metropolis; where the mode of living and the dearness of coal (caused by local and public tax), leave the inhabitants no alternative but the consumption of brewers' beer: and to this circumstance may be partly attributed the greater prevalence of spirit drinking in London.

* See statements drawn from public documents at the end of this chapter for a confirmation of the facts mentioned in the text.

† These are not exactly the duties payable on beer; under 6 Geo. IV. c. 58, they were nominally reduced to accommodate them to the new imperial gallon, which is of less capacity than the old standard ale gallon, of 282 cubic inches, nearly in the proportion of 59 to 60. The excise-duty on strong beer is 9*s*. 10*d*. per barrel; on intermediate 4*s*. 11*d*. on table beer 1*s*. 11½*d*.

We have thus endeavoured to place before the reader the more important facts connected with the history and present state of the beer-trade in the Metropolis. It only remains shortly to advert to the recent measures of the Legislature, intended to ameliorate the evils which have been shown to result from the brewster-monopoly—from undue and corrupt influence in the licensing of publicans—from the insecurity of the victuallers' property—and from vending a weak and unwholesome beverage for general consumption. Government has been actuated by the most praiseworthy motives, and if more effective measures have not been introduced, it may be ascribed to the difficulty of grappling with abuses of enormous magnitude, and of interfering with property, which, however hurtful in its management to the public, could not be suddenly disturbed without being productive of extensive loss and suffering.

The Licensing Act of 1822, though introduced by a member fully master of the subject, did not effect any substantial improvement: its more important objects were to lessen the influence of brewers in obtaining licenses, and to guard against the admission of improper characters as publicans, by requiring a certificate of fitness from the parish where the applicants had resided the preceding six months; the provisions for both these purposes did not prove of great practical utility.

Ministers, however, were convinced of the policy of opening the beer-trade, and, in the year following, introduced the 4 Geo. IV. c. 51, to allow the brewing and sale of beer of an *intermediate strength*, between strong beer and table beer, subject to a proportionate excise-duty. Under this act, beer brewed of the proportion of not less than five barrels, nor more than five and a half barrels, from one quarter of malt, is liable to a duty of 5*s.* per barrel. Such beer, if sold in any quantity of nine gallons, not to be charged to the consumer at more than at the rate of 27*s.* per barrel, and so in proportion for any greater or less quantity than a barrel; and, if sold in quantities *less* than nine gallons, not to be charged more, under a penalty of £50, than at the rate of 10*d.* per gallon, and so in proportion for any quantity greater or less than a gallon. Persons entering to brew beer under this act, having any other beer of greater or less strength, to be charged with a duty of 10*s.* per barrel; and using any other ingredient in the brewing of such intermediate beer than water, malt, hop, and yeast, subjects the beer to be forfeited, and a penalty of £200. When malt or hop rises in price, the Treasury may authorise an advance of the price of intermediate beer. The beer may be retailed on the premises, but not consumed there, nor in any yard, orchard, or outhouse adjoining, under a penalty of £100. By section 12 no intermediate beer brewery is to be set up within the distance of *one hundred yards*, in a direct line from any licensed brewery of beer, ale, or porter, established three months preceding; nor within *twenty yards* of a licensed victualler.

If the limitations of the last section were adopted from a reluctance to invade the *soke* of the great brewers, they might, we think, have been spared; the large capital and long-established trade of these monopolists afford sufficient advantages in defending their seignorial rights; and, by furnishing their houses with better liquor for a season, they possess a ready resource for meeting and crushing any new competition in their neighbourhood. The act, however, is an extremely judicious measure, affording to working people and others some of the advantages of private brewing, by enabling them to have constantly in their houses a barrel of cheap, wholesome, and refreshing beverage; in the consumption of which there is no fear of swallowing *coculus Indicus, quassia, nux vomica,* or other deadly ingredient. Could the duty be lowered, so as to admit of a greater proportion of malt and hop in the manufacture, it would be still more palatable to the consumer.

In 1824, the provisions of an additional Beer Bill were suggested by Mr. Brougham, and adopted by ministers, in the 5 Geo. IV. c. 54, and was intended to promote the retail of strong beer for the use of families. As the retail brewer was likely to compete with the licensed victualler, he has been placed under particular restrictions. He must first obtain an excise license; his beer must not be consumed upon the premises, under a penalty of £100; it must be retailed from the place where it has been brewed, unless such place be out of a city or market-town, in which case he may enter *one* house, room, cellar, or other place for retailing his beer in any *one* adjoining city or market-town. No other kind of beer than that charged to the duty of strong beer is to be retailed, nor shall the brewer consume any less quantity than 16 bushels of malt at one brewing; and, by a subsequent Act, 9 Geo. IV. c. 68, he is not permitted to retail his beer at a later hour than ten o'clock in the evening, and earlier than four o'clock in the morning.

Both the Intermediate Beer Act and the Retail Brewers' Act have contributed to the beneficial purposes for which they were intended; they have raised a little opposition, in most parts of the Town, to the monopoly of the great brewers, and the public are not confined, as formerly, to take either the slender beverage of the overgrown houses or none at all.

The Alehouse Licensing Act, of last year, 9 Geo. IV. c. 61, cannot be reckoned among measures likely to open the beer trade; it is calculated more for the benefit of the brewer, distiller, and victualler than the community. Among the new provisions of this statute it extends the period for granting licenses, and requires greater publicity in the transfer of licenses. The principle of exclusion, where magistrates are supposed to have any interest in licenses, is extended. In every case an appeal is allowed against an act of the magistrates, and, to secure a more impartial decision, the appeal is to be to the county at large. The necessity of publicans obtaining certificates before they apply for licenses, and finding sureties for maintaining order in their houses, is dispensed with; both which obligations, it was alleged, had been found vexatious to the parties, and of no security to the public. A great many statutes and parts of statutes, intended to prevent idleness, drunkenness, and low gaming, in public-houses, are repealed; among others, 30 Geo. II. under which publicans, permitting journeymen, labourers, servants, or apprentices to game in their houses, are subject to a penalty of 40*s.*, and, upon a subsequent offence, to £10. Had this act been framed by a committee of brewers and distillers only, it could not have been better calculated to promote their interests, and less for the benefit of society.*

More regard for the public welfare was evinced in the protection afforded to *Hotel-keepers*, who, from overlooking the provisions of an act of parliament, had become the prey of informers. It is known that houses

* The statutes repealed by the Licensing-Act are 5 and 6 Edw. VI. c. 25; 1 Jac. I. c. 9; 4 Jac. I. c. 4 and 5; 7 Jac. I. c. 10; 21 Jac. I. c. 7; 1 Car. I. c. 4; 3 Car. I. c. 3; of 9 Geo. II. c. 23, ss. 14, 15, 20; of 24 Geo. II. c. 40, s. 24; of 26 Geo. II. c. 13, s. 12; 26 Geo. II. c. 31; of 28 Geo. II. c. 19, s. 2; of 29 Geo. II. c. 12, ss. 23, 24; of 30 Geo. II. c. 24, s. 14; of 5 Geo. III. c. 46, ss. 20, 21, 22; 32 Geo. III. c. 59; of 38 Geo. III. c. 54, s. 13; 39 Geo. III. c. 86; of 48 Geo. III. c. 143, ss. 7, 10; and of 4 Geo. IV. c. 125, ss. 1–6. [Middlesex Local Act.]

for the accommodation of strangers, which bear the name of "hotel," in contradistinction to "coffee-house," are the class of London inns to which individuals and families resort who wish to be comfortable and not annoyed by the drinking and promiscuous society found at the generality of taverns and victualling-houses. The hotels thus necesssary to the enjoyment of respectable persons coming for short periods to the Metropolis, continued, for a number of years, in the practice of supplying their customers with wine, &c. under licenses from the Board of Excise. This was contrary to the 32 Geo. III. c. 59, s. 11. which prohibits any person selling wine by retail, to be drank in their houses, unless they have a magistrate's license to sell ale and beer in the same house. And it expressly declares, that justices and other officers shall exercise the same power over such retailers of wine as they do over persons licensed to sell ale and beer. The object of which provision had been to prevent any person becoming a retailer of wine, to be consumed on the premises, without having first entered into such securities, for the maintenance of order, as were required of the publican. The licensed victualler certainly sustained an unfair competition by the non-enforcement of the act; since a vast number of persons had opened *wine-rooms, shades, and oyster-rooms,* in the Metropolis, for the sale of wine and spirits to be drank on the premises, though they had not a justice's license for the sale of beer or other exciseable liquor. For the protection of these no legislative interference could be reasonably expected; but the regular hotel-keepers formed a class of an entirely different description. Accordingly, the hotel-keepers, under the 9 Geo. IV. c. 46, were discharged from the penalties they had incurred under the 32 Geo. III., and two or more justices were empowered, *if they thought fit,* (a puzzling phrase this at the Mansion-house and Bow-street,) to grant a license to any hotel-keeper, who had kept an hotel from Jan. 1, 1828, to keep such hotel as a common inn or alehouse for the residue of the year, and till the time when the general licenses for that purpose are renewable.

Having gone through the laws affecting the victualling trade and the abuses therein, from the earliest period to the present time, we shall conclude the chapter with offering three suggestions, which we think might be gradually incorporated into any future legislation affecting this important interest of the community, and which would be productive of incalculable benefits to the inhabitants of the Metropolis.

Our *first* suggestion refers to the police of public houses. An ill-regulated alehouse is one of the greatest nuisances in society, and, by the habits of drinking and disorderly life it tends to promote, fills the streets with beggars, and the hospitals, gaols, and workhouses with the miserable victims of intemperance. Under the present system of licensing, no authority can be said to exist likely to be exercised solely for the purpose of suppressing such a pregnant source of depravity and crime. In London, the brewers are omnipotent, and no one would think of either losing or obtaining a license without the powerful intervention of a member of this unchartered combination. Every day their influence is extending; it grows with the growth of the Metropolis, and not a piece of building-ground is anywhere to be seen in the suburbs without a "big brewer" having got his foot upon the most eligible site for a porter-shop. As a counterpoise to this spirit of monopoly, a power ought to be vested in the Home-Office, or in the Board of Police, which it has been proposed to establish, of opening, in any part of London, a new public-house, or of promptly suppressing an old one that had become justly objectionable. Such authority it would, perhaps, be unnecessary frequently to exercise; but a knowledge that it existed would have the most salutary influence in furthering the ends of police, in the accommodation and security of neighbourhoods, and in controlling the conduct of publicans, brewers, and licensing magistrates.

Our *second* suggestion refers to Retail Breweries. It has been the laudable policy of Government to encourage these establishments, but we fear they have hardly allowed them sufficient opening to guarantee their ultimate success. It would not be too much, we apprehend, to allow them, under an excise-license, to retail beer, within certain hours, to be *consumed on the premises*, and to open more than *one* place, to which they are now restricted, for the purpose; such license not to be compatible with a wine or spirit license. The exclusion of a spirit and wine license would afford protection enough to old-established interests; a vast number of victualling-houses are carried on merely as spirit-shops, in which they are careful not to keep a glass of beer fit for any human being to drink, lest it should interfere with the more profitable trade in GIN: they are the very reverse of what alehouses were intended to be; instead of places of rest and refreshment, many of them do not afford the convenience of a chair or bench, the only object being to exchange, with all possible despatch, the half-filled glass of poison for the last pence of the ignorant and miserable creatures by whom they are frequented. Every disinterested observer of such comfortless pick-pocket places must rejoice in their decline; their proprietors, for the most part, are a set of unprincipled, low-minded, and mercenary wretches, who, to amass wealth, would, without compunction, fill the whole country with disease and beggary.*

* It has been stated of the late Mr. Ricardo that he realized an

Our *last* suggestion refers to the hours of closing public-houses at night, and the observance of the Sabbath. As a simple regulation of police, nothing could be more successful, in the maintenance of order and sobriety, than the power exercised, by the magistrates, of closing public-houses after eleven o'clock; from that hour intoxication mostly ensues, and foolish people are deluded out of their money by worthless liquor. Under the late regulation they were protected, and the streets and outskirts of the town effectually cleared at a seasonable time. Under the new Licensing Act, it seems, magistrates have no power to fix the hour of closing public-houses; as the publican is merely under obligation, by the tenor of his license, to keep good order therein, without restriction as to time.

The scenes of drunkenness, quarrelling, and riot, which prevail in low parts of the Metropolis, through the whole of Sunday, caused by early drinking in the morning, are disgraceful to a Christian community. We notice this not only as a gross violation of the sanctity of the Sabbath, but from its injurious tendency on the morals and comforts of the labouring classes. During

immense fortune, on the Stock Exchange, by "watching the *turn* of the market." Many persons, we doubt not, in London, are gathering money quite as fast, by watching "the turn of the glass," as it is called; that is, taking care every glass of spirits sold shall be a small fraction short of full measure. Mr. Alderman Wood informed the Police Committee that some public-houses take in as much as 10 or 1200 gallons of strong spirits per month. The profit on this, from the turn of the glass and adulteration, must be immense. Besides this, the retailer gains greatly from selling much of the liquor *twice over;* the counter over which the tippler is served is drilled full of holes, through which all slops pass, to be vended a second time. In the sale of beer, profit is made by the same indirect means; the commission, per butt, allowed by the brewers to their tenants, is too small to pay rent and taxes without the publican helping himself, by dilution and by the "turn of the pot," in serving both in-door and out-door customers.

the late hours of Saturday night and on Sunday morning the week's earnings of numbers are dissipated in drink, and families are left, for the remainder of the seven days, with no alternative but the pawnbroker, theft, or starvation. The butchers' and bakers' shops we would suffer to be open, but the publicans' we would close every Saturday night at ten o'clock, and not suffer them to be opened on Sunday till after the morning-service. By so simple an expedient, the *loaf* and *joint*, at least, would be saved from transmutation into gin, and thousands would enjoy a luxury they are now deprived of in the enjoyment of a comfortable Sunday dinner. There are many working people, we are aware, too intelligent to require such protective legislation, but it is far otherwise with multitudes. Exhausted by toil, and suffering from the want of substantial fare in the latter part of the week, they rush, in a state of inanition, to the liquor-shop, unusual excitement is induced, and all thought of their families or food for them is stifled in the stupidity or madness resulting from sudden intoxication.

We subjoin the documents referred to, page 321, and which complete our exposition of the brewing and victualling trade. They also illustrate many remarkable facts in public consumption; indicating nearly a stationary consumption of malt, beer, and wine, though the population has increased nearly 70 per cent. within the last forty years. The increase in the quantity of beer brewed, is unaccompanied with a corresponding increase in the quantity of malt used. The consumption of spirits has increased within the last three years, solely from a reduction in the duties. As a set-off against the diminished consumption of liquors of all kinds, there is a gradual increase in the consumption of tea, sugar, and butchers' meat; and it might have been shown, from the returns of Mark-lane and the Custom-house, that the consumption of corn, and flour, and fuel had increased in a corresponding proportion. These facts do not show a diminution in the power of purchasing by the people, but a change in national manners, either from the vicissitudes of fashion, or from the wider diffusion of intellectual pursuits having superseded former habits of drinking to excess.

STATEMENT *of the Number of Barrels of different Kinds of* BEER *chargeable to the Duties of Excise, in One Year, in Great Britain, and by whom brewed; and the Barrels of Strong Beer exported.*—[Parl. Paper, No. 160, Sess. 1828.]

	PUBLIC BREWERS.		VICTUALLERS.		RETAIL BREWERS.		INTERMEDIATE BREWERS.	Number of Barrels exported.
	Strong.	Table.	Strong.	Table.	Strong.	Table.		
Country Collections	2,315,082	725,068	2,328,067	478,683	142,968	34,069	1,178	9,651
London, within the Limits of the Chief Office	1,582,198	274,828	6,001	9,333	19,095	18,762	15,975	49,222
Total, England & Wales	3,897,283	999,896	2,334,068	488,016	162,063	52,831	17,153	8,8735
Scotland	102,928	188,336	4,598	48,813	4,493	4,412	—	2,505
Grand Total	4,000,208	1,188,262	2,338,666	536,829	166,556	56,943	17,153	61,378

STATEMENT *of the Bushels of* MALT *and Barrels of* BEER *charged with Excise-Duty in England; the Quantity of* TEA *and* SUGAR *for Home Consumption; and the Number of* CATTLE *and* SHEEP *sold in Smithfield-Market, in the Forty Years from* 1789 *to* 1829.

Years.	Bushels of MALT.	Barrels of BEER.	Lbs. of TEA.	Cwts. of SUGAR.	Number of CATTLE.	Number of SHEEP.
1789	24,250,510	6,196,777	16,707,612	1,547,108	93,269	693,700
1790	22,669,579	6,354,367	16,693,670	1,537,837	103,708	749,660
1791	27,923,505	6,681,416	17,262,227	1,403,214	101,161	740,360
1792	28,604,962	7,109,423	18,137,108	1,361,597	107,348	760,859
1793	24,453,901	7,202,313	17,373,687	1,677,083	116,848	728,480
1794	25,595,351	7,044,813	19,112,013	1,555,976	109,448	719,420
1795	24,715,955	7,067,704	21,307,609	1,336,229	131,092	745,640
1796	28,142,015	7,549,213	20,577,894	1,754,067	117,152	758,840
1797	30,923,923	7,942,561	18,780,031	1,273,724	108,337	693,510
1798	26,967,361	7,954,101	22,813,271	1,476,859	107,470	753,010
1799	31,766,690	7,982,601	24,070,340	2,772,438	122,986	834,400
1800	14,492,537	6,759,803	23,378,816	1,506,992	125,073	842,210
1801	18,573,251	6,427,529	24,470,645	2,773,797	134,646	760,560
1802	30,360,133	6,714,693	25,144,177	2,250,315	126,389	743,470
1803	30,493,707	7,244,403	25,401,468	1,491,294	117,551	787,430
1804	22,542,859	7,045,193	23,087,607	2,144,270	113,019	903,940
1805	22,347,999	7,188,938	24,926,560	2,076,112	125,043	912,410
1806	27,492,395	7,215,256	22,887,530	2,801,747	120,250	858,560
1807	24,920,289	7,309,886	24,027,844	2,277,670	134,126	924,030
1808	22,411,138	7,281,603	25,901,451	2,842,813	145,042	1,015,280
1809	22,818,143	7,196,010	21,920,052	2,504,507	137,600	989,250
1810	24,288,426	7,388,097	24,958,257	3,589,314	132,155	962,750
1811	26,801,614	5,625,646	23,058,096	3,226,758	125,112	966,400
1812	18,663,708	7,454,263	24,856,913	2,604,020	133,854	953,630
1813	22,385,492	6,838,705	25,895,005	2,384,500	137,770	891,240
1814	26,118,612	7,056,744	29,597,054	2,003,214	135,071	870,880
1815	27,073,982	7,667,846	27,787,239	2,078,078	124,948	962,840
1816	26,260,459	7,497,246	23,408,209	2,096,930	120,439	968,560
1817	17,139,712	6,672,008	25,428,188	2,123,809	129,888	1,044,710
1818	26,432,962	6,793,127	27,370,026	2,270,322	138,057	963,250
1819	22,344,271	7,089,344	26,235,021	2,774,830	132,226	949,900
1820	24,535,005	6,740,991	26,111,451	2,404,385	135,933	947,990
1821	28,697,057	7,015,800	27,638,031	2,610,942	142,133	1,107,230
1822	25,151,507	7,205,210	27,880,565	2,594,830	142,033	1,340,160
1823	26,873,937	7,569,854	27,753,550	2,807,856	149,552	1,264,920
1824	25,628,016	7,743,708	23,908,629	3,005,056	163,615	1,239,720
1825	28,485,567	8,113,769	24,150,372	2,750,282	156,985	1,130,310
1826	30,504,576	8,278,317	25,238,006	3,702,235	158,920	1,485,020
1827	27,335,792	8,618,255	26,043,227	4,098,448		
1828	25,096,336	7,944,746	—	3,895,763	134,214	1,484,330

COMPARATIVE STATEMENT, *in Gallons, of the Consumption, in Great Britain, of* FOREIGN WINES, *and* BRITISH, IRISH, *and* FOREIGN SPIRITS, *in the Years* 1801–2–3, *and the Years* 1826–7–8.—Parl. Paps. Nos. 320 and 556, Sess. 1828.

	1801.	1802.	1803.	1826.	1827.	1828.
WINES.	7,965,877	6,663,156	8,461,043	7,376,453	5,510,677	6,254,310
SPIRITS.	9,341,978	11,166,357	11,342,730	12,478,335	17,651,216	16,052,104

STATEMENT *of the Number of Public Brewers, Retail Brewers, Victuallers, Intermediate Brewers, and of Victuallers who brew their own Beer, in Great Britain.*—Parl. Pap. No. 159, Sess. 1828.

	PUBLIC BREWERS.	RETAIL BREWERS.	VICTUALLERS.	INTERMEDIATE BREWERS.	VICTUALLERS who brew their own BEER.
Country Collections	1,472	893	44,962	13	23,074
London, within the Limits of the Head Office of Excise	99	67	4,397	4	31
	1,571	960	49,359	17	23,105
Scotland	211	8	16,695	—	300
Total	1782	968	66,054	17	23,405

Number of Ale, Wine, and Spirit Licenses, issued in England and Wales, in the Years 1810 *and* 1827.

In the Year 1810.

	ALE.	WINE.	SPIRITS.
London	4,371	2,410	4,325
Country	44,690	10,101	32,686

In the Year 1827.

	ALE.	WINE.	SPIRITS.
London	4,303	3,084	4,297
Country	45,024	13,636	38,302

CHAPTER XIV.

CONCLUDING REMARKS ON METROPOLITAN POLICE, CRIMES, FRAUDS, AND MANNERS.

Frauds in London.—Mock-Auctions.—Swindlers and Cheats who defraud Tradesmen of their Goods.—Cheats who take genteel Lodgings and assume false Names.—Discharged Servants who obtain Goods from their former Employers.—Cheats of the Society of Jews.—Fraudulent Bill-Discounters and Money-Brokers.—Adulteration of Food.—Short Weights and Measures.—Vulgar Sports—Prize-Fighters, and Impropriety of Persons of this Description holding Victuallers' Licenses.—Charity to the Poor.—Responsibility of the Police.—Proposal to establish a Gradation of Salary among the Police-Magistrates.—Defects in the City Magistracy.—Remarks on the slow Increase of Female Delinquency.—Futility of certain Expedients for embarrassing Thieves—Stopping light Carts and Chaises—Registering Lodging-Houses.—Marine Store-Shops.—Proposal for Registering convicted Thieves.—Apple-Women and Street-Hawkers.—Suffering Dogs to be in the Streets of the Metropolis.—Superior Morals of the Middle Orders questioned.—Talent and Accomplishment of some well-known Thieves.—Newspapers Auxiliaries to the Police, and the Advantages of rendering them more accessible to the industrious Classes.—The French Police an Example of the Futility of a complicated System of Preventive Justice.—Police Reporting—Want of Decorum in the Public Police-Offices.—Dress and Discipline of Watchmen.—Transportation and the Establishment of the Hulks.

In closing our exposition of the Police, Crime, and Protective Institutions of the Metropolis, we find we have still a few observations remaining, which had either escaped notice, or did not properly fall into the body of the work, though of the same nature as the staple material; and we think we cannot do better than throw these remnants into a kind of *omnium gatherum*, forming the concluding chapter to the whole.

FRAUDS OF LONDON.

Though the frauds of London are so numerous, there are few which ordinary prudence will not enable any one to avoid. Sobriety, keeping from places clearly immoral, seasonable hours, guarded intercourse with strangers, and trusting neither persons nor property in the hands of those with whom you are unacquainted, are obvious precautions. If people will get tipsy, frequent brothels, give their confidence to strangers, and receive apparent advantages from those to whom they are unknown, what can be expected but deception and loss! It is astonishing how the stalest devices often succeed; *ring-dropping* and *duffing* are centuries old, yet they are still practised with success in the streets of London. The race of dupes will certainly never be extinct, no more than that of sharpers for whom they are the natural prey. A genteel exterior, a demeanour apparently artless, and a good address, still form the usual qualifications of the host of swindlers, sharpers, and cheats, who infest the Metropolis. Their mode of doing business, too, has undergone little change or improvement; the frauds most rife now in London are the same as those described by Colquhoun upwards of thirty years since, as will be seen from the following descriptions of the most common classes of swindlers in his time:—

Swindlers who take out Licenses as Auctioneers, and open shops in different parts of the Metropolis, with persons at the doors, denominated *Barkers*, inviting strangers to walk in. In these places various articles of silver plate and household goods are exposed to sale, made up on a slight principle, and of little intrinsic value; associates, denominated *Puffers*, are in waiting to bid up the article to a sum greatly beyond its value, when upon the first bidding of the stranger it is knocked down to him, and the money instantly demanded; the goods, however, on being carried home and examined, are generally found to be very different in reality from what their appearance exhibited, and, upon close examination, the fraud is discovered.

Cheats and Swindlers who conspire to defraud Tradesmen of their Goods.—One of these sharpers generally assumes the character of a merchant; hires a genteel house, with a counting-house, and every appearance of business. One or two associates take upon them the appearance of clerks, while others occasionally wear a livery: and sometimes a carriage is set up, in which the ladies of the party visit the shops in the style of persons of fashion, ordering goods to their apartments. Thus circumstanced, goods are obtained upon credit, which are immediately pawned or sold, and the produce used as a means of deception to obtain more, and procure recommendations, by offering to pay ready-money, or discount bills. When confidence is once established in this way, notes and bills are fabricated, as if remitted from the country, and applications made to their newly-acquired friends, the tradesmen, to assist in discounting them. Sometimes money and bills upon one another are lodged at the bankers', for the purpose of extending their credit, by referring to some respectable name for a character. After circulating notes to a considerable amount, and completing their system of fraud, by possessing as much as possible of the property of others without the risk of detection, they move off, assume new characters, and, when the bills and notes become due, the parties are not to be found.

Cheats who take genteel Lodgings, dress elegantly, and assume false Names.—These pretend to be related to persons of credit and fashion: produce letters familiarly written to prove an intimacy; enter into conversation; and shew these letters to tradesmen, and others, upon whom they have a design—get into their good graces, purchase jewellery, wearing apparel, and other articles, and disappear with the booty.

Cheats who have been formerly in the service of Milliners, Mantua-Makers, Tailors, and other Tradesmen who have occasion to send to Shopkeepers and Warehousemen for Goods.—Swindlers of this class, after being discharged from their employment, get into the company of sharpers and thieves, while out of place, and teach them how to personate their former employers; in whose names they too frequently succeed in obtaining considerable quantities of goods before the fraud is discovered.

Cheats of the Society of Jews are to be found in every part of the Metropolis, who, under the pretence of purchasing old clothes and metals of different sorts, prowl about the houses and stables of respectable persons for the purpose of holding out temptations to the servants to pilfer and steal small articles, which they purchase at about one-third of the real value.

Swindlers who raise Money by pretending to be Discounters of Bills, Money-Brokers, &c.—These chiefly prey upon young men of property, who have lost their money at play, or spent it in expensive amusements, and are obliged to raise more upon any terms until their rents and incomes become payable; or who have fortunes in prospect, as being heirs to estates, but who require assistance in the meantime. Another class, having some capital, advance money upon bonds, title-deeds, and other specialties, or upon the bond of the parties having estates in reversion; by these and similar devices large sums of money are extorted from the dissipated and thoughtless, who, eager in the pursuit of criminal pleasures, are ready to make any sacrifice.

Frauds by pretended bill-brokers and discounters have greatly multiplied since Colquhoun wrote, and have not been limited to the gay and dissipated, but have been practised to a great extent towards merchants and tradesmen, both in the Metropolis and the country. The usual plan of this class of swindlers is to assume respectable mercantile names, and take a counting-house or warehouse in the most trading part of the town; they then, by the aid of Directories or information derived from other sources, address circulars to trading firms in the country, representing themselves as houses of great business and capital, and offering to take goods on commission, or to accommodate them with acceptances, on condition the parties send goods against the time their bills become due. If the bait take the goods are received, sold, or pawned, and the drawer perhaps left to take up his own bill. Several gangs of this description have been recently broken up by the activity of the police, and their schemes of depredation exposed in the newspapers.

Obtaining money, under pretence of procuring situations for persons under Government, in the East Indies, or in mercantile houses, has lately formed a common trick of London swindlers. And, as advertising for wives has become frequent, it is not unlikely some of the fraternity may open offices for negotiating the sale of this description of commodity as well as register-offices for servants out of situations.

The most serious frauds, however, are those practised towards our food, either by *adulteration* or by vending it by short weights and measures. These affect every member of the community, but more especially the poorer classes, the rich having the means, and often adopting precautions to guard against impositions of this description; but the poor, in their bread and beer, tea, sugar, and every article of consumption, are the victims of the most shameless depredation. Laws have been made expressly for punishing bakers who mix improper ingredients in their flour, or use false weights, and, generally, every kind of cheating in trade is punishable; but, either from the difficulty of executing these laws, the supineness of individuals, or defects in the police, they afford little protection to the public.

The juries of the Court-leet anciently used to regulate this department of civil economy; but their functions having been found ineffectual, and in many respects inapplicable to the present state of society, three acts passed in the last reign, (35 Geo. III. c. 102; 37 Geo. III. c. 143; and 55 Geo. III. c. 43,) empowering magistrates, in petty sessions, to appoint examiners of weights and measures, and to authorise them to visit shops, mills, &c. and seize and destroy those deficient or fraudulent: a majority of the inhabitants, in vestry, may nominate examiners for their respective parishes, subject to the approval of the justices. These laws are still in force; but, either from the smallness of the penalties they inflict, (20*s*. being the highest,) or the difficulties of proceeding by information before a magistrate, which the acts require, they are seldom resorted to.

Penal statutes, for the protection of the community,

must always prove unavailing, unless the execution of them is made an express part of the duties of the general police. Individuals, who only suffer in common with others, will not subject themselves to the loss of time, odium, and inconvenience of preferring complaints against their neighbours; the task, at best, is an invidious one, and, as the advantage to be derived is public, it ought to be discharged by a public officer.

VULGAR SPORTS—PRIZE-FIGHTING.

There are two sorts of "Life," both unnatural and inimical to happiness: the one would stifle the passions, the other give them a pernicious development; it is the object of true wisdom to do neither. Youth cannot be expected to submit to the regimen of age; in spite of the adage, old heads do not sit gracefully on young shoulders, and one is apt to view them as a good thing somewhat too premature. In early life, there is a propensity to amusement, gaiety, and adventure, and, where neither marriage, nor business, nor politics supervene to demand more sober cares, they may be indulged, without compromising more important social duties. While, however, we would leave youth to its congenial pursuits, we would not recommend the discipline of the modern school of vulgar sports, under the pretext of "seeing life." Every rank and condition in society have their peculiar amusements, style of conversation, diet, and demeanour. A person with the education of a gentleman, and the sentiments and discourse belonging to the station, can have no sympathy with the humours of a cock-fight, a boxing-match, the slang of a fishwoman, or stage-coachman. It is proper a gentleman should have his recreations as well as the plebeian; but it is quite out of keeping he should seek them in a dram-shop, the prize-ring, or Westminster-pit. There may be gentlemen who prefer such divertisements, but they form the exception, not the rule of their class; they are a sort of monstrosities, who, from unnatural perversion of taste, prefer the offal and garbage,—like those of whom we sometimes read, who feed on *caviare* and carrion in preference to more choice and wholesome viands. However such non-descripts may be set off in fine clothes, or in highly-finished engravings, they can only be esteemed well-dressed blackguards, having the souls of scavengers and nightmen, for which offices Nature clearly intended them.

Prize-fighting has fallen too low to be an object of animadversion, and we only notice it to remark on the inconsistency of allowing so many of this fraternity to hold victuallers' licenses. The first duty of a publican is the maintenance of order in his house; but the trade of a prize-fighter is one continued violation of the peace, and the encouragement of its violation by others. Besides, the general character of these men ought to place them entirely out of the pale of magisterial countenance; many of them are known to be thieves or the associates of thieves; their houses are mostly the resort of the vilest characters in London, and the sham fights they are continually getting up, to "fright the isle from its propriety," are only some of the frauds by which they live. Nothing evinces more strongly the corrupt influence exercised in licenses than the readiness with which these persons obtain them, or even (as some of them do) keep houses without a justice's license: it shows any one, however disreputable, provided he is likely to draw company, and procure a vent for the brewer's or distiller's beverage, may keep a liquor-shop.

CHARITY TO THE POOR.

It has been the fashion, of late years, to decry charity,

as tending to multiply objects of distress rather than diminish human misery. We have felt the force of the reasoning whence this conclusion has been derived, but we have since seen reason to qualify our opinion. The good we do, by relieving one destitute object, is certain, but the evil which may arise from our benevolence, in raising up other claimants, is at most only contingent. It seems extraordinary that a single person should ever die of absolute want in London, abounding as it does in so many resources for the indigent. Yet, that such is the fact, is attested by coroners' inquisitions, and hundreds, we doubt not, perish every year in obscure retreats, whose wretched fate never meets the public eye. Some of these, at least, are the victims of unavoidable calamity, and have sunk under an adverse fortune which no prudence could avert, and what a pity one such should be left to perish, from an apprehension of prospective evil, or because there are impostors who abuse the intentions of benevolence! It may be expected the rich should listen favourably to a principle which absolves them from all care about the poor; but, even supposing the latter the authors of their own misfortunes, still this does not relieve the former from the obligations of humanity. The rich are the natural guardians of the poor, and this duty is imposed not only by the ties of a common species, but their superior intelligence, greater political power, and the very advantages they enjoy from the prevalence of the vices they lament. Besides, before the principle of non-relief can in fairness be acted upon towards the poor, it ought to be first shown they knew better and worse have followed; for, if their distress has resulted from involuntary ignorance, it is as much their misfortune as if it proceeded from unavoidable physical privations.

For our part, it is more from the interference of the

rich than the exertions of the poor themselves we anticipate any great improvement in their condition. Popular education will always be limited in its empire, and a dense mass remain beyond its power to reclaim. For example, can we ever hope that those who delve in mines, or the class of mere labourers, or that numerous portion of the population scattered in the agricultural districts can ever become educated? The scantiness of their leisure and the severity of their toil preclude such a hope, and, in their estimation, the pleasures of intellect will never compete with those of sensual ease and appetite. Certainly even those might be orally taught the few truths most essential for them to be acquainted with, if those who ought to be their teachers would condescend to instruct them. But it is chiefly, we apprehend, from a sort of coercive legislation, which places them out of the reach of temptation and withholds from them the power of self-injury, that they can be protected from distress and indigence.

RESPONSIBILITY OF THE POLICE.

A good salary attached to any service tends to elevate it in public estimation, and to draw into the employment men of character, probity and education. But a good salary alone affords an insufficient guarantee for an efficient discharge of duty, unless a scale of contingent rewards and punishments be superadded. If the emoluments of an office be fixed, and not capable of increase by extraordinary exertion, the official is content with the bare discharge of his duties, and the avoidance of such flagrant derelictions as may incur the forfeiture of of his situation. Rewards stimulate to exertion, as punishment deters from negligence. No branch of public service is so ill-paid as the naval and military, yet, aided by a severe code of discipline, no service is so faithfully and strictly performed. The emoluments of the police should be considerable, to engage in the employment competent persons; but, as the trust and responsibility are great, they ought to be severely punished for a betrayal or inefficient discharge of their duty. A principle cause of the inefficiency of the existing system is, that the officers are without prospect of reward, either from pension or promotion, if they do well, and are exempt from punishment if they do ill. Two improvements in police, therefore, would consist, first, in allowing a pension to every retainer in this department who had served faithfully a limited term of years; secondly, the duties of every functionary, patrol, watchman, police-constable, and clerk, ought to be specifically described, and precise punishments annexed to any practices, in contravention of them.

The police magistrates, as well as the subordinate officers, have too few objects of lucre or ambition in view to be excited into extraordinary exertion. Among the twelve judges, as well as among the right reverend bishops, there are many temptations to which they may individually aspire; but the whole twenty-seven police-magistrates have only one—namely, the office of chief magistrate, at Bow-street, to which greater emolument is attached than the rest. If all three magistrates at Bow-street had higher salaries granted them, and the next office in the magnitude of its establishment and business had the same distinction; or if the leading magistrate of each office received a higher salary than the other two, the field of promotion and inducement to exertion would be enlarged.

DEFECTS IN CITY MAGISTRACY.

The aldermen who attend in rotation at the Mansion-House and the Justice-Room, Guildhall, receive no salary; nor are the hours of attendance regulated by act of Parliament or of the Common Council. From one or both these causes a great failure of public justice ensues in the City. The time of the magistrate's attendance is uncertain; or he comes too late to get through the business of the day; or, as sometimes happens, he never comes at all, nor appoints a brother alderman to come for him: in which case, after waiting four or five hours in fruitless expectation of his worship's arrival, witnesses, accusers and accused, clerks, door-keepers, reporters, &c. are obliged to retire with a kind of "call again to-morrow," and the whole business of the day, night-charges included, is postponed to next morning. Such occurrences might pass over like a summer's cloud among the unpaid of the country, but they are quite incompatible with the economy of the first mercantile city in the world.

But this is not the only blemish in city justice. Frequent mistakes are committed in the interpretation of the law; such as mistaking trover for theft, or confounding some other obvious distinction of civil and criminal justice. It cannot be expected that gentlemen, not professionally educated, and who have their private affairs to manage, can always be *au fait* to the matters brought before them; and while their services continue gratuitous it hardly appears reasonable to subject them to severer discipline. The corporation supports a paid magistrate in the Borough, and, we think, two barristers ought to be appointed to act in the City, and the hours of attendance to be fixed. The magistrate on the rota might still be required to attend in the latter part of the morning, to assist in the double duty.

An inconvenience is sometimes felt, of the same nature, at Bow-street, from that office being exempt from the regulations to which the other offices are subjected, as to the hours of magisterial duty.

SLOW INCREASE OF FEMALE DELINQUENCY.

Since concluding the Chapter on the Causes of the Increase of Crime we have been struck, in turning over again the criminal returns laid before Parliament, by a result that we had not remarked, and which, as far as we know, has not been any where noticed. The result to which we refer is the different ratio of increase in crime in males and females; in the former, since 1811, the commitments have nearly trebled, in the latter they have only increased about one-fifth or twenty-five per cent., which is probably not more than the increase in population. Nearly a similar result is obtained from inspecting the criminal returns in the country during the same interval. The following are the commitments in London, Westminster, and Middlesex, in 1811, 1818, and 1827 :—

	1811.	1818.	1827.
Males	974	2108	2719
Females	508	557	662*

Now this appears to us a more conclusive argument that society has recently undergone no moral deterioration than any we have seen advanced, and that the greater development of crime, as exhibited in the criminal calendar, has chiefly resulted from the long continuance of peace, the increase in mercantile transactions, the avidity of speculation, the operation of the debtor laws, and those other causes which have principally acted on the male part of the community. Had there been any growing depravity it must have been shared in by the women as well as the men, and the existence of it would have been demonstrated by a corresponding augmentation in the number of female offenders.

* Report on the Police of the Metropolis, 1828, App. A. p. 289.

FUTILITY OF CERTAIN EXPEDIENTS FOR EMBARRASSING THIEVES.

On every suggestion for the improvement of the Police an important consideration is—Whether the advantages it would yield are such as would compensate for the sacrifices it would require. It is easy to devise expedients for augmenting the efficiency of the civil power, but the additional security they would afford would, probably, be a disproportionate equivalent for the abridgement of personal freedom, the annoyance, inconvenience, and expense, they would entail. For instance, it would tend much to embarrass thieves, coiners, and delinquents, generally, were magistrates armed with greater authority, promptly to enter and search houses or places suspected of concealing stolen property, or harbouring persons engaged in criminal practices. But the possibility such additional authority might be abused—the arbitrary power it would give over every one's dwelling—and the likelihood that 500 innocent persons might be disturbed for one guilty enterprize defeated, are strong objections against its adoption.

It is thought that *light carts* and *one-horse chaise* are much used by theives in transporting their booty; and, as a preventive, it has been proposed to authorize the turnpike-keepers (many of whom are as great depredators as any who pass through them) to examine every vehicle of this description. Perhaps, by this means a dozen robberies might be detected or frustrated in the course of a twelvemonth; but what an indequate advantage for the thousands of innocent persons who would be annoyed, irritated, and unjustly suspected, in the same time: for it is known that honest people as well as thieves use light carts—to go to market, to see their friends, to collect money, and sometimes to go to church. Authority vested in the police to stop and examine any hackney-coach or cart, travelling in the night, after a certain hour, is a precaution that could not be objected to. But there are people who would frame plans of police as if the entire community were delinquent; but the truth is, thieves still form a very inconsiderable minority, and the spoil they acquire at every risk—great though it may be—forms a very insignificant fraction of the immense mass of property possessed, comfortably enjoyed, and securely transported by the reputable portion of society.

Of the same nature are suggestions for registering *lodging-houses*, and for *licensing* certain traders; as purchasers of old rags and bottles, keepers of draught-carts, vans, and trucks for removing goods, dealers in metals, &c. The advantages likely to result from such preventive expedients are at best doubtful, while the suspicion and inconvenience to which they would subject many honest people are certain evils.

A great deal of suspicion has been excited in respect of *marine-store-shops*, and the late Dr. Colquhoun was much haunted about the dealings of these obscure retreats. But the fact is, these places are no longer what they were thirty years since, during the war, when the King's dock-yards and the line of river, from Blackfriars to Woolwich, formed a continued field of depredation. It has been calculated that the West-India ships and other vessels, which then unloaded in the Thames, were plundered, to the amount of half a million per annum, by thousands of thieves, under the denomination of *river pirates, light horsemen, game watermen, game lightermen, lumpers, mudlarks, and scuffle-hunters.* The public stores were shamefully embezzled, and the custom of perquisites, which was tolerated among the workmen in the royal yards and arsenals, encouraged an extensive system of pillage. The dealers in marine-stores were among the principal receivers of the plunder derived from these different sources. All this, however, has been changed; the alterations introduced by Lord St. Vincent effected a complete reform in the dock-yards; and the erection of the London, West-India, and other docks, aided by the establishment of the Thames police, have nearly exterminated the host of river plunderers. With the decline of these the marine-store dealers declined also; and we apprehend, from what we can observe of them at present, they are not very extensive dealers in stolen goods: no doubt they will purchase, as far as their capital admits, any article offered for sale, *without asking questions;* but we suspect the chief booty obtained in London is either sent out of the kingdom or disposed of in the country, by the intervention of *fences* possessing greater resources. The name of dealer in *marine stores* sufficiently indicates the origin of this species of chapmen, and the causes which must have operated a decline in their calling.

If a measure could be devised for registering the name, abode, and occupation of *convicted thieves*, after their term of punishment had expired, and to compel them to give securities for their future good behaviour, it might impose a salutary restraint upon their conduct. It seems a little preposterous, after being at the trouble and expense of hunting down and capturing a depredator, and, after his criminal pursuits and character have been ascertained by trial and conviction, to let him again loose upon society, without taking any precaution against his return to his old haunts and vocation, or placing him under any kind of surveillance by which the civil power may be apprised of his future residence and movements.

APPLE-WOMEN AND STREET-HAWKERS.

One often hears complaints of the hardship of driving from the streets a few poor apple-women, sellers of oranges, &c. without any attempt being made to determine the limits within which the practice of offering articles for sale in the open thoroughfares becomes a nuisance or public convenience. It would be inconsistent with municipal order to permit persons, without restraint, to assemble on the pavement for traffic; this would be a return to the times when the draper, mercer, and almost every dealer offered his wares for sale in the open streets, and would have the effect of ultimately superseding the regular shopkeeper by a species of interlopers, who pay neither rent, taxes, nor poor-rates. At the same time there are articles which may be vended in the streets without serious detriment to the regular dealer, and of public accommodation; such as fruit, flowers, vegetables, and mackerel. These are all of a perishable nature, they are only in season during short periods, and, unless a sale for them could in some measure be forced, they would cease to be produced; whereas, by thousands of persons being employed in hawking them, a vent is obtained and the consumption promoted when it is most conducive to the public health. But the same reasons cannot be urged for exposing in the streets, for sale, commodities of a more durable kind, as hardware, toys, books, and stationery; the sale of these the police ought to prohibit, it interferes with the established dealer, and no pretext of loss or public utility can be urged for its toleration. It is unnecessary to remark that, even venders of fruit, &c. should not be allowed to assemble in numbers tending to impede the thoroughfares; the public pavements being made for the convenience of passengers, not for a market-place.

KEEPING OF DOGS.

Suffering dogs to go loose, in a populous city, is a nuisance which ought to be abated. During the hot months of summer, the alarm of hydrophobia is very great, and many people are afraid to stir abroad, lest they should be bitten by a mad dog; and the confusion often caused by the populace hunting down those supposed to be in that state is an interruption to business and annoyance to the passenger. When there is a rumour of mad dogs, the magistrates usually order all dogs to be tied up; but this is a precaution for which, in the present state of the law, the magistrate has no legal authority to enforce. A person bit by a savage dog has a remedy by action; but in this he may fail, unless he can prove the owner had notice of the dog having bitten somebody at least once before. Suffering a *mischievous* dog to go loose or unmuzzled is indictable as a nuisance; but this is too vague a description, and the remedy too difficult. We submit that no dog (drovers' dogs excepted) at any time should be suffered to appear in the streets of the Metropolis, unless *held in a string*, under pain of being seized or destroyed by the police. The number of dogs trained for fighting, and other blackguard purposes, and the assemblages that take place, in the fields, on Sunday morning, in the environs of the Metropolis, are matters not unworthy attention.

MORALS OF THE MIDDLE ORDERS.

It is certainly a vulgar error to ascribe exclusive virtues to any section of society, for no one can have lived thirty years in the world without having observed an assortment of good and bad in every class of the community. Whether a man be born a prince or a peasant, or a haberdasher, can, *per se*, have no influence on individual character, which must depend on the subsequent education, society, and associations acting on the natural dispositions. Those born to the enjoyment of an independent fortune, and those born to acquire one, will receive different impressions and training as their future vocations demand; but it is not easy to decide which, upon the whole, will develope the greatest moral excellence. The vices as well as the virtues of the mercantile classes necessarily differ from those of the proprietary orders; among the former is observed greater decorum, order, punctuality, and industry; among the latter more frankness, sincerity, and independence: the first may justly pride themselves on their piety and stricter sexual purity; but the higher classes are not generally so obnoxious to the imputation of hypocrisy, disingenuousness, and fraud. These diversities result from differences in their social position, and, perhaps, MINOS himself would be at loss to which to assign the palm of entire superiority.

It is a vulgar error, of the same kind, to attach great moral importance to a man's profession, politics, or religion. History and experience attest that neither corruption nor purity is the exclusive attribute of any party, sect, or calling. If we wished to choose a steward, an executor, or person for any confidential employment, we should certainly like to be apprised of his natural dispositions and former history; but, should no more think of inquiring whether he were a Whig or Tory, Churchman or Sectarian, than whether he were a partizan of the Vulcanian or Neptunian theory of the Earth.

We have been drawn into these unpleasant comparisons from observing the common practice of holding up the middle classes as the type of human perfection. The truth is, they have their failings as well as those above and those below them. The unprincipled schemes and speculations of 1824–5 shew they are not immaculate, and the practices of select vestries, and the numbers constantly being brought before the tribunals for selling adulterated provisions and using short weights and measures, have lowered them in our estimation. In the City of Westminster, not long since, 150 tradesmen were summoned and fined for using fraudulent weights and measures.* Upwards of 200 were brought up a short time previously, in the Borough of Southwark, for similar practices. Shame on such doings! If the assessed taxes press too heavily upon them, they ought to petition the Legislature for their repeal; but weight and measure are due to every one, and a " false balance is an abomination to the LORD."

ACCOMPLISHMENTS OF THIEVES.

The late Parliamentary Committee, in their able Report on Criminal Commitments, after remarking the less-proportional increase of crimes against the person than those against property, make the following important observations:—

" This view of the subject is important, for two reasons: the one as it tends to shew that, with some remarkable exceptions, the state of society is not one of remarkable depravity; the other that it gives to the operations of Government a body that may be acted upon by law. Gangs of pickpockets, pilferers, and even housebreakers, may be, to a great degree, controlled and restrained by means of preventive police and exemplary punishment; their crimes are not the result of

* *Morning Advertiser*, April 12, 1828.

blind passion, which is satisfied to satiate itself and suffer for the enjoyment, but the result of a calculation of unprincipled men on a cool view of their interests. If you can make the hazard greater than the probable gain, you may rest satisfied you will diminish crime. On the other hand, it must be confessed that the *art of crime has increased faster than the art of detection.* The improvement of communication, the employment of young thieves by the older and more practised, the crowded state of our gaols, and other causes, have tended, in many parts of the country, to make the plunderers of property a species of organized society, having their division of labour, their regular leaders, and premeditated means of escape."—*Parl. Report, No.* 545, *p.* 5. *Sess.* 1828.

The mode of conducting depredations in the Metropolis, the caution with which they are planned, the dexterity with which they are executed, the arrangements for disposing of the plunder when obtained, and the corrupt *liasons** which the heads of the fraternity are

* Some of the retainers of the Police do their business in a very quiet way, and maintain, to the letter, the designation of peace-officers, by often interfering to settle, by amicable negotiation, the differences which arise among the King's lieges. In process of time we may expect that such cruel implements as handcuffs, staves, and cutlasses—except for poor rogues—will be dispensed with, and the only equipment of a thief-taker be a cash-box or long purse. In illustration of the modern practice, we will mention an occurrence that happened only a few weeks since:—A gentleman, well known in the City, attended the late Epsom meeting on the Catholic question; passing through the crowd, and thinking some of those present might be none too good, he thought he would place the appendages of his watch out of the way of temptation; but, on feeling for them, they were gone, some rascal, having cut the waistband of his small-clothes behind, had anticipated him in the object of his anxiety. Next morning he called on one of the officers belonging to Union-Hall, relating his disaster, and giving a description of the persons he observed about him at the time. The officer said he knew the parties, and had no doubt who had stolen his

known to cultivate with the police, to elude justice, evince a combination of means to an end which might successfully carry through the most laudable and difficult enterprise. It was ascertained, by the Police Committee, that some of the principal thieves were pains-taking money-getting men, who, after amassing large fortunes, died and left them to their descendants. One of the most noted *fences* now in London is precisely a character of this description; he is a shrewd, industrious, persevering man, who follows the business of receiving, as the shortest and easiest way to wealth. When C—y was employed in the City, he was a most exemplary servant; he was mostly the first at his desk in the morning, and was prompt to remonstrate at any remissness in others. His exhibition, in a court of justice, for picking pockets, came upon his fellow-clerks like a thunder-clap, never having remarked in him, what Shakspeare calls, an "itching palm:" he was then a first-rate penman, and wrote as fine a hand as Porson, the late celebrated Grecian.

NEWSPAPERS AUXILIARIES TO THE POLICE.

Newspapers have contributed, far more than gas-lighting, to expose and defeat the designs of unprincipled persons. They are the proper *hue and cry* of

watch; "but," said he, "it will cost you £20 to recover it; you must advertise." Accordingly the watch was advertised for as "LOST," and, next day, a note was brought by a little boy, stating it would be returned, on the reward mentioned being paid to the bearer: which was done, and the watch restored to the owner. These practices are now so frequent and notorious, in the Metropolis, that we apprehend few persons who have been robbed of valuable property, which they are more anxious to recover than promote the ends of public justice—which is the case with most people—think of applying to the magistrates, but resort privately to a police-officer, or to a "well-known solicitor."

delinquency, and, by circulating in victualling-houses, taverns, and private houses, everywhere make known frauds and robberies—the way in which they have been perpetrated, and put society on the alert against the practices of swindlers and thieves. This is only one of their uses. They have been justly termed the "best public instructors;" they are not only such, but the most agreeable of schoolmasters, possessing that variety which interests the most careless of scholars, and communicating the knowledge most essential for every person to possess. They do not transport the reader out of the world, neither carrying him into the regions of imagination, like poetry or romance, nor abstracting him from the duties of this life, by involving him in the mazes of unprofitable scientific inquiries. They just communicate the information which comes home to the "business and bosoms of men;" and we verily believe Government could not adopt any course more conducive to public morals and popular education than by adopting measures to render them more accessible to the industrious classes. It has been shewn, we think satisfactorily, that a reduction in the newspaper-duty would be compensated by increased circulation. But, if this were not so, an additional tax on spirituous liquors (now so much abused) would make up the deficiency.

As to any political consequences from the greater circulation of the public journals, Government is well fortified against them: we are convinced more men inquire and reflect, and more abundant reason will they find for contentment with the institutions under which they live; the improvements of late years must have demonstrated to every one that there is a principle of renovation in our establishments which gradually accommodates them to the wants of society—that industry and talent have a fair field for development—that personal liberty and the enjoyment of property are nowhere more secure against lawless power—and if they do not possess greater theoretic perfection and wiser measures have not always been adopted, it may be ascribed rather to prejudices among the people themselves than to any defective responsibility in their Rulers—and to the growth of interests which, though hurtful, could not, either with justice or safety, be suddenly disturbed. In short, we foresee, in the measure, the best antidote to the growth of Atheism and Sectarianism, and the encouragement of that rational piety and freedom of discussion essential to a reduction in poor-rates and the advancement of social improvement.

There is another reason for reducing the newspaper-duty, and which would operate upon another class of interests, like the encouragement afforded to the retail breweries in counteracting the monopoly of the great houses. It cannot be denied that the engrossing of any article of general consumption, whether of intelligence or food, is dangerous to the general interests of the community. The incomparable ability with which the principal newspapers are conducted—their able advocacy of every salutary measure—and their devotion to sound morals and good government—every one must admire; still, as everything sublunary is liable to change, it is impossible to foresee into whose hands they may ultimately pass, and one cannot think without alarm of the consequences which might ensue from such powerful engines being perverted by wicked men to purposes either hostile to the Government or the people. Affording an opportunity for the establishment of minor journals, to which a reduction in the stamp-duty would tend, might have the effect of lessening the serious responsibility now resting upon the great newspaper proprietors, and the evils which might result from the few great lights to which the public are now restricted, being darkened or controlled by malign influence.

THE FRENCH POLICE.

The system established by Fouché and Savary, and continued under the administration of M. de Villèle, is quite sufficient to disgust us with refined and complicated organizations of preventive justice, and cannot have the most distant resemblance to any establishment required in this country. These persons had mingled their myrmidons through every grade of the community,—from that of artizans to the highest classes; persons were found of all ranks mean enough to accept the regular pay of the minister for reporting the conversations of every saloon, every club, and every society, to which they were admitted on terms of equality and confidence. The sanction Bonaparte gave to this vile *espionnage* detracts from the magnanimity of his character; his prying curiosity into domestic life was such, that, according to his own expression, he was desirous of "*cooking every man's dinner*." His object appears not only to have been to frustrate any conspiracy against the state, but to ascertain every idle comment on his own personal character and actions, evincing the spirit of Tiberius united to the busy meddling of a village gossip. After all, this Paul Pry system was productive of no advantage to the Imperial government; plots really dangerous escaped its vigilance, while a mass of names and details were accumulated in the bureaus not more valuable for state purposes than the "annals of P. P. a parish-clerk." The best political police is a free press; which at once discovers all conspiracies, all discontents, and every fluctuation in public sentiment and feeling.

POLICE REPORTS—MAGISTERIAL DECORUM.

Reports in the newspapers of proceedings at the public police offices were given in a very different form from what they now are, fifteen or twenty years since; they then consisted of a brief notice of what had taken place before the magistrates, without comment, burlesque, or embellishment. They communicated the information most useful to the public, neither amplifying nor distorting facts, nor indulging any unseemly levity at the follies or crimes of individuals. The ingenuity of modern artists produces a very different manufacture: police reports are now frequently thrown into a sort of dramatic dialogue or one-act farce, in which, by justices, reporters, clients, plaintiffs, and witnesses, clubbing their wits into a joint-stock, a pungent refection is got up for the news-room or next morning breakfast-table.

This is a practice liable to abuse, but which we are not disposed absolutely to condemn. We have observed many follies chased from society by a satirical exhibition of them in the journals; and, no doubt, frivolous complaints are kept from before the tribunals by a dread of being held up to ridicule in a newspaper report. On the other hand, without the exercise of a severe judgment (which is not always found in greatest perfection in the most clever scribes of this description) subjects not proper for burlesque may be exhibited in a light in which they ought not to appear; and even persons having serious complaints to prefer may, from an apprehension of being *shown up*, be deterred from appearing at a police office, which operates as a real obstruction to public justice. Upon the whole, we cannot think the general business of a public office affords much food for merriment: the matters generally audited there are chiefly those of distress, ignorance, and depravity, which are any thing but laughable incidents in human affairs.'

Another circumstance has grown out of this Comus vein of reporting, not unworthy of notice: some of the justices appear infected with the spirit of drollery, and the decorum of the place occasionally sacrificed to a desire to shine in a smart or humorous repartee. This, it must be confessed, is very "pitiful ambition," and almost as unseemly on the bench as the cap and bells in the pulpit. The stipendiary magistrates, through the medium of the press, have the means of rendering important services to the community; they may communicate much useful information, and often read a salutary lesson, drawn from actual experience of the frailities of humanity, in which they have the advantage of the minister of religion—for they have the "gall'd spirit" before them; —but the other must launch his bolt at random among the crowd.

These remarks are not meant in disparagement of the London magistracy, whose ability and integrity must be generally admitted. What has chiefly attracted our notice in the qualifications of these gentlemen is, the result of their examination before the late Police Committee. Though possessing such favourable opportunities for observation, and the subject constantly before them, scarcely one had formed any definite idea of the causes of the increase of crime, or of the manifold defects in metropolitan police, nor of any alterations by which they could be remedied. Their attention appears to have been strictly limited to the discharge of their official duty; and, as is not unusual in men actively engaged in a laborious vocation, they seem to have been too much oppressed and satiated with the performance of their daily functions, to have had any relish for afterwards indulging, in their private leisure, in gratuitous speculations on their general character, or by what means the administration of them could be improved.

From these observations one or two magistrates ought to be excepted. Mr. Dyer, in particular, after his attention had been awakened by the Committee, submitted, on his second examination, some valuable suggestions: especially those relating to the extortions and compounding of penal suits by the common informer—to the inadequate penalties imposed on the public drunkard and on furious driving—to the difficulties of enforcing the law against the owners of carts guilty of offences—to the impediments to the prompt execution of search-warrants—and to the very important improvement that would result from substituting a simple summons in place of written informations, in proceedings against that numerous class of offences over which a power of summary conviction is given to one or two magistrates.* The necessity of employing a lawyer to draw up an information—the great technical accuracy required—and the expense attending it are such as to operate as a denial of justice in complaints under the *Pawnbrokers' Act*, the *Weight and Measure Acts*, and other salutary statutes intended for the protection of the community.

HINTS ON THE NIGHTLY WATCH.

The invention of clocks has superseded the utility of a watchman *calling the hour* while on duty, and it only serves to apprize thieves of his approach. As a check afforded to the inhabitants over him it is not of much

* Report on the Police of the Metropolis, Sess. 1828, pp. 173–9

use, and the uncertain rounds of an inspector through the different watch stations would be far more effectual for keeping him on the alert.

The parish of Islington, and some others, employ a *double watch*, and this, we apprehend, is the most judicious system. It is physically impossible one man can watch with effect through the whole of a long winter-night; besides, by dividing the night-duty there is sufficient time for rest during the twenty-four hours, and for following some other occupation in the day time. Upon this plan, too, a more vigilant and strict watch may be enforced; in the first place, there is no pretext for *watchboxes* for intervals of rest; and, in the next, which we esteem an important principle in night-police, the watchmen may be required to be always in motion, not going their rounds at stated intervals of a quarter or half an hour, but continually patrolling their beat at uncertain times; by which means depredators could have no knowledge when they would be at any particular spot.

A lantern we deem an essential part of a watchman's equipments; and those called *bull's eyes* are well contrived. The light can be concealed if necessary, while it affords an opportunity for examining any suspicious person, and for inspecting courts, alleys, and areas, and looking to the fastenings of doors and windows.

The clothing of a watchman ought to be such as to protect him from the most inclement weather, so that he may have no pretext for the indulgence of rest, shelter, or absence from duty, at any time.

Where a *day-patrol* is kept there ought to be no interval between the time they withdraw from duty to the coming on of the nightly-watch.

The general duties of the police partake more of a

military than civil character; and, as Chelsea and Greenwich pensioners have proved the most efficient watchmen, it is not improbable officers on half-pay, and those accustomed to military-duty, would make the best superintendents; and, should a general and consolidated police for the Metropolis be established, their services could not fail to be of the utmost utility in the subordinate departments.

In conclusion, we may remark, that an inefficient or ill-regulated watch is worse than none at all; for people trust to the guardians of the night, and neglect those precautions which, without them, they would adopt.

TRANSPORTATION AND THE HULKS.

The punishment by transportation was first authorised by Parliament in the year 1718, when the general plan of sending convicts to the American plantations was adopted. This system continued for fifty-six years; during which period, and until the commencement of the American war, in 1775, great numbers of felons were sent chiefly to the province of Maryland. The rigid discipline which the colonial laws authorised masters to exercise over servants, joined to the prospects which agricultural pursuits, after some experience was acquired, held out to these outcasts, tended to reform the chief part, who mingled in the society of that country, after the expiration of their servitude, under circumstances highly beneficial to themselves, and even to the colony. Possessed in general (as every adroit thief must be) of good natural abilities, they availed themselves of the habits of industry they acquired in the years of their servitude—became farmers and planters on their own account, and, many of them succeeding in these pursuits, not only attained the respectability which is attached to property and industry, but, also, in their turn, became masters, and purchased the services of future transports sent out for sale.

By the Transport-Acts, 4 Geo. I. c. 11, and 6 Geo. I. c. 23, the persons contracting for the conveyance of convicts to the colonies, or their assigns, had an interest in their services for seven or fourteen years, according to the term of transportation. But, for some years previous to the rupture with the colonies, the adjudged services of convicts became so valuable, in Maryland, that contracts were made to convey them *without any charge to Government*, who had before allowed £5 each for their passage; the services of the convicts being preferred, for the reason already assigned, to those who voluntarily engaged to emigrate to America.

The convicts having accumulated greatly in the year 1776, and the intercourse with America being closed, it became necessary to resort to some other expedient; and, in the choice of difficulties, the system of the *hulks* was suggested and adopted, under the authority of the 16th of George the Third.

As is generally known, the hulks are large vessels without masts, which have been line-of-battle ships or frigates, and are moored near a dock-yard, or arsenal, so that the labour of the convicts may be applied to the public service. The present establishment consists of 10 vessels, on board of which have been usually confined, at one time, for some years past, between 3000 and 4000 convicts. The average number daily, during the year 1826, was 3609, and, in 1827, 4262. The principal stations are at Deptford, Woolwich, Chatham, Sheerness, and Portsmouth. One ship, the *Euryalus*, is appropriated exclusively for the reception of boys not exceeding 16 years of age, most of whom are taught trades—shoemaking, tailoring, bookbinding, &c. Very few of the adults work at trades, they are employed in everything the most laborious the Navy-Board and Ordnance Department can find them to do, in removing ballast out of and into ships, cleaning the ships out, taking up the mooring-chains, clearing the mud from the docks, and, since the disuse of horses, in removing and drawing all the timber.

It is only the convicts sentenced to short terms that are usually kept on board the hulks; those for life and fourteen years are sent to New South Wales; unless, under peculiar circumstances, the Secretary of State orders their detention in this country. On their arrival at the hulks, from the different gaols, they are immediately stripped and washed, clothed in coarse grey jackets and breeches, and two irons placed on one of the legs, to which degradation every one must submit, let his previous rank have been what it may. They are then sent out in gangs of a certain number to work on shore, guarded by soldiers. A strict account is kept of the labour performed by each gang, there being a scale by which it is calculated, and out of each shilling earned for the Government, by the convict, he is entitled to a penny, which is carried to his credit; but of this he receives only one-third part weekly, the remainder being left to accumulate until the expiration of the term which he is doomed to serve; thus it sometimes happens that a man who has been six or seven years on board the hulks, on his discharge is put in possession of £10 or £12, and is also supplied with an additional sum of money to defray his travelling-expenses home. The diet of each, for one week, is barley 1lb. 12oz., oatmeal 1lb. 5oz., bread 8lb. 12oz, beef 3lb. 8oz., cheese 12oz., salt 3½oz., small beer 7 pints. Those whose behaviour is exemplary are favoured by their term of punishment being shortened, or their irons lightened, or promotion to little offices, which relieves from severer labour. The number of convicts annually returned upon society from this source, by pardon or otherwise, amounts to about 600.

In the opinion of a member of the "Society for the Improvement of Prison Discipline," the evils which prevail on board the hulks are the result of a defective system of management, necessarily arising from the prison being a vessel afloat, and considered and regulated by law as a temporary place of confinement for convicts sentenced to transportation. The hulks have, however, for some years past, been converted into permanent prisons, and for the confinement of offenders for long periods. The vessels are not subjected to those salutary rules which the Legislature has provided for the government of gaols. The hulks are not visited by the magistrates, and a large body of criminals are therefore placed exclusively under the jurisdiction of the Home Secretary of State; they are only visited occasionally by the superintendent appointed by him, and who resides in London, and reports twice a-year, to the Secretary of State, upon the condition of the convicts.

The captain of each vessel has the privilege of recommending, as deserving of free pardons, a certain number of the prisoners (viz. two in 100) every three months. This extraordinary power has never been extended to the keeper of any gaol, nor should such a privilege be vested in any single officer. In the hulks it is customary to allow convicts to receive money from their friends, and to purchase therewith food of a better description than that afforded by the regulations. No such indulgence is permitted in a county gaol, except in particular instances, at the discretion of the magistrates. The convicts on board the hulks are allowed a portion of their earnings to be similarly expended.

The want of classification and of proper inspection are, however, the principal defects of the hulk system, if considered as a system, for the punishment and reformation of offenders. Various efforts have been made to introduce better discipline and management, but, from the limited space and construction of ships, these advantages do not appear to be attainable. Without classification any place of confinement must necessarily be a school of vice, and prisoners discharged from the hulks are manifestly *hardened in depravity*. The fact is too notorious to require any statement of individual cases.

Upon the concluding remarks of the Prison Discipline Society we may observe that the failure of the hulks to reform the convict's character is only a result they share in common with the public penitentiary, transportation, and the house of correction. The chief advantages we anticipate, from the most improved system of discipline and classification, are the prevention of criminals becoming *more* hardened and expert in the arts of depredation; but of any lasting reform, should they be allowed to rejoin old connexions, and be exposed to old temptations, we have already expressed our despair. Of transports being made good citizens in New South Wales the examples are abundant; but to such regeneration in the mother-country is superadded to natural turpitude the almost insurmountable obstacle of obtaining a livelihood—hard enough frequently to honest persons—but greatly augmented to those suffering from the opprobrium, suspicion, and loss of character inflicted by criminal punishment. Under this impression we have strenuously recommended *perpetual exile*, coupled with limited probationary treatment, according to the offence in a penal settlement, as a substitute for terminal punishments, and as holding out the best chance of reform and a diminution in the number of offenders. We remarked above the benefits which resulted from transporting convicts to the American plantations—how they gradually amalgamated with the community to which they were banished—and how Government was ultimately relieved from the expense of transporting them. The number of settlers who have lately gone out to New South Wales, and the increased demand for labour in the colony, hold out hopes of a similar issue to our settlements in that country.

APPENDIX.

MR. PEEL'S BILL FOR THE IMPROVEMENT OF THE POLICE OF THE METROPOLIS AND ITS VICINITY.

SINCE concluding our work a Police-Bill has been introduced, in which we recognize the commencement of a better system of protective justice, and an attempt to introduce that energy and consolidation of power which we have shown to be essential to public security. Though the new measure of the Right Hon. Secretary of State is of limited extent, and intended to operate gradually, we apprehend the powers it confers, if fully and judiciously executed, will accomplish important improvements in the metropolitan police. The chief points in the proposed measure are,—

1. The establishment of a new office of police, consisting of three magistrates, whose duties are to be chiefly ministerial; they are to act as justices of the peace within the counties of Middlesex, Surrey, Hertford, Essex, and Kent, and execute such *other duties* as the Secretary of State may direct; but they are not to act in any court of general or quarter sessions, nor in any matter out of session, except for the "preservation of the peace, the prevention of offences, and the detection of offenders;" they are not required to take any *oath of office* or landed qualification; and are to have the entire control, regulation, classification, and discipline of the police force intended to replace, within certain districts, the present nightly watch and police.

2. The City and Liberties of Westminster, and certain other parishes and places mentioned, are to be constituted into one district, called "*The Metropolitan Police District;*" within which limits the substi-

tution of the new police is at first to be restricted; but his Majesty may order any *other parish or place, within twelve miles* of Charing-cross, to be added to the metropolitan police district, and placed under the charge of the new establishment. The new system is not to be introduced into any parish till after public notice has been given on the two preceding Sundays; from which time all parochial powers for levying a watch-rate are to cease; and all watch-houses, watch-boxes, accoutrements, and other necessaries, provided at the public expense for the night-police, are to be surrendered to the new authorities.

3. The men forming the police are to be empowered to act as *constables* within the five counties, and to be entitled to all the privileges and subject to all the duties and responsibilities of that office. They are, also, empowered, in certain cases of petty misdemeanour charged before them in the *night-time*, at any watch-house within the police district, to accept bail for the appearance of the accused next morning.

4. As soon as the new police begins to act in any parish, the justices appointed under the statute may issue their warrant to the overseer, commanding him to levy, within *forty days*, to the amount therein mentioned, a *police-rate* upon all the property rateable to the relief of the poor, and according to such valuation as, for the time being, may be acted upon in fixing the poor-rate.

Lastly, a receiver or treasurer is to be appointed to the new establishment.

With such powers, it must chiefly arise from a defective execution of them if greater security be not obtained both for persons and property in the Metropolis. There are, however, we think, a few omissions and defects in the new bill, as it now stands, and which we beg leave shortly to enumerate:—

First, it does not appear the new Police-Board is to act in concert with, or exercise any control over, the public offices already established: without this, we fear, there will remain some of the disunion and conflict of authorities now lamented, and an absence of that general superintendence, unity, and subordination of parts essential to an effective police. The police offices, at present, require control, and a more vigilant superintendence, we suspect, than is compatible with the multifarious duties of the Home Secretary.

Secondly, the utility is somewhat questionable of disqualifying *all three* magistrates from a seat in Parliament: we are aware of the motives that have dictated this exclusion, and that it is in conformity with the regulations of former police-acts; but, in our opinion, the interrogatory system to which public servants are occasionally subjected in the House of Commons, affords a salutary check on their conduct, and far more than counterbalances any contingent danger which might result from the addition of a fraction of $\frac{1}{658}$ part to the influence of the Crown in that assembly.

Thirdly, the new bill appears principally directed to the improvement of the *nightly* watch and police, leaving the *day*-police, as heretofore, to those very inefficient functionaries the parish-beadles, street-keepers, and constables. We were in hopes the duties of the two last, at least, would have been absorbed in the new establishment; above all, that such reform or substitute would have been devised for the parochial constabulary, as would have prevented its functions clashing with those of the regular officers; especially as it is intended to impose on the parishes a rate levied expressly for their protection and police.

Lastly, we do not discover, in the proposed measure, a sufficient guarantee for the faithful discharge of their duty by the new police constables. As to fining a publican £5 who suffers them to drink in his house—which is proposed in the bill—it is a most futile expedient, and inflicts punishment on one who, in fact, is not the offender. Dismission from employment also affords inadequate security to the public;—an officer of police possesses great power, and an important trust is confided to him; and, in our opinion, when he is guilty of any act in dereliction of his duty (the cases of which might be specified) he ought to be subjected to criminal punishment in a similar manner to servants in the Post-Office or Excise.

We have little doubt this important bill will receive considerable improvements before it passes into a law, and we also flatter ourselves that Mr. Peel has some measures in reserve that will be brought forward in due course, for superseding the whole race of common informers by a responsible agency—for bringing within some limits the great nuisance of Mendicity—for checking the compounding of felony and lesser offences—and for dissolving those disgraceful ties which are known to subsist between notorious depredators and the retainers of the stipendiary force.

INDEX.

THE END.

Patterson Smith Reprint Series in
Criminology, Law Enforcement, and Social Problems

1. Lewis: *The Development of American Prisons and Prison Customs, 1776-1845*
2. Carpenter: *Reformatory Prison Discipline*
3. Brace: *The Dangerous Classes of New York*
4. Dix: *Remarks on Prisons and Prison Discipline in the United States*
5. Bruce *et al: The Workings of the Indeterminate-Sentence Law and the Parole System in Illinois*
6. Wickersham Commission: *Complete Reports, Including the Mooney-Billings Report.* 14 Vols.
7. Livingston: *Complete Works on Criminal Jurisprudence.* 2 Vols.
8. Cleveland Foundation: *Criminal Justice in Cleveland*
9. Illinois Association for Criminal Justice: *The Illinois Crime Survey*
10. Missouri Association for Criminal Justice: *The Missouri Crime Survey*
11. Aschaffenburg: *Crime and Its Repression*
12. Garofalo: *Criminology*
13. Gross: *Criminal Psychology*
14. Lombroso: *Crime, Its Causes and Remedies*
15. Saleilles: *The Individualization of Punishment*
16. Tarde: *Penal Philosophy*
17. McKelvey: *American Prisons*
18. Sanders: *Negro Child Welfare in North Carolina*
19. Pike: *A History of Crime in England.* 2 Vols.
20. Herring: *Welfare Work in Mill Villages*
21. Barnes: *The Evolution of Penology in Pennsylvania*
22. Puckett: *Folk Beliefs of the Southern Negro*
23. Fernald *et al: A Study of Women Delinquents in New York State*
24. Wines: *The State of the Prisons and of Child-Saving Institutions*
25. Raper: *The Tragedy of Lynching*
26. Thomas: *The Unadjusted Girl*
27. Jorns: *The Quakers as Pioneers in Social Work*
28. Owings: *Women Police*
29. Woolston: *Prostitution in the United States*
30. Flexner: *Prostitution in Europe*
31. Kelso: *The History of Public Poor Relief in Massachusetts: 1820-1920*
32. Spivak: *Georgia Nigger*
33. Earle: *Curious Punishments of Bygone Days*
34. Bonger: *Race and Crime*
35. Fishman: *Crucibles of Crime*
36. Brearley: *Homicide in the United States*
37. Graper: *American Police Administration*
38. Hichborn: *"The System"*
39. Steiner & Brown: *The North Carolina Chain Gang*
40. Cherrington: *The Evolution of Prohibition in the United States of America*
41. Colquhoun: *A Treatise on the Commerce and Police of the River Thames*
42. Colquhoun: *A Treatise on the Police of the Metropolis*
43. Abrahamsen: *Crime and the Human Mind*
44. Schneider: *The History of Public Welfare in New York State: 1609-1866*
45. Schneider & Deutsch: *The History of Public Welfare in New York State: 1867-1940*
46. Crapsey: *The Nether Side of New York*
47. Young: *Social Treatment in Probation and Delinquency*
48. Quinn: *Gambling and Gambling Devices*
49. McCord & McCord: *Origins of Crime*
50. Worthington & Topping: *Specialized Courts Dealing with Sex Delinquency*

Patterson Smith Reprint Series in
Criminology, Law Enforcement, and Social Problems

51. Asbury: *Sucker's Progress*
52. Kneeland: *Commercialized Prostitution in New York City*
53. Fosdick: *American Police Systems*
54. Fosdick: *European Police Systems*
55. Shay: *Judge Lynch: His First Hundred Years*
56. Barnes: *The Repression of Crime*
57. Cable: *The Silent South*
58. Kammerer: *The Unmarried Mother*
59. Doshay: *The Boy Sex Offender and His Later Career*
60. Spaulding: *An Experimental Study of Psychopathic Delinquent Women*
61. Brockway: *Fifty Years of Prison Service*
62. Lawes: *Man's Judgment of Death*
63. Healy & Healy: *Pathological Lying, Accusation, and Swindling*
64. Smith: *The State Police*
65. Adams: *Interracial Marriage in Hawaii*
66. Halpern: *A Decade of Probation*
67. Tappan: *Delinquent Girls in Court*
68. Alexander & Healy: *Roots of Crime*
69. Healy & Bronner: *Delinquents and Criminals*
70. Cutler: *Lynch-Law*
71. Gillin: *Taming the Criminal*
72. Osborne: *Within Prison Walls*
73. Ashton: *The History of Gambling in England*
74. Whitlock: *On the Enforcement of Law in Cities*
75. Goldberg: *Child Offenders*
76. Cressey: *The Taxi-Dance Hall*
77. Riis: *The Battle with the Slum*
78. Larson *et al: Lying and Its Detection*
79. Comstock: *Frauds Exposed*
80. Carpenter: *Our Convicts.* 2 Vols. in 1
81. Horn: *Invisible Empire: The Story of the Ku Klux Klan, 1866-1871*
82. Faris *et al: Intelligent Philanthropy*
83. Robinson: *History and Organization of Criminal Statistics in the United States*
84. Reckless: *Vice in Chicago*
85. Healy: *The Individual Delinquent*
86. Bogen: *Jewish Philanthropy*
87. Clinard: *The Black Market: A Study of White Collar Crime*
88. Healy: *Mental Conflicts and Misconduct*
89. Citizens' Police Committee: *Chicago Police Problems*
90. Clay: *The Prison Chaplain*
91. Peirce: *A Half Century with Juvenile Delinquents*
92. Richmond: *Friendly Visiting Among the Poor*
93. Brasol: *Elements of Crime*
94. Strong: *Public Welfare Administration in Canada*
95. Beard: *Juvenile Probation*
96. Steinmetz: *The Gaming Table.* 2 Vols.
97. Crawford: *Report on the Pentitentiaries of the United States*
98. Kuhlman: *A Guide to Material on Crime and Criminal Justice*
99. Culver: *Bibliography of Crime and Criminal Justice: 1927-1931*
100. Culver: *Bibliography of Crime and Criminal Justice: 1932-1937*

Patterson Smith Reprint Series in
Criminology, Law Enforcement, and Social Problems

101. Tompkins: *Administration of Criminal Justice, 1938-1948*
102. Tompkins: *Administration of Criminal Justice, 1949-1956*
103. Cumming: *Bibliography Dealing with Crime and Cognate Subjects*
104. Addams *et al: Philanthropy and Social Progress*
105. Powell: *The American Siberia*
106. Carpenter: *Reformatory Schools*
107. Carpenter: *Juvenile Delinquents*
108. Montague: *Sixty Years in Waifdom*
109. Mannheim: *Juvenile Delinquency in an English Middletown*
110. Semmes: *Crime and Punishment in Early Maryland*
111. National Conference of Charities and Correction: *History of Child Saving in the United States*
112. Barnes: *The Story of Punishment.* 2d ed.
113. Phillipson: *Three Criminal Law Reformers*
114. Drähms: *The Criminal*
115. Terry & Pellens: *The Opium Problem*
116. Ewing: *The Morality of Punishment*
117. Mannheim: *Group Problems in Crime and Punishment*
118. Michael & Adler: *Crime, Law and Social Science*
119. Lee: *A History of Police in England*
120. Schafer: *Compensation and Restitution to Victims of Crime.* 2d ed.
121. Mannheim: *Pioneers in Criminology.* 2d ed.
122. Goebel & Naughton: *Law Enforcement in Colonial New York*
123. Savage: *Police Records and Recollections*
124. Ives: *A History of Penal Methods*
125. Bernard (Ed.): *The Americanization Studies*
    - Thompson: *The Schooling of the Immigrant*
    - Daniels: *America via the Neighborhood*
    - Thomas *et al: Old World Traits Transplanted*
    - Speek: *A Stake in the Land*
    - Davis: *Immigrant Health and the Community*
    - Breckinridge: *New Homes for Old*
    - Park: *The Immigrant Press and Its Control*
    - Gavit: *Americans by Choice*
    - Claghorn: *The Immigrant's Day in Court*
    - Leiserson: *Adjusting Immigrant and Industry*
126. Dai: *Opium Addiction in Chicago*
127. Costello: *Our Police Protectors*
128. Wade: *A Treatise on the Police and Crimes of the Metropolis*
129. Robison: *Can Delinquency Be Measured?*
130. Augustus: *A Report of the Labors of John Augustus*
131. Vollmer: *The Police and Modern Society*
132. Jessel: *A Bibliography of Works in English on Playing Cards and Gaming.* Enlarged
133. Walling: *Recollections of a New York Chief of Police*
134. Lombroso: *Criminal Man*
135. Howard: *Prisons and Lazarettos.* 2 vols.
136. Fitzgerald: *Chronicles of Bow Street Police-Office.* 2 vols. in 1
137. Goring: *The English Convict*
138. Ribton-Turner: *A History of Vagrants and Vagrancy*
139. Smith: *Justice and the Poor*
140. Willard: *Tramping with Tramps*